Western Allegan County

Pioneer Days

Henry Hudson Hutchins at his desk in his attic study in the 122nd Avenue farmhouse about 1930.

By Henry Hudson Hutchins

PAVILION PRESS
P. O. Box 250
Douglas, Michigan 49406

THE HUTCHINS'
(IMPROVED)
Fruit and Vegetable ASSORTER.

(The above Illustration represents the Assorter as arranged for Peaches, Plums, etc.)

FOR ASSORTING

Apples, Peaches, Plums, Potatoes, Etc.

Manufactured by

H. H. HUTCHINS, Ganges, Mich.

International Standard Book Number
1-877703-07-9

LC # 95-068819
Published in 1995

Henry Hudson Hutchins

1853 - 1933

Henry Hudson Hutchins was born in Ganges Township, Allegan County, Michigan, December 14, 1853, the third son of Harrison and Laura (Hudson) Hutchins. His father was the first settler in Ganges Township, arriving in 1837 from New York State. Although the elder Hutchins worked at many tasks, roadbuilding, logging, mill construction, etc., he was primarily a farmer and one of the first in western Michigan to plant fruit trees. Henry's mother, Laura (Hudson) Hutchins, came to Allegan County in 1847 as a school teacher. She enjoyed writing poetry, usually long narrative poems designed to be read at picnics and other social gatherings. Laura also wrote about her experiences as mistress of the boarding house at Singapore 1848-49 shortly after her marriage. Her son later used some of her narratives in his historical letters. Henry attended the Veeder school near Fennville and studied at Kalamazoo College. He was married in 1877 to Hattie Robertson. The couple had four children, but no grandchildren.

In 1873 he established a fruit farm on 122nd Avenue, east of Ganges. He was never a success at fruit farming, but he added to the family income with his inventions including a mechanical fruit and vegetable sorter and a portable buggy light. For many years he was an officer in the Ganges Pomological Society, and was secretary of the Western Allegan County Pioneer Society. He also was a founding father, and longtime manager, of the Saugatuck and Ganges Telephone Company, said to have been the first cooperative telephone company in the nation.

About the turn of the century he began interviewing the "old timers" of the area and writing up their recollections along with some of his own. In 1919 "since no one has appeared on the scene to use my notes," Hutchins wrote a series of 16 articles which were published in the *Commercial Record* in Saugatuck and the *Fennville Herald*. In 1925 he followed the original 16 with additional "letters." For the rest of his life he continued to write on topics that interested him, or on which others brought him special information. Many of these articles were published in the local newspapers.

Henry Hutchins died in 1933 and his papers, still in his attic study in the 122nd Avenue farmhouse, were cared for by his nephew, Evert Olney Hutchins, son of Henry's brother David. Here as late as 1976 the original interview notes were still carefully filed away along with a vast collection of letters, pictures, and documents related to some of his many business efforts. Some of this material was later given to the Bentley Historical Library, University of Michigan, Ann Arbor. Some remains with the family.

* * * * * * *

When the articles were first published in 1919 the local editor advised his readers to make scrapbooks of the material for future generations. Many of them did. In addition Hutchins himself made a number of scrapbooks which he donated to Michigan libraries. At least one typescript of the columns was made and is now in the state library, and in 1976 the *Commercial Record* reprinted the original 35 in a book entitled *Recollections of the Pioneers of Western Allegan County*, a publication which is now out of print. The remaining 14 "letters" in this volume are being reprinted for the first time.

Persons using these articles for research are advised to consult the index for all of the references on a single topic. The letters were written by Hutchins over a period of 26 years and there are several instances of a fact being revised in a later letter as information was recalled or brought to his attention by others.

Table of Contents

	Henry Hudson Hutchins, 1853-1933	3
1	Interview with D. H. Hall	5
2	Interview with J. D. Billings	5
3	First Settlements	7
4	W. A. Dressel's Recollections	8
5	Singapore	9
6	Singapore Continued	10
7	Singapore Businesses	11
8	Singapore Bank	12
9	Singapore Concluded	13
10	Reminiscences of J. P. Wade	15
11	Wallinville	16
12	Saugatuck Mills	18
13	Shipping	19
14	Douglas also Plummerville	21
15	Pier Cove	23
16	Pier Cove Continued	25
17	Ganges Township	27
18	Allegan County Organization	27
19	Subdivision of Newark	29
20	Wildlife of the Forest	31
21	Bears and Indians	34
22	Early Settlers	36
23	Schools	39
24	Building Roads	42
25	Early Steamboats	45
26	The Plummers	48
27	Address by E. A. Fenn	51
28	Fennville	54
29	Fennville Continued (also Bravo)	57
30	Pearl (also Pullman, New Richmond)	59
31	Fruit Industry	60
32	Apples and Pears	62
33	Local Phone Company	63
34	Pioneering	65
35	Pioneer Cooperative Work	66
36	Saugatuck's Other Names	68
37	Kalamazoo, Then Saugatuck	68
38	One More Chapter About Singapore	69
39	Oshea Wilder, Founder of Singapore	76
40	Founders of the Village of Fennville	77
41	Founders of Fennville Continued	78
42	Rogers & Bird Transportation Co.	80
43	Ganges Roundup	81
44	Early Bands in Western Allegan County	82
45	Some Historical Errors Corrected	83
46	The Slaughter of the Pine	85
47	Rural Telephones	88
48	My History in Business	90
49	Meditations of Henry Hudson Hutchins	91
	Index	92

[*Commercial Record*, October 16, 1919 -- Arrangements have been made for a series of articles on the early settlement and history of this region, to be published in this paper at an early date, probably beginning next week. These articles are from the pen of H. H. Hutchins of Ganges, than whom we know of no one better qualified by personal participation, knowledge and research for this interesting task. Doubtless many readers will wish to preserve these articles in their scrap books. Mr. Hutchins has spent much time and effort over a period of several years gathering and arranging the material for these articles, and has heretofore furnished some valuable data to the State Historical Society, and it is at the request of that organization that the present work is undertaken. It is purely a labor of love on the part of Mr. Hutchins.]

1
Interview with D. H. Hall

The late Mr. D. H. Hall, in an interview of February 15, 1914, told some of his early observations here as follows:

"My first recollection of wild birdlife was that the birds were here without number. While living with mother at Wallin's tannery, northeast of Saugatuck, I woke up one morning and heard the darnedest racket entirely, and was told it was wild pigeons that had just come in. They nested there, and the people would cut down a tree and get from forty to fifty squabs. The habit of these birds was to hatch a nest of two, then lay more eggs in the same nest and let the first brood hatch the second pair. The crops of the squabs would be filled with little beech sprouts just started to grow from the beech trees. We cleaned the young pigeons and put them down in brine for future use. We did not disturb the older ones, as we did not want them, though they could have been had by the thousands.

"When the pigeons were migrating the flocks were so dense that they would cast a shadow on the ground, and were almost sufficient to hide the sun. The flight would continue for probably half an hour, likely to be followed by another. Pigeon hunters made it their business to trap them with nets. They would strew grain on the ground, tie a few birds to stakes, and pull a string attached to the stool pigeon to make him flutter and attract the flock that was flying over. When the ground was well covered with birds they would trip the net by pulling another string, the net being so arranged that it would fly over and cover the lot. The trapper concealed himself under a booth made of green brush. The birds were killed by pinching their heads, were packed in barrels without dressing, and shipped to what market I don't remember.

"Migration south, I should say, began about September, and the northern flight began about May. Ducks, geese and blackbirds migrated in great numbers but not to the extent in numbers as did the pigeons.

* * *

"Indians, too, were migratory in the early days. They came around in their canoes from Mackinaw in the fall, would hunt, fish and trap all winter and in the spring they went back north. The old buck would go out on a hunt, and when he killed a deer he hung it up, went to camp and sent the squaws out to bring it in.

"The Indians brought in calico and beads to trade for provisions. They no doubt got the merchandise in exchange for their furs. When a white girl got a squaw calico dress she was attired in pleasing style. The women wore their dresses in Mother Hubbard style of make, and a blanket or shawl as a covering for the head and shoulders.

"The Indian name for corn was *opin*; flour, *napanee*; meat, *weos*; deer, *sucsee*. To explain, deer, as stated was *sucsee* and venison *sucsee weos*; hog was *cucuss* and pork *cucuss weos*, or deer meat and hog meat, emphasis on the last word.

"The Indians always made maple sugar before going north in the spring. By stirring continuously they would make a sugar quite similar to our brown sugar. When the whites bought sugar of the Indians they melted it to cleanse it, as the Indian boys used to swim in the storage trough before the sap was boiled down. Small packages were put up in birch bark dishes called *mokirks*. Sugar was *sisbouquette* (accent on the last syllable). In their migrations they always traveled in Indian file -- in a row, one behind the other."

* * *

Mr. Hall was born October 31, 1842, and was the second white child born in Ganges township. He was the nephew of the late Harrison Hutchins and his home was here until 1871, when he migrated to Kansas. He died in December, 1916, at the home of his son Homer at Horatio, Arkansas.

2
Interview with J.D. Billings

To persons now living, who were here during the fifties and early sixties and earlier, these stories bring nothing new, but the best time to take note of happenings is while those scenes are fresh in memory. The object is to secure the facts and set them down so they will be available in time to come, when no doubt they will be of interest. We trust the readers born in more recent years may be interested even now.

Mr. J. D. Billings, now living at Akron, Iowa, born in 1838, and coming with his parents, who settled on the farm now owned by V. A. Kenter, section 3, Ganges, in February, 1839, said in an interview of October 3, 1917:

"While living west of where Fennville now is (on the farm now owned by Mr. E. D. Wadsworth) the wild pigeons roosted just north of the corners west of town. Their nesting grounds covered acres, and their singing or merriment was so noisy that they could be heard for a mile distant, and when under a tree full of nests we had to yell to be heard. When the squabs were just ready to fly my father went to the nesting grounds, cut down a tree well filled with nests, and when it fell we boys gathered the squabs, pinched their heads and put them in baskets, frequently getting several bushels at one cutting. Those we could not eat at once were dressed and salted down for further use.

"Later, after the squabs were mature and before they migrated south, they roosted in the woods farther east, no doubt to feed on acorns in the oak and pine lands, also huckleberries, wild sunflower, etc., and we went there for them. By getting under a tree at night and shooting up into the top with a shotgun we could bring down several at a shot. I was about 10 or 11 years old at the time (about 1848 or 1849).

"In their migrations north in the spring and south in the fall these birds went in tremendous flocks, a constant string would go over, and from woods to woods and across the fields they went in such masses that for some time one could see neither end of the flock. Not only one flock, but others would be seen in one direction or another, or both.

Wild ducks, geese and blackbirds migrated in large numbers, but in no such quantity as did the pigeons."

The writer has a very vivid recollection of these migrations, and remembers well of seeing pigeons caught in large numbers with nets. As soon as the net was sprung it would be in a perfect flutter from end to end by the birds in their efforts to escape.

Mr. Hall and Mr. Billings speak of pinching the heads of the squabs (young pigeons) but my observation in netting older birds the men crawled over the net, drew the head up and bit it with their teeth   not an inviting task, as it appeared to a small boy.

The statements are borne out by the following:

Kalamazoo Telegraph, May 16, 1860: "Three men who have been engaged in pigeon shooting for the last six months, following their various migrations, were in town Wednesday. Since spring opened they have barreled and sent to eastern markets 130 barrels of pigeons. About a week since one of them brought down at one shot 120 pigeons. Of course these pigeons were not on as many different trees, but on a single roost These sportsmen are not given to telling big stories."

Grand Rapids Eagle, May 22, 1860: "Osborn & Co. are the pigeons hunters spoken of in the above items, and they bagged their game with nets in the vicinity of this city. Abundant as has been their success they have been beaten by M. H. Littin, who alone has taken 28,000 pigeons near this city since March 26 last. He has shipped to the eastern markets 164 barrels averaging over 300 to the barrel, and has now over 3,000 pigeons which he is keeping and feeding with grain. He has spent over $1,500 for express charges and dressing the birds. Goodhart & Co. also have sent 52 barrels, making a total of 347 barrels of pigeons shipped from this city so far this season. All these would make a flock of 111,500.

Mr. H. H. Goodrich, who came with his parents to western Allegan county in about 1844, called me up to state that in 1847 and 1848 they lived at Manlius, about a mile south of where New Richmond now is, and he remembers well how his uncle, Dan Shed, and others would stand on the brink of a hill and as the wild pigeons, flying high over the valley, came near the ground on approaching the hill, they could knock them down with a club.

I remember hearing of like occasions, but was too young to witness them.

Mr. Goodrich also tells of visiting in Laketown, north of Saugatuck, in 1858 or 1859, and the woods there were alive with them for miles around. As near as we can recollect they ceased coming very suddenly along about 1870. Why this was so or what became of them we have never learned.

3
First Settlements

On January 13, 1829, Mr. H. E. Blackman, then a lad of 19 years, started from Hudson, Ohio, with a team of horses, and arrived at Allegan, Mich., on the 26th of the same month. From him I got the following interesting statement of Allegan, in a talk while at his home on the 24th of September, 1907:

"Alexander Ely had secured some land on the Kalamazoo river, and hired Alonzo Prouty to work for him a year, for which service he was to pay him $12 a month. As there was no road except the Indian trail, the only way to transport goods was via the river, and as no other boat was to be had a raft was in order. So Mr. Prouty bought lumber at Pine Creek, built a raft and loaded his scanty supplies of household goods, tools and provisions, among which were a barrel of pork and a plow.

"On June 6, 1834, he started on his voyage accompanied by his wife, Eber Sherwood and a Mr. Crittenden. They had floated twelve or fifteen miles from Pine Creek and were yet about eight miles from their destination when their conveyance snagged and was wrecked to some extent. They lost the plow in the river -- but secured it afterwards. Late in the evening they landed for the night, and Mrs. Prouty was very much frightened by the howling of the wolves near their camp. Next day they built a cabin where they passed the night, and here they lived the following year. This was the first white man's dwelling on the present site of Allegan, as well as the first settlement between Pine Creek and the mouth of the Kalamazoo.

"Mr. Prouty cut a wagon track the same fall from his home to Pine Creek, found land that suited him, and later bought there.

"Mr. Hull Sherwood came to Pine Creek from Rochester, New York in 1829. When he arrived he found the land was not yet in the market. He brought his daughter, Mrs. Scott, and family in 1830, and squatted. In 1831 he brought his family, and later, when land was on sale, he bought there. His grandson, Chauncey Scott, who came with the others in 1830, said William G. Butler came on horseback about 1832 from Indiana. There was no road down the river below Pine Creek at that time, so he left his horse with Mr. Scott, who took care of it while Mr. Butler went on to the mouth of the river prospecting. Later Mr. Butler went back to Indiana and moved his family to where Saugatuck now is, via St. Joseph and the lake."

(Mr. Blackman stated that he was well acquainted with both Mr. Scott and Mr. Butler, though he got this information from Mr. Scott, and from information gotten from the earliest settlers he is certain the white man first settled at or near the mouth of the Kalamazoo in 1832 or 1833.)

* * *

"In November or December, 1834, Alexander Ely, accompanied by another man, came to Pine Creek. When they arrived they found the inhabitants raising a barn, and as whiskey was furnished at the raising some were considerably under its influence. So Mr. Ely and his companion did not feel safe to remain there for the night, and about four in the afternoon they started by boat for his place twenty miles below. When they were just above the present site of the dam above Allegan they struck some flood wood, their boat was capsized and both were thrown into the river. The other man drowned, but Mr. Ely swam to the north shore and made for his destination as best he could. There was no road, it was dark, and his clothes were frozen. Finally he heard a dog bark, and went toward it until he saw a light. he called and an Indian came across the river to his aid and took him in for the night. Next day they found the man who was drowned and buried him.

"The Indian was going north the next fall, and Mr. Ely fitted him out for the trip. Again in the spring when he returned Mr. Ely gave him considerable and finally when the Indian died, he buried him."

Mr. Blackman told of a case where an Indian befriended a white man (he knew them both, but withheld the names for good reasons). The white man lived in Kalamazoo county, was sick and in need, and the Indian brought him food -- venison and other eatables such as an Indian could provide. When the whites were transporting the Indians west to the Indian Territory this man was hired to help hunt them. This Indian did not want to go, because the Indians west were his enemies, but the white man persisted in hunting for him. So one morning the Indian went to the white man's home and said: "Two mornings I have seen you in the woods looking for me. If I see you again I will shoot you." But he never had occasion to shoot.

* * *

The late Mr. B. B. Born said (Sept. 25, 1907): "Mr. Blackman's account of Mr. Prouty's coming to Allegan is correct." He was familiar with the circumstances and said that Jeanette E. Prouty, eldest daughter of Leander S. Prouty, was the first white child born in Allegan. She married William A. Gibbs of Portage township, Kalamazoo county, on May 10, 1854, and Mr. Born attended the wedding.

* * *

On May 17, 1908, the late Alvin H. Stillson of Saugatuck, who came to Allegan in 1837, when a lad of 9 years said:

"The Indian who helped Judge Ely was Macsaube. Mr. Ely gave his two sons, Joe and Louie Macsaube, a good education (common school was the best then). They considered themselves above the others of their tribe, and engaged in speculating in furs. By their education and being naturally bright they had a considerable advantage over their tribesmen."

Mr. Stillson was well acquainted with the Macsaube boys.

I might say that the general understanding on the lake shore is that Mr. Butler first came to the mouth of the Kalamazoo in 1830, instead of 1832 as Mr. Blackman said. I told him this, but he insisted that he had related the story just as it was told him.

At this late date a variation of one or two years matters little, and it would seem that Mr. Scott, having come to Pine Creek in 1830, would remember whether it was the same year or two years later that Mr. Butler came to his home and left his horse while he went down to the river's mouth.

By the way, the English for the Indian word *Saugatuck* is river's mouth.

4
W.A. Dressel's Recollections

Mr. W. A. Dressel came from Saxony, Germany, to America in 1834, and to Ganges, Mich., in October, 1838, and settled on a parcel of land one half mile south of where Ganges Grange Hall now stands.

When he came here the road through what is now Fennville was a floating corduroy. The principle business here at that time was getting out tan bark, stave bolts, shingle bolts and cord wood. Three shillings per cord was the price paid for the work of cutting and piling four-foot wood, which was hauled to Pier Cove and shipped to Chicago.

When he quit the wood business he went to work for Mr. Perrottet (pronounced Pa-ro-ty) in the tannery at Plummerville. This was in 1859. From there he went to Singapore to work in the saw mill where he worked one month for $5 per week, then began loading ship at 20 cents a hour. Flour at this time was $15 a barrel.

At some time during this period he lost his pocketbook, which contained $7. So S. A. Morrison trusted him for 100 pounds of corn meal. This he took on his back and started for his home in Ganges by way of the ferry and the lake shore road. He got lost, and after a long time, going through brush and over logs, he came to the road on the Kenter hill, on the west side of Kalamazoo Lake. Though it was dark he managed to keep to the road, and finally reached home with his load. The only road leading to Saugatuck from the south at this time was by the lake shore.

While working at Singapore he came home on Saturday nights, and was back on the job again Monday morning. On one occasion he came home over a trail which followed what we now know as the Baragar road. He came to the creek near where the Baragar school house is, and while crossing the creek on a fallen tree he heard two wildcats scream in the creek bottom nearby. They seemed to be in a fight, but it frightened Mr. Dressel. He hurried on, but they did not disturb him.

Wildcats used to kill sheep occasionally. Jake Miller caught one in a trap, and Mr. Dressel shot it. It measured five feet from tip of nose to end of stub tail. Mr. N. W. Lewis killed a very large one on the place now owned by the writer. Mr. Dressel went cooning one night in company with Jake and Adam Miller. The dog treed what was supposed to be a coon. They cut the tree, and the animal got to a second tree, and in like manner to a third tree. This time the dog got so close that the animal snarled and scared the dog. Then they discovered it was a wildcat, but it got away.

Hedgehogs caused much damage in the corn. They would climb the stalk and if it did not break over they would get hold of the ear and let go of the stalk, and their weight would break the ear off. These animals made a very peculiar noise -- a strange squeal. Mr. Dressel said he heard a strange squealing noise one night soon after he came into the woods. He got up, went out and followed the noise until he came to a hemlock tree from the top of which it proceeded. He cut the tree down and killed the hedgehog. Squirrels were so thick they would come up to a shock of corn he was husking on for feed. After cutting timber in winter deer tracks would be seen all about the fallen tree tops in the morning, where the deer had been during the night feeding off the green brush -- or browsing as it was called. Deer were quite plenty up to and including the sixties, and wolves would howl at night in the woods near the house.

The principle interest in this interview is that it names some of the conditions in western Allegan county at the dates given, and shows how different life was then from the present. Mr. Dressel came here just twenty years after the first white man moved into the township in 1838. Note the wages paid -- and a day's work was from sun to sun, summer and winter.

The lack of roads and the mode of travel stand out in broad contrast to the present. And of course the wild life has disappeared.

Mr. Dressel was a respected man in the community, was a member of the Baptist church, and any statement he would make could be relied upon.

5
Singapore

In its original channel the Kalamazoo river, on leaving Kalamazoo lake at Saugatuck, took a course almost due north for about a mile, then made a fine curve to the northwest, west and southwest for perhaps half a mile, when it took a course nearly south for about half a mile, then turned abruptly west and emptied into Lake Michigan after another run of half a mile to the west from the last turn.

The explanation is to record the original course of the river, as the double bend -- known as the Ox-Bow on account of its resemblance to the bow used in harnessing or yoking oxen -- is done away now, since the new channel, completed in 1906, leaves but one bend in the river between Saugatuck and the lake, instead of the three bends as formerly. The old channel is rapidly filling with sand, so that there is slight trace of the old bed in sight at the present writing.

* * *

Here it was that the first white man, William G. Butler, located. Local tradition has it that Mr. Butler came here in 1830 to establish a fur trading post with the Indians, though from the statement of Hon. H. E. Blackman, noted in article No. 3, it was not until 1832 that Mr. Butler came.

In a talk on May 17, 1908, with Fred Plummer, who came here with his parents in 1835, he said the first saw mill built in this section stood on the north bank of the river at the lower end of the Ox-bow, and was put up the same year they came by an eastern company, ran for a year or two, when the company went bankrupt, the mill was deserted and finally burned down.

J. P. Wade substantially corroborated Mr. Plummer's statement as follows. He said (December 6, 1906):

"Jonathan Wade -- no relation -- and Asa Bowker built and operated this mill and boarding house at the same time the bank was started, and owned the entire milling interest, having hired the money of a Mr. Carter with which to finance the venture.

"The contract under which the money was secured provided that Mr. Carter would take their lumber at $5 per thousand feet, mill run, for a given time after which the price would be less, until finally it would be but $4. They ran the mill for perhaps a year, but were unable to repay the borrowed money according to contract, so Mr. Carter took possession of the property under the terms of the contract."

Wages at this time for common labor were $16 a month, with board. Mr. Wade continued:

"About 1846 this mill burned down. The fire was supposed to have been of incendiary origin. Another mill was built on the same ground by Mr. Carter and Francis B. Stockbridge, which was operated for several years." [Mr. Wade came from Boston to Singapore in 1844 to clerk in the store. More of him later.]

M. B. Spencer, one of the very earliest to locate here, was quoted in 1888 as saying:

"The Boston company here built a large saw mill costing $44,000. It was a failure. In 1842 a new mill was built, ran two years and burned down. In 1844 the old mill was again started, and again failed. The property then changed hands, and a new mill was built on a large plan, ran two years, and burned."

Captain A. A. Johnson who came from Maine to the mouth of the Kalamazoo with F. B. Stockbridge in 1846, and who commanded lake boats in the early lumber trade here, and who at one time was foreman over the Singapore mill, told the writer that much unnecessary expense was put out in the construction of the first Singapore mill. All the timbers in the frame were planed smooth as a floor, and much of the other work in its construction was equally expensive.

* * *

Again quoting Mr. Spencer (June 12, 1888): "In 1844 a mill was put up by Carter Brothers of Boston and run on a large scale, but lumber was low and money scarce, so it did not pay.

"In 1856 O. R. Johnson & Co. bought all of Singapore and all the pine land worth having in the county and began the manufacture of large quantities of lumber. This industry they carried on for twenty years, making millions of dollars, and then removed the machinery to Point St. Ignace, when Singapore was deserted, and has since so remained."

The Singapore mill was but a small part of their holdings in the county.

In a talk with Darius and Charles Billings, who were born in those early days and raised here, they agreed it was about 1875 that the mill above mentioned was dismantled and removed to St. Ignace, Jay Myers having charge of the work.

6
Singapore Continued

W. G. Plummer, son of Daniel Plummer, said (April 2, 1917): "When I was sawyer in the O. R. Johnson mill they had two saws, one circular and one muley, capacity about 6,000 feet per day each. This was in the late forties and early fifties." Mr. Plummer understood that the first mill was built in 1835 and the second about ten years after. He was said to have been one of the most skilled lumber sawyers in this section during his time.

The name "Singapore" was given to this town -- if it could be called a town, for it was never more than a lumber milling camp. Though I have not learned definitely, it is my belief that the bank established there about 1837 or 1838 took that name, and as was natural the place was known by the name.

Quoting from the *Moderator* of June 22, 1888: "It is difficult, as one looks at the elaborate map made by O. Wilder, the surveyor, nearly fifty years ago, to realize that this town, with its broadly and regularly laid out streets bearing the names Broad, Detroit, Cherry, River, Oak, Chestnut, Walnut and Beech, is no more, and that as the semi-centennial of its 'boom' approaches nothing but a few deserted, decaying houses mark the spot with the sands blowing over them as if to bury the last vestige of the place, while the wild waves breaking on the beach a few roads away chant its requiem."

* * *

We have read in articles on Singapore how it had its banks, its stores, mills and hotels, and a population estimated at from 500 to 1,000, but consider such stories unworthy of notice. They are misleading and a damage to the real history of western Allegan county at this time. While it has three or four mills during the forty years of its existence -- 1835 to 1875 -- there never were more than two standing at a time and never more than one doing much business, and from W. G. Plummer's statement as above the rate of cut was only about 12,000 feet per day when at the best. There never was a hotel there -- only the mill boarding house, where transients were accommodated -- and never more than one store at a time, I believe. The population was just sufficient to manufacture and ship 12,000 feet of lumber per day, run the boardinghouse and store and such other businesses as accompany that extent of manufacture.

As stated above, the first mill stood at the lower bend of the Ox-Bow. The other mill site was nearer the upper end of the bow, about half a mile east of the first, and all on the north side of the river or on the outer margin of the bend. The boarding house and the bank were just back of the east mill.

* * *

We have never heard of a "meeting house" (they did not have churches at that time) nor school house in the place, though what is yet known as the Singapore school still stands to the east of the place on the road to Saugatuck. This school house was built about 1838, and will be mentioned in a later article, as also will be the stores, the bank, etc.

In article No. 3 we find Leander Prouty came to the present site of Allegan in 1834, and the Singapore mill was built the following year. There was not a white man at Holland or South Haven for twelve or fifteen years later, so this town formed what might be termed an oasis in the woods, and was really the only white settlement this side of Pine creek, twenty miles up the river from Allegan.

7
Singapore Businesses

Leaving the life of Singapore as a lumbering town to previous letters, we find almost at the same time the milling business was started in 1835, the Bank of Singapore was established in 1836 or 1837 and, too, the general merchandise store must have been stocked up during the same years. In other words we feel safe in saying that the entire business proposition of the place was established within the years 1835 to 1838.

In a talk December 16, 1906, John P. Wade said "Oshea Wilder and Co. came to Singapore in about 1836 or 37 and built the Singapore Bank. The money for the bank was furnished by the Lancaster Bank of Lancaster, Massachusetts, and James G. Carter of the same place was its President."

We have already learned that the saw mill was built in 1835 and the Bank in 1836 or '37. Now Mr. Wade says, "In 1844 I was hired by the Massachusetts Banking company to come to Singapore and work as a clerk in the store owned and operated by Mr. Carter and was to report back east occasionally on the business situation. It developed later however that I was intended as a spy on Carter and his business for the eastern people, tho I was only requested to give general information."

By this last statement we find the store in full operation previous to 1844 and the same man that was President of the Bank owned the store. Also Mr. Wade was hired by the eastern people who seem to have financed, Mr. Carter, so it seems safe to presume this store was started at about the same time as the Bank or previous to 1840.

Mr. Wade said that when he arrived in Allegan there were but 2 stores there and at the point where Saugatuck is now there were but 3 families. They were Mr. S. A. Morrison, Samuel Underwood, and James McLaughlin.

It would seem Saugatuck was at a standstill at this time, Mr. Wade came to Singapore in 1844 and found but three houses on Kalamazoo lake at the present site of Saugatuck, while we read elsewhere in an article written in 1907 where the writer says, "Edward Johonnett and R. R. Crosby are mentioned as the next settlers after Butler. They established the first industry, a tannery, and from this time for over half a century tanning was one of the leading industries of the west portion of the county. With the establishment of the tannery in 1834 other settlers came to the place.

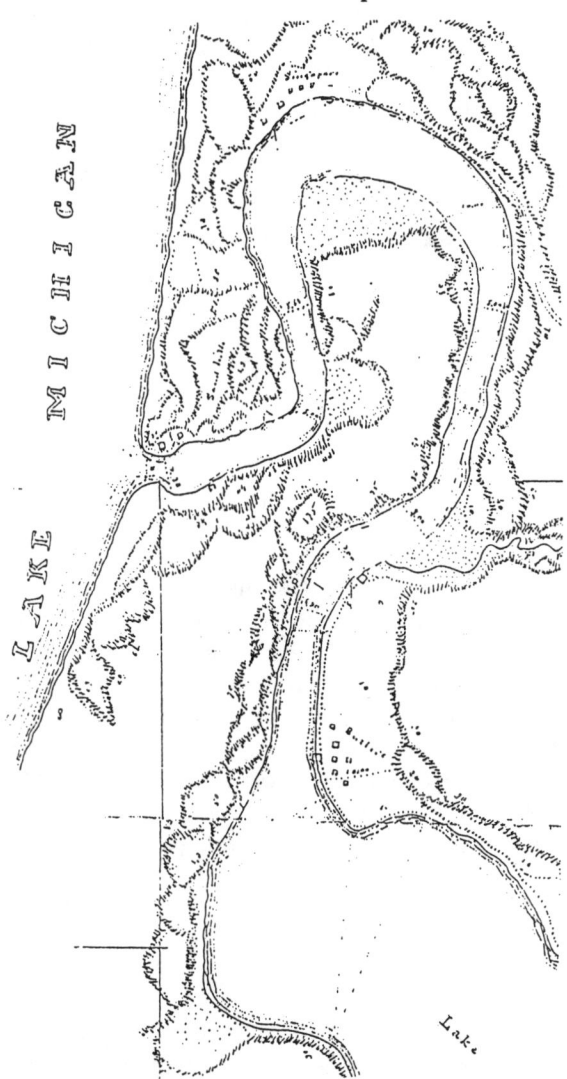

An 1837 map shows five buildings at Singapore at the top of the bend, and six buildings at "Butler's" just north of Lake Kalamazoo.

"The tannery and three dwellings stood on the low shore on the east side of the river in July 1834, when Stephen D. Nichols and H. H. Comstock came up the river on a prospecting trip, having come up the lake by boat." The writer says further, "Nichols besides taking up a quarter section of land on section 17 made a contract with his partner to erect a warehouse and piers at the mouth of the river, after deciding on his location and plans Nichols brought his family from the east and in the same year made settlement on the north bank of the river near the mouth. The construction of the warehouse and dock was begun at once. It is an interesting fact that all the sawed lumber for this and other structures at Saugatuck and the mouth of the river up to this time were brought down to the river from the sawmill at the mouth of Pine Creek."

It would seem from 1834, when this writer found but three families here, until 1844 when Mr. Wade came there had been no addition to the population at this point, since each give an account of but three families there, tho the personnel of the population had entirely changed in the 10 years. That writer says further that Mr. Butler built his cabin on the site of Saugatuck village in 1830, and established a store in it, and being the only white settler there for several years he was engaged in trading with the Indians. He also says that Mr. Nichols built a store near his warehouse and his location took on a commercial aspect that excited some jealous fears in Butler and his associates up the river, who feared the rivalry of the enterprise at the mouth. Finally Butler built a warehouse on the south bank of the river, opposite that of Nichols, hoping to share in the warehouse business.

It seems the mouth of the Kalamazoo formed a transfer point at this early date between river floats that brought freight and produce down river and lake carriers. That is natural, but it is hard to understand just what use there would be for extensive docks and warehouses at so early a date as 1834 -- the year Leander Prouty came to the present site of Allegan and there was not a clearing for 20 miles up river from Prouty's landing place and very thinly settled beyond that point. Nor was there a clearing between Prouty's landing and the mouth except the abode of the three families at Saugatuck.

* * *

We do not desire to carry on a controversy, but prefer to harmonize the statements, so from the above we conclude that but little was accomplished at the foot of Kalamazoo lake during the ten years from 1834 to 1844 and no doubt the statements quoted and those made to me by Mr. Wade are all substantially correct. I well remember hearing mention of "Steve Nichols store" in pioneer talks, but never was sure where it was located but from the above it seems to have been at least a mile below Singapore and right near the lake.

In November 1842, when the ship **Milwaukee** was wrecked two miles north of the river some of the survivors of the crew came to Nichol's place, at the mouth and in freezing condition. The first lighthouse was built in 1838 and Mr. Nichols was the first keeper and from those times discussed by the people who took part in the transaction of those days I have presumed those shipwrecked seamen went to the lighthouse and am of that opinion. I have not been informed as to how long the docks and warehouses remained in operation at the mouth and it would be interesting to learn from someone who happens to have that information.

8
Singapore Bank

We read in Dr. Thomas' *History of Allegan County* (1907, page 34) that Oshea Wilder & Sons of New York were the promoters of Singapore; that they built a saw mill and founded a bank, etc. And from an interview in 1906 with the late John P. Wade, who came here in 1844, that Oshea Wilder & Co. came here in 1836 or '37 and built the Singapore bank which was financed by the Lancaster Bank of Lancaster, Massachusetts, and James G. Carter of the same place was president of the bank. But, as stated in a previous letter, it was Jonathan Wade and Asa Bowker who built the mill in 1835. These differences are immaterial, as the real object of the research is dates and doings and extent of advancement from time to time.

I have never known the extent of business transacted by the Singapore Bank, nor on what financial basis it was established, but the purchasing power of wildcat money can be better understood when we know that people had to be informed at all times as to the standing of a bank before the money could be accepted in trade. My grandfather paid $40 in Singapore bills for a darning needle and had accepted those bills a short time before at par. I was told by men who were boys in 1837 that they had pockets full of Singapore bills after the bank failed, and used to trade with it as play money.

* * *

The late Levi Loomis told an interesting story of the Singapore bank. Mr. Loomis was born in New York State in 1810, and in 1835 came to Singapore, and I understand he helped to construct the first mill there. His sister Emily was the wife of the Indian trader and first while settler William G. Butler, before mentioned.

There was a scarcity of boots here, and Mr. Loomis though a carpenter by trade, decided to send back east for a supply. When the goods came the men offered him bills issued by the local bank when he refused to accept and demanded "good money" or no sale. There were about 200 men at the burg and in the woods who wanted boots, and there was no other place where they could be supplied, but Mr. Loomis preferred to hold the goods to receive good money in exchange.

This state of affairs did not suit the officers of the bank, so they arranged to redeem their bills with eastern money in time for Mr. Loomis to remit to the eastern dealers. To this he agreed, and the whole stock was sold out, amounting to about $600.

The day was fixed on which the bank was to redeem the money, but as might have been expected the bank was not prepared, and put him off four days. Then a draft was made on an eastern bank, and after a short time it came back as worthless. Things went on until more than another month had passed and Mr. Loomis became desperate. His credit and honor depended on the payment of his debt, and he resolved to have good money at any cost.

Hill, the cashier of the local bank, slept in the chamber of Loomis' house with other boarders, but in a separate bed, and did not rise as early as the others. Mr. Loomis suspected that Hill carried with him the good money of the bank and slept with it under his pillow. So he formed his plan, and one morning after the others had gone down, Mr. Loomis went to his room, entered and locked the door, then wakened Hill, laid the wildcat bills on the bed, drew a pistol and told him that the exchange must be made then and there.

Hill was surprised and indignant and began to protest, saying he could do nothing until he went over to the office.

"I know better," said Mr. Loomis, "and you will not go down these stairs until you are carried down unless you fulfill your promise and make the exchange."

These words, with the look of determination and the pistol were sufficient and without more ado Hill raised his pillow and took from a roll containing about $1,000 -- the total genuine capital of the bank -- the $600, and received his bank's bills in exchange.

Mr. Loomis said that one evening in the winter of 1838 he and a man by the name of Moulton were invited to the home of one of the officers of the Singapore bank to witness the destruction of the bills on hand at the bank at the time of its suspension. When they arrived they found a table about three and a half by four feet in size covered with bills in packages, lying in piles from three to six inches deep. These they were requested to burn in a stove. This was the closing chapter of the famous Singapore Bank.

We are indebted to Mrs. Flora Loomis Goodrich, eldest daughter of Levi Loomis, for the foregoing story. Aside from the amusing incident, it furnished the only account of the date of suspension of the Singapore bank we have been able to secure.

Capt. A. A. Johnson who was at one time foreman at the Singapore mill, told the writer that the brick with which the vault of the bank was built were shipped around the lakes from Massachusetts at considerable expense. They were costly brick, and my impression is that they were glazed, but it might have been they were pressed. My memory fails me there.

9
Singapore Concluded

The banking laws in the time of the wild cat banks provided that each bank should have constantly on hand a required amount of specie reserve, and I well remember hearing my parents, in conversation with other old settlers tell how it was arranged among a chain of banks along the Kalamazoo that a reserve fund should be held at a bank up the river where the state examiner would call first in his round of inspection. As soon as the reserve was counted at that bank the specie was sent on to the next bank in the chain by special messenger. So when he arrived at the place the

reserve was sure to be on hand ready for counting and so on the length of the chain. Each bank using the same specie reserve. I asked Mr. J. P. Wade if he ever heard of it and he said he had, and recited an incident I had heard earlier but I will repeat his narration.

"On one occasion an Indian was taking the sack from Allegan to Singapore in a canoe and when between the present site of New Richmond and Singapore the canoe was capsized and as a result said specie reserve went to the bottom of the Kalamazoo.

"The examiner was detained at the place where New Richmond now is and feasted and treated until men could go with the Indian and fish out the bag, so that when the examiner finally arrived at Singapore the bank there had the required amount of specie reserve."

The late V. R. Wadsworth in his letters entitled, "The Days of 1836," printed years ago said: "One time when said specie basis, a little ahead of the bank inspector, was coming down the river in a canoe just above Saugatuck, the canoe got wrong side up, and James Harris, the village blacksmith was called upon to make a sort of drag hook to fish up the said specie basis, while the indulgent inspector was grandly entertained at some not far distant place."

* * *

An important epoch in the life of the earlier settlers here was the "hard winter" of 1842 and '43, at the beginning of which happened the wreck of the three masted schooner **Milwaukee**. This story has been printed here some time ago but to make these letters more complete we beg to repeat. In speaking of this occurrence, Mr. Wade said: "Late in the fall of 1842 the schooner **Milwaukee** lay anchored off the mouth of the Kalamazoo taking on flour which had been floated down from the inland sections. A terrible storm came up from the NorthWest and she was wrecked. Both whites and Indians hearing of the wreck, secured ample supplies of flour for present use. As the flour was in barrels it was not damaged by water. That flour was the means of saving much distress and hunger during the following hard winter and probably prevented starvation among the Indians.

The late Capt. Charles Link said: "I remember well the storm that blew the schooner **Milwaukee** ashore at Singapore on November 26, 1842, loaded with high wines and flour. The captain wanted to make sail and get out to sea when the storm came on but the crew mutinied and would not move the ship. The Indians indulged too freely in the high wines and some died as a result.

Mr. Wadsworth said (we omit what others have said): "Wm. G. Butler, after the wreck of the **Milwaukee** came round and told the people that he wanted men and teams to get the flour off that wreck. They were thus well supplied with flour to last thru this very long winter." And again he said, "This was certainly the most horrid winter I ever saw or heard of."

I quote in part from a talk with A. H. Stillson. "In January a little thaw came and I went with Uncle Harrison Hutchins 4 1/2 miles East of where Fennville is then to Richmond where we crossed the river and to the mouth, where we got two ox team loads of flour. I think he paid 75 cents a barrel, then the hard winter closed right in and there was no chance to get anywhere. Not a track to Allegan and no road anywhere until late in April, then the snow all went off in about two weeks. I remember well the first Monday in April 1843 at the close of the hard winter, the voters went to the Singapore school house to town meeting on snow shoes over snow four feet deep."

Mr. Wadsworth said, "The men came to town meeting on snow shoes. Stephen D. Nichols -- the light house keeper, S. A. Morrison, William G. Butler, James C. Haile, Harrison Hutchins, John Billings and James Wadsworth comprised the voters present in the town known by the name of Newark, consisting of 8 township of land to wit: Casco, Ganges, Saugatuck and Laketown and the four adjoining townships on the East."

The hard winter and "the cold new years" were two dates from which old timers have recalled events. I remember the cold new years but do not know the date, tho it were not far from 1860.

* * *

My understanding is that but one boat of a seaworthy size was ever built at Singapore. And Mr. Wade said of it, "The schooner **Octavia** was built by Carter & Stockbridge in about 1848 at Singapore, and was first commanded by Capt. A A. Johnson."

Mr. A. H. Stillson said, "The schooner **Octavia** was built at Singapore by F. B. Stockbridge, most of her ship's carpenters were brought from Maine. Joe St. Germain and his brother Jim worked on her. I hauled lots of her timbers. She was built in the winter of 1848 and '49, The old gal and I danced on her deck before and after she was launched and were aboard her when she went in."

Capt. C. M. Link said a Mr. Short of Maine got the schooner started on the ways at Singapore and she was finished by Joe St. Germain.

At this late date I do not know why the **Octavia** stood so prominently in the minds of the old settlers, but she seems to have formed an epoch in the early history here, and no doubt was a very fine ship, and the first one of her class built on the Kalamazoo, tho Saugatuck has turned out a good many since, but none stand out like the **Octavia**.

* * *

An amusing incident back in the early days of Singapore, tho not of a historical nature, is somewhat interesting. A lumber dealer came from Chicago to buy supplies for his trade, and one of the mill hands at the boarding house took occasions to impose upon him at times. This went on for a time until finally another burley young fellow, known as Hank Elliot asked the dealer why he didn't trash the tough. The dealer said he had wanted to do so but didn't think himself man enough to accomplish it. Hank said he had been tempted to do it himself but it was none of his business so he did not interfere. After some talk it was arranged that the next time the fellow should carry his amusement beyond the point of common decency Hank would take it up for the dealer and thrash the mill hand, and next time he went to Chicago he would bring Hank a gallon of whiskey. Shortly afterwards the mill hand renewed his antics and Hank suggested that he had carried that kind of treatment of a good customer far enough. This brought on words until the two went out doors to settle it. It was a very even match and for some time it was a question which would prove the better man but finally Hank got in a knockout blow and sent the fellow sprawling to the ground, and made him agree to let the Chicago gentleman alone thereafter. True to his word that gentleman brought the whiskey, and managed to turn it over to Hank secretly. After a while Hank was wanted and could not be found. A messenger was sent to find him. Finally he and the fellow he had whipped were discovered off behind a slab pile, both dead drunk, with the jug of whiskey between them.

* * *

In our earlier letters we have been considering the old pioneer Singapore from 1835 to about 1855. The last mill operated there by O. R. Johnson and Co. was capable of sawing 65,000 to 75,000 feet of logs per day. That was the mill that was removed to St. Ignace in 1875, at which time the old town became a thing of the past.

Since last writing a few corrections have been brought out by referring to men who have known all about the place for the past 60 to 70 years and we learn that the Nichols store was in operation at the mouth for about two years, then Mr. Nichols built in Saugatuck and moved his goods there, and a Mr. A. B. Titus ran a boarding house in the building for a number of years.

The first lighthouse only stood a short time when it was undermined by the changing channel in high water and toppled over into the river and a new one was built farther north.

At a meeting of men from the mouth and from Pine Creek money was subscribed for the construction of the first dock at the mouth known as the Nichols dock.

Our informants had never heard of Mr. Butler owning dock property at the mouth.

There was no harbor at the mouth of the Kalamazoo until 1870, except the lighthouse. In the *Commercial* of Aug. 7, 1869, we read, "The stone scows have made their appearance at the mouth of the river, and but a short time will elapse before the harbor work will be well under headway. The contract for furnishing the stone was let to a man in South Haven and the other branches of the work to practice in Chicago."

I well remember going to the mouth on the river boat **Aunt Betsey** in the late 60s, and there were no harbor works there at that time.

10
Reminiscences of J. P. Wade

In the telling of the early days in Western Allegan County Mr. J. P. Wade said:

"In the early years of the white man's life in Western Allegan County there were no regular roads overland, so mail was received but once in two weeks, and at irregular intervals. Sometimes it was taken down the river from Allegan by Indians in a canoe, and at other times it would come down on a lumber raft. Also a man named Fairchild made special trips from Allegan on foot or horseback. The postage was 25 cents per letter paid by the receiver, and each extra sheet in the letter was subject to extra postage. To avoid this extra postage a sheet of foolscap paper was used as wrapper. (There being no envelopes as yet.) The extra was written on this, using skim milk in place of ink, this would not been seen until heated by the fire, when it would come out and be readable."

Saugatuck did not have daily mail before 1870, for in *The Commercial* of July 2 of that year we read, "Congressman Stoughton writes to Postmaster Ellis that the department has not put mail service on the railroad to Holland, but as soon as this is done they will take measures to give us a daily mail. With a daily mail to Holland and return Saugatuck will have no great need to growl about need of more facilities of communication. As we have now a better chance than most of our sister lake shore towns, and almost every week we have to tell of some new route opened up, or old ones changed and improved."

J. P. Wade drove some fire insurance men up the lake beach to St. Joseph in 1846, and had to cross the rivers on the bar. There was no human habitation at the mouth of Black River where South Haven now is. Not a white man's hut nor an Indian wigwam. As the water at St. Joe was too deep to ford they left their team with the only man at Benton Harbor, a farmer who took care of the horses and set the men across the river in a canoe.

"In 1852 Mrs. Wade drove through the woods from Singapore to Kalamazoo with a six months babe in her arms. The only house between Singapore and Allegan on the road she traveled was the Old Pine Plains Tavern, located 4 1/2 miles East of where Fennville is. She saw deer, squirrels and other wild animals." (On an interview on May 17, 1908.)

Towns and trading centers do not precede the settlement of a country but are a result of such settlement and so it was that the country along the lake shore at the times of Mr. Wade's drive up the beach with the insurance men was dotted in here and there with pioneer settlers though no towns were as yet established. A mill, a store, or a shipping point makes room for clerks and helpers, and thus a nucleus is formed around which the town grows. So it was that during the thirty years from 1830 to 1860 the Western part of Allegan County found settlers dotting in as time went on, and as they became sufficient in numbers to warrant, or we might say demand, community centers for the transaction of business, trade and transportation, so it was not until about the fifties that either Holland or South Haven were established as trading centers.

Dr. Van Raalte came to the Holland section in 1847 and established the colony, and for years it was known simply as "the colony," though it did not become a commercial center until some years after the first settlement, and as we have seen above, not a blow had been struck at South Haven in 1850.

11
Wallinville

Wallinville is a place that exists as much in the past as does Singapore.

Mr. Benjamin Plummer built a raft at Pine Creek, on which he placed his family and floated down the Kalamazoo to its mouth in 1834, and his son Fred N. Plummer gave the following history in an interview May 17, 1908.

"My father built a sawmill on the outlet to Goshorn lake in 1836. It was a water mill and he run it about ten years. It was torn down later. About 1848 Wells and Bartlett built a tannery just below the sawmill. They run the tannery about ten years when they sold it to Frank B. Wallin. He operated it until about 1875 and it was then abandoned on account of the tan bark playing out.

"Mr. Geo. P. Heath built a grist mill there about 1880 but this only run about two or three years, and proved to be the last effort at milling at what became known as Wallinville.

"Miss Mary Elizabeth Peckham taught the first school in Saugatuck township in a room in our house just west of the Plummer mill, on a farm owned by my father in about 1836. I think she taught three months and she boarded at our house at the time. The house was built on the old style barn frame plan, with big timbers, and is now used as a barn.

"The Singapore schoolhouse was built about 1838 two or three years after she began at our place, after which she taught there several terms. I think until she got married."

Mr. Plummer said he remember well how S. A. Morrison and his brother were rivals for the hand of Miss Peckham but Mr. S. A. won out.

With the closing down of the Heath grist mill, about 1883 the burg known to this day as Wallinville became a thing of the past.

Goshorn lake, located on the townline between Saugatuck and Laketown. On section three of Saugatuck and 34 of Laketown and is about two miles north and east of Saugatuck, has for its outlet small creek which leaves the southern point of the lake, runs due south for three fourths of a mile and thence takes a south westerly course and empties into the Kalamazoo river just below Saugatuck. Wallinville was located on this creek about half a mile below the lake and it was the water from this creek that furnished the power to operate the machinery.

Saugatuck, having a better harbor and dockage facilities and being more accessible to the surrounding country survives the decline and decay of the two competing sister towns of former days.

The Singapore schoolhouse, the first school established in western Allegan County which was built in 1838 stood and still stands at a point about a mile South and East of the site of Singapore village, on the road to Saugatuck, and is still used for school purposes, tho on a road over which there is very little travel at the present time.

Wallinville, sometimes called Dingleville, was located north and east of Saugatuck on the stream that connects Goshorn Lake with the Kalamazoo River. This map is from an 1873 atlas.

By way of a correction I may say, I learn from several persons interested in these letters, that the cold new years was on January first 1864. This day being left in doubt in a former letter. Also by way of answering inquiries it seems best to go back and get the history of the organization of Newark and its subdivisions.

The work of surveying Allegan County was begun in 1825 and was not completed until 1836. It was first laid out in blocks six miles square, and these were numbered, then these blocks were run off into sections of one mile square, so the map stood blank except for the surveyor lines and showed four blacks East and West, each block six miles square, and twenty-four in all and each designated by number. The four blocks, or six mile square along the East line of the county making a strip of land six miles east and west and 24 miles north and south were set off and named Plainfield township in 1836. The next row of four blocks along the adjoining Plainfield on the west was named Otsego. The next two rows of blocks, lying between Allegan township and Lake Michigan was named Newark township. Each of these eight squares that formed the township of Newark in 1836 were later cut off from Newark, and became a separate township by itself as the population increased.

There is no complete record of the township of Newark, since they were lost, but we get from persons who lived here in the earliest days, the history of the first township meeting.

Dr. Thomas says all that is known is that Daniel A. Plummer was its first supervisor. But as seen in our last letter Mr. V. R. Wadsworth (he was at this time a lad of 18 years, and his father attended that meeting, and no doubt he did also) named seven men as the voters present at the town meeting at the Singapore School house on the first Monday in April 1843, tho he does not mention Mr. Plummer nor does he say who was elected to the town offices, however we read in *Portrait and Biographical Record* that: "Daniel A. Plummer came to Saugatuck in 1834 and was the third family to settle at the mouth of the Kalamazoo," so no doubt he was at the meeting and was elected supervisor of Newark.

I have often heard my father speak of the first town meeting at the close of the hard winter. That it was held at the Singapore School House, and how they went (he and others) on snow shoes, over snow four feet deep.

Like Newark, the early records of the township of Saugatuck were destroyed, tho it had a civil history from 1836. It held the name of Newark until 1861 at which time it took the present name.

Manlius was set off from Newark in 1838 and held its first town meeting at the home of Ralph R. Mann on April 1, 1839. John Allen was supervisor.

Ganges was first settled in 1837 when Harrison Hutchins first began on section one, but not set off from Newark until 1847, and at that time embraced the present Casco. Held first town meeting at the home of Orlando Weed, April 5, 1847, 27 voters present. A. H. Haile elected supervisor.

Fillmore was a part of Manlius until 1847. Its first town meeting was held in April of that year, and Isaac Fairbanks was elected supervisor.

Casco was separated from Ganges in 1854 and was organized in 1855, Timothy McDowell elected supervisor.

Lee was a part of Newark until 1841, when it became a part of Manlius. In 1850 it became a part of Pine Plains, and by April 1859 it had been organized into a township and held its first town meeting under the name of Lee, and Thomas Raplee was elected supervisor.

Clyde was first settled in 1837 by Leonard and Jacob Bailey, but was not organized into a township until 1859, and held its first town meeting April 2, 1860.

Laketown was set apart in October 1858, and held its first town meeting on April 4, 1859, and so it was that Newark disappeared from the map when Saugatuck adopted its present name in 1861.

12
Saugatuck Mills

Louis Campau, a Frenchman, had a trading post at the mouth of Rabbit River, east of New Richmond, and the American Fur Company established a trading post at Macks landing in 1825. By the way, Macks landing was a point on the river where Purdy's landing is now, and was so named because James McCormick tied his boat at that place, and that name became a designation in that locality. Mr. McCormick came to the southwest corner of Manlius in 1837, and was the first white settler in the town. Like most of the frontiersmen he was a hunter and trapper and enjoyed a feast on fish. These lines called for a canoe, and his landing on the river was three miles almost due north of his home. The canoe also came in use in going to Singapore for trade.

The traders mentioned above did not become settlers, however, Mr. Butler, mentioned earlier, who came about 1830 remained and entered into commercial lines when other families moved in, and his home was here until several years later when he was killed while loading logs.

In 1833, and while Mr. Butler was the only white man here, he had a village plat surveyed where Saugatuck now stands. This was while Allegan County was yet a township of Kalamazoo County. The city of Kalamazoo, as it is now, was then know as Bronson, in honor of its found, Titus Bronson, and Butler's map of this unnamed village was recorded at Bronson, the county seat on July 17, 1834.

The first business enterprise here aside from the Butler trading post was the tannery before mentioned built in 1834. This tannery was operated by a large dutch windmill. It was bought in 1837 by Mr. S. A. Morrison, who operated it until the tan bark played out, or perhaps until 1880. But right here is where Saugatuck came to a standstill, and it remained for about fifteen years. At one time, it is said, only the family of S. A. Morrison, and a few Indians lived here. During this time Singapore started, in 1835, and with its sawmills and store, and bank while it lasted, held supreme, with the exception of such activities as were carried on at Plummers mill, the S. D. Nichols dock and store at the mouth were in operation just a short time and were over a mile below Singapore, so are not here included when treating the place.

In 1846 Mr. M. B. Spencer built a steam sawmill in what is now Saugatuck, and from this date the place began to show signs of life. Wells and Johnson succeeded Mr. Spencer in 1850, and another sawmill was built by Dunning and Hopkins in 1852. We will let two of the boys of the early forties name the succession of mills as they came in.

Darius and Charley Billings, born and raised here and both veterans of the civil war, agreed to what follows, in a talk on Oct. 17, 1917.

"Next after the Spencer mill and built in the fifties [they overlooked the Dunning mill of '52] came the J. B. Judson sawmill which stood about 20 rods below the ferry. This mill burned later. H. D. Moore's sawmill, about 100 rods north of the ferry. Ebmeyer and Smiths shingle mill, north of the pavilion, Blanchard's Shingle mill, above the ferry, built about 1860 on the west side of the river. This mill was bought in the late sixties by Bird and Smith. Lew Shed and Ed Densmore Shingle mill, on the site of the Judson mill, this mill burned later also.

"George Heath built a grist mill about 1865. It run 12 or 13 years and burned. Porter and Co. built a grist mill where Hotel Butler now stands, the hotel being the mill built over. It was financed by subscription in the early nineties, run six or seven years and the machinery was taken to Allegan."

In about 1856 J. D. Billings scored the timbers and A. H. Stillson hewed them for the old Saugatuck house built by Mr. A. O. Smith in that year. Mr. Smith was drowned at the Richmond bridge while it was in the course of construction in 1856. It was said a case where whiskey and water were rivals and water came out victorious.

* * *

The starting of the first ferry at Saugatuck was told as follows:

"The bridge that had been used to cross the river at Saugatuck stood right about where the ferry is now, and was abandoned because the schooners, in passing thru the draw would bump against it and knock the spiles loose, so in 1857 the ferry was built and established. Darius Billings wanted the job of running the ferry but was only 19 years old, and not responsible on a contract on account of being under age, so his father bid in the job from the town at $300 and turned it over to Darius and he came to be the first ferryman on the job. He operated the ferry during the season of 1857."

* * *

The following taken from *The Commercial*, will show something of the growth of the town during the last 25 years after Mr. Spencer built the first sawmill here.

"Feb. 27, 1869. The building of the bridge was let to Ed. Densmore, he having made the lowest bid, which was $5,500.

"Aug. 7, 1869. Geo. E. Dunn has moved his Sash, Door and Blind factory into a portion of Mr. Henry's tannery at the head of Lake Street, near the new bridge."

"Sept. 11, 1869. The bridge will soon be completed."

"The work on our harbor does not progress very rapidly."

"The vessel being built by Mr. Elliot will have 118 feet keel, 26 beam, and the capacity for carrying 180,000 feet of lumber."

"At O. R. Johnson & Co.'s mill one day last week 56,000 feet of lumber was sawed. This is the largest amount of lumber that has been cut in the same length of time at any one mill in Saugatuck or Douglas."

"Oct. 9, 1869. There are in Saugatuck five shingle mills, two sawmills, one grist mill, one sash, door and blind factory, and planing mill. There are seven general stores, besides one drug store, two jewelry stores, one news room and book store and two millinery stores."

"The village affords two hotels, the Sherwood house kept by Geo. Sherwood and the Saugatuck house kept by Whitney and Strong."

"There are four doctors. Lawyers do not seem to flourish here: two daguerrean rooms, one music school, two billiard saloons and restaurants, two insurance offices, one tailor shop, two bakeries, three butcher shops, three paint shops, two wagon shops, two fisheries, one brewery, one livery stable, one brick yard."

A sketch of Saugatuck about 1910, the ferry is just crossing the river in the left hand corner.

"Nov. 20, 1869. The completion of the new bridge brings more teams to town every day."

Let us say here that credit should be given the late Mr. Thomas Gray Sr., for the shade trees along the bridge. As all the old timers will remember the bridge was first built by piling slabs and edgings from the mills and covering them with sawdust. When completed, and the bridge was open for traffic, Mr. Gray, who was in business in Douglas at the time, became a self-appointed agent to set in some very small willow slips along the edges of the fill. There was no soil in which to plant them, just the slabs and edgings, but he wedged them in some way and to the wonder of many, they grew, and if those who jollied that wise gentleman about his experiment are still living they have an example of his foresight in the refreshing shade those trees now provide on a hot summer day.

* * *

Saugatuck was nearing the peak of her business advancement at the time of the following. From the *Commercial*, June 10, 1871:

"During the month ending May 15, there was shipped from this port 4,135,000 feet of lumber, 3,135,000 shingles, 993 cords of wood, 9,600 railroad ties, 40,000 pickets, 48,000 lath, 86 cords bark, 25,000 pounds hair, 50 barrels flour, 121 pkgs. fish, 66,000 lbs. leather."

And again: "Among the shipments from this port for the month ending Oct. 15 were: Lumber 3,232,000 feet; shingles, 2,207,000; lath, 252,000; wood, 2,169 cords [This would mean four foot sticks, or what was known as cordwood or 6500 cords of stove wood.]; Ties, 5000; staves, 20,000; leather, 62,559 lbs; fruit, 5206 pkgs; fish, 27 pkgs." (*Commercial* 11-4, 1871)

Figures are dull at best, however, these are given to show that up to this date the traffic of the community was largely from the timber in one form or another. In following letters we aim to show the line, by dates, where the forests became exhausted, and agriculture and fruit took its place in the activities of the inhabitants.

13
Shipping

On one day in June, 1870, there were counted nineteen vessels loading in Saugatuck harbor, and several more loaded and waiting a fair wind, and the following figures given out by Samuel Johnson, deputy collector of customs, show that the exports for that year exceed those of any port on this shore except Grand Haven.

"In 1870 672 vessels entered and 670 cleared. The principal articles of shipment were 30,000,000 feet of lumber, 31,000,000 shingles,

2,000,000 lath and pickets, 1,500,000 pounds of leather, and 8,050 bushels of potatoes." No mention is made in the above of the quantities of cord wood and ties, staves and heading, etc. that were going in a constant stream out from the Kalamazoo. Some of the enterprises furnishing this freight are reported as follows:

"The O. R. Johnson & Co. sawmill at Singapore capacity 60,000 feet per day, and another in Saugatuck, turns off 50,000 feet of lumber. 10,000 lath and 25,000 shingles per day. The two together manufacture 22,000,000 feet of lumber, 1,000,000 shingles, and 2,000,000 lath per year.

"Johnson & Co. kept three schooners plying between Saugatuck and Chicago and Ebmeyers shingle mill turns out 8,000,000, H. D. Moore's sawmill 6,000,000 feet of lumber, Densmore Barber & Co.'s stave mill 4,000,000 staves and heading. At Douglas T. Gray & Co.'s mill manufactures about 6,000,000 feet of lumber and 6,000,000 shingles per annum; H. B. Moore's mill has a capacity of 5,000,000 feet of lumber and 6,000,000 shingles per year."

The Gray & Co. mill of 1870 was formerly the Dutcher mill, and the H. B. Moore mill had previously been owned by Mr. Gerber.

It may be noticed that previous to 1860 the place was called Newark, but now in 1883 it is Saugatuck.

We feel quite safe in saying that 1870 was the turning point in quantity shipped from the port of Saugatuck. The Lake Shore and Michigan Southern railroad came into Allegan at about this time, and traffic was begun on the Michigan and Ohio (now Michigan Central) railroad in November, 1883. Previous to this the river had furnished the only outlet for freight this side of Kalamazoo, and daily boats had been in operation between Allegan and Saugatuck.

The following account of a shipwreck, while of interest in itself, will bear out the above statements. We quote from *The Allegan Journal*, dated December 27, 1858:

"Loss of the Schooner **Globe** -- After our paper had gone to press last week we received from F. B. Wallin Esq. of Newark the particulars of the loss of the schooner **Globe**. It appears that this vessel left the mouth of the Kalamazoo River Saturday night, Dec. 14, with the captain and owner, Nelson Olsen and his brother of Newark; one seaman; a single man and a married man with wife and two children, as passengers aboard. She had as freight lumber and lath belonging to Mr. Parish of Silver Creek and about $800 worth of leather from the tannery of C. C. Wallin & Sons. S. A. Morrison also had placed $100 in the captain's care for some person in Chicago. As soon as fears were entertained for the schooner's safety Mr. Wallin started a search along the beach for the wreck, and after he had proceeded a short distance he found fragments of the vessel which had washed ashore. It is though the vessel must have been unseaworthy, though the captain supposed she was strong and tight. All the circumstances seem to indicate that she split during Saturday night or Sunday morning, as the wreck was on the beach Monday morning."

The conversion of natural resources of western Allegan county into commercial properties was about completed by 1880. First the cordwood played out, then the tan bark, and last the good lumber, though there was some timber cutting going on for some time after, where people picked out culled logs and brought them in to make a poor grade of lumber. There is a small sawmill in Fennville still in 1920 where odd trees and second growth logs are cut up, but does not begin to satisfy the local demand.

I worked at lumbering with my father 1880 or '81 by which time there were no more tracts worth a contract. In all our jobbing we took nothing that would cut less than two-thirds good lumber, and it was generally understood that a poorer grade was not worth the expense of cutting, hauling and milling. What was left in the first cut became more valuable as soon as the supply of good timber was gone and we had to ship timber back from the north. It was this low grade stuff that kept a few mills in operation later than 1880. Very little if any of this was shipped away, however.

The lumber men came in, stripped the country of desirable timber, and moved on to fresh fields. The tanners used all the bark they could, and shipped the rest away as fast as they could and they, too, moved on, each and all of the large operators, and they all took their money away with them.

Aside from giving temporary employment to a large number of men, and furnishing a market for the material taken off by the settlers in clearing their land, they were a damage to the country. They bought large tracts of timber land for very low prices, stripped the timber and bark off and sold the land for what they could get and often they got as much for the land as they paid for timber and all, and had the rake-off as clear gain. They left no gift or improvement to the community, built no buildings and constructed no roads as a gift in appreciation of what they had received. They simply came in grabbed all they could lay their hands on and took it away. True, they were within their rights, but it seems to some of us that the conditions were radically wrong that will permit men with money to go in and rob the community of all natural resources, and leave no compensation.

But we digress. The Chicago and Michigan Lake Shore railroad ran its first train through New Richmond and Fenn's Mills (now Fennville) in April, 1871, and this headed off the most of the up river freights. Also Holland on the north and South Haven and the piers to the south were taking freight, all of which lessened the shipping from the port of Saugatuck.

As timber products grew less in quantity, farm products, and especially fruit, increased at a rapid rate, which held the freight shipments to some extent though probably not as great in volume. This however, will be considered in a later letter.

14
Douglas

Jonathan Wade settled on the south side of Kalamazoo lake, where Douglas now stands, at an early date, and his brother Nelson came soon after. They were the only white settlers there for some time. Frank W. Wade, son of Nelson, was the first white child born there -- January, 1853.

In 1851 Jonathan Wade laid out a village plat on that portion of the town south of the main street (or Center street, as it is called) on section 16, and called it Dudleyville. William F. Dutcher platted that portion of the town north of Center street, and called it Dutcherville. These names held until about 1870, by which time the inhabitants had increased in number until they decided to incorporate the village and the very important subject of a name satisfactory to both sides of the street arose. Col. Frederic H. May, son-in-law of Mr. Dutcher, suggested Douglas, and this proved satisfactory. When the board of supervisors incorporated the village October 14, 1870, the name was legalized, and Douglas held its first village election on December 5 of that year.

About 1851 Jonathan Wade built a saw mill just south of what is now the west end of the bridge. This mill was later acquired by William F. Dutcher, Thomas Gray and Jonas S. Crouse later controlled the property. During the early seventies it was turned into the manufacture of fruit packages and is now known as the Weed & Co. basket factory. For perhaps twenty years it has been the only important manufacturing plant near the mouth of the Kalamazoo.

About 1861 another saw mill was built by a man named Conger on the river bank a little to the south of the east end of Center street, owned by Horace B. (Harry) Moore later on.

At its best the Wade mill is quoted as having a lumber capacity of 6,000,000 feet and 6,000,000 shingles and the Moore mill 5,000,000 feet of lumber and 6,000,000 shingles. This property also changed owners before being dismantled.

Daniel Gerber built a tannery on the creek at the southeast portion of the village in the early sixties and operated it for several years until it was sold to Wallin & Sons. This, like tanneries in Saugatuck, Wallinville and Plummerville, closed down when the local supply of hemlock bark became exhausted about 1880.

In 1868 Crawford McDonald built a grist mill at the east end of Center street. This mill was 26 x 36 feet in size and two and a half stories high, with an engine room 20 x 20 feet, two run of stone, and a capacity of 250 bushels of wheat per day. This mill was later owned by J. S. Payne & Co. T. B. Dutcher also owned it, and it was under his ownership when it burned in the late nineties and was never rebuilt.

Robert M. Moore was active in the lumber business here for a number of years and until the saw timber played out.

Douglas was at the peak of its development at the end of twenty years, for we read, June 10, 1871: "In Douglas there are two stores, two saw mills, two shingle mills, one grist mill, one tannery, one planing mill, two carpenter shops, three shoe shops, three blacksmith shops, one wagon shop, one paint shop, two meat markets, three millinery and dressmaking shops, one church, one school, and one hotel. The census of 1880 gives Douglas a population of 522. The M. E. Church was built in 1870. The post office was established in 1868 with Dyer C. Putnam as postmaster.

* * *

Plummerville

Benjamin Plummer moved from Newark (now Saugatuck) to section 8, Ganges in 1846 and built a saw mill on the creek there, near the lake. W. H. Plummer thinks Orlando Weed had an interest in it, but sold out to Plummer in a year or two. He also says: "The mill was in operation until 1862 or '63."

O. R. Johnson Co. built a tannery right away after the saw mill was built. No doubt the two joined forces in constructing the dam.

The pier was built by a stock company of which Mr. Plummer was a member, in about 1854. F. B. Wallin succeeded O. R. Johnson in the tannery, and Mr. Perrottet succeeded Wallin. Theodore Perrottet, his son, now of Chicago, is interested in these letters and has been kind enough to give us an account of his father's work here, which we quote as follows:

"In the early part of 1857 A. H. Perrottet purchased the Plummerville tannery from S. A. Morrison of Saugatuck, and it was in the spring of the same year he put his furniture aboard the small schooner **Falcon**, of which he was part owner, and with wife and young son, they sailed from Chicago, bound for Plummerville Pier. It was a week before they were able to land owing to storm. They were obliged to turn back three times, each time making St. Joe harbor for shelter. The tannery at time of purchase was a small water power plant. In a short time Mr. Perrottet installed a boiler and engine. At this time about ten men were employed and the output was about 25 hides a day. This for shoes and harness. Hides were purchased from farmers around the country and some were shipped in from Chicago and delivered at the pier, now known as Perrottet's Pier. Leather in summer was shipped by boat from the pier, and in winter was hauled by farmers to Kalamazoo, at that time being the nearest railroad. The first stop was Allegan, and then on to Kalamazoo. During the winter farmers brought hundreds of cords of wood and piled it up on what was known as pier ground. The boats were loaded with this during the summer and carried it to Chicago.

"In March 1860, the tannery burned to the ground. Mr. Perrottet rebuilt it at once and increased its capacity to 100 hides a day, and at this time being tanned for sole leather. Thirty-five men were employed, but skilled labor was hard to find in Ganges township, so Mr. Perrottet brought from Canada the following families: Lackie, Elliott, Purcey and Drought, names still familiar in Allegan county. The tannery at this time was using from 3,500 to 4,000 cords of hemlock bark a year. The cost of the bark was $3.50 to $5 per cord. (At the time of writing it is $18 a cord and hard to get.) Bark was brought in from Casco and delivered at the tannery during the winter, as many as 30 and 40 teams a day hauling bark. This work was given to farmers.

"During the summer bark was towed to the pier on scows by tugs from Saugatuck or Mack's Landing and was purchased by Mr. Purdy. In the early seventies F. B. Wallin bought an interest in the tannery. In 1876 the enterprise was given up, owing to the shortage of bark and the plant not being large enough to compete with larger tanneries.

"Farmers were paid about $4 a day for hauling the bark."

Capt. Charles Link said of the place: "The pier at Plummerville was built in 1854 by Taylor & Co. Teams could not drive out on this pier as at Pier Cove so the load was driven onto the foot of the pier and run to the outer end by hand. The schooners **Jane, Louisa, Arabella** and **A. P. Dalton** were among the first to take cargoes here.

"An amusing incident happened in the early days as follows: Dr. Goodrich, while hunting, heard some thing coming down the runway. Supposing it to be a deer he shot at it, but when he went for the game found he had killed Mr. Plummer's old ram. This caused considerable amusement in the community. The doctor fixed it up with Mr. Plummer right away as he was the last man to harm anybody."

We are in receipt of an interesting letter from A. D. Goodrich, now of Holland, but who was born and raised here, from which we quote in part:

"One thing I have in mind at Plummerville was the pier, that was kept up for so many years. I think it first was built for the cordwood business.

"Between Saugatuck and South Haven at one time there were five cordwood shipping piers,

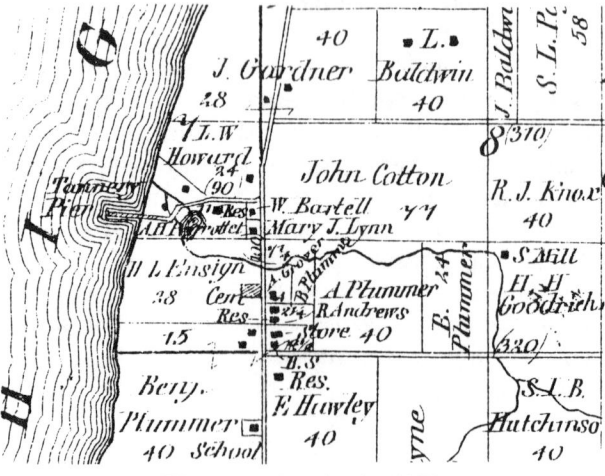

Plummerville pier in 1873.

known as Pier Cove, Plummerville, Webster's, Packard's (now Glenn) and McDowell's piers, and there was a regular traffic in this commodity between them and Chicago, as the farmers were clearing up their land and cut most all good beech and maple into cordwood and all cut with an ax.

"But about the Plummerville pier. At one time it was rebuilt by Mr. Perrottet, and he received hides and shipped leather over it to Chicago via the steamer **Ira Chaffee**, that plied between Saugatuck and Chicago and would call at the pier on her trips.

"Another incident comes into my mind in connection with the cordwood days. The schooners that loaded at the piers would drop anchor out in deep water, and by a long line haul themselves in to the side of the pier, paying out their anchor chain, which when the boat was loaded, would be used to haul the boat out by means of the windlass on the boat. They would then set their sails, lift anchor, and away they would go. The vessels could not lay at the pier if the wind or a storm came up that made a rough sea, but they would have to watch the weather, and if they saw a storm coming pull out and put to sea and wait until the sea subsided again.

"At one time, I think it was the **Josephine Dresden** loading at Plummerville, a storm came up and for some reason they failed to get out, so she pounded a hole her length through the pier and went onto the beach. The cordwood that was already loaded was thrown out and the boat pulled off again.

"Other boats I remember as trading there were the scow **Three Bells**, scow **Frederick** and scow **Trio**. The **Trio** was built at Pier Cove by Link and the Tourtellottes of Glenn.

"The Plummer saw mill stood just below the dam on the north bank of the creek, just across from the Perrottet tannery. Was operated by water power, and consisted of the old fashioned sash-saw that 'went up today and came down tomorrow.' I never saw this mill in operation, but it stood there with some of its machinery in place at my earliest memory.

"There was another tannery there in the early days, known as the Peckham tannery, It was before my day, but the vacant building stood there. It was located on the main north and south road on the east side, and south side of the creek, jut below the south hill."

The writer referred to W. H. Plummer about this tannery, and he said it was built later than the Johnson tannery, did not do an extensive business, and was in operation but a short time. The building was later moved south about two miles and is now used as a barn on the Harvey James farm.

The Plummerville store stood and still stands on the east side of the lake shore road, on top of the south hill and opposite the cemetery.

Barnard Bidwell established a brickyard here in about 1858. It was located on the north side of Plummerville creek and on the west side of the lake shore road. The dry sheds were on the east side of the road, opposite the yard. He ran it until about 1865. At this time he was marching in a political parade and dropped dead. The brickyard was never operated again.

There was a store established by John Taylor on the southwest corner of the road about 1851 or 1852, and Amos C. Haile clerked for him, and may have bought the store later. Mr. Haile died soon after and the store was closed.

The above is from a talk with J. T. Henderson, and later Charlie Haile, son of A. C., corroborated the statement.

A. D. Goodrich said of the burg: "There were a half a dozen houses stood around the Perrottet tannery grounds where employees lived, and single men boarded at what was called "Plummerville Proper" with Uncle Ben Plummer and Rufus Andrews, the little man. The store was operated by various persons. Uncle Ben, I think at one time, and later by John S. Payne, Caleb Ensign and others."

With the closing of the tannery in 1876 all commercial enterprise ceased. The pier was soon washed away by the sea and winter ice jams, and the buildings were either torn down or moved away and some years before the close of the 19th century this bustling little center, created for the disposal or use of bark and cordwood gradually shrank away with the disappearance of the causes of its first existence, and we are reminded of little Paul Domby when he said, "Floy, what are the wild waves saying?"

15
Pier Cove

Harrison Hutchins became the first settler in Ganges township when he moved into his cabin on section 1 in December, 1838. Others followed by ones, twos and threes in a season, so that within about ten years there was need for shipping facilities, and the only way, out or in, for freight was over the sand road down the lakeshore to Saugatuck and the river.

Coal did not come into general use for heat and power until about the 80's, so Chicago and the west furnished a demand for wood, and the settlers on the shore of Lake Michigan had wood to burn while clearing their land -- so if transportation could be provided they could realize a profit from

A plat of Pier Cove published in 1873.

their hardwood timber by cutting it into cordwood. Marcius Sutherland came here and noticed the conditions, interested himself to the extent of financing the construction of a pier at the mouth of a creek which emptied into Lake Michigan at the west end of the quarter line of section 5, Ganges Township, and the project was completed and put in operation in 1849.

Lake Michigan forms a long curve inland here, and when the pier was built the place took on the name of Pier Cove.

This pier was so planned that teams could drive to the outer end, unload, and turn around for the shore trip, and the cordwood and tanbark business flourished from that time on. This was the first of five piers built between Saugatuck and South Haven, and the task was not an easy one, as it was all done by man power. Power pile drivers were not in use here at that time, according to statements of the early settlers.

In the early fifties Sidney Squires owned and operated a water power saw mill at Battle Creek, and sold it to a Mr. Cranson. About 1852 it was moved to Pier Cove, but steam power was applied. Mr. Squires came with the mill to set it up and put it in operation.

In arriving at the correct date, one of Mr. Squires' daughters told it as follows: "Father moved the mill here previous to the family coming. I remember mother telling of being left alone there while father was here putting up the mill. The family came in 1854. They moved into the woods, and father had to go to Allegan to get wheat ground, Mother was afraid to stay alone nights while he was gone as the wolves were howling around the house, so she carried rails into the house to prop the doors shut."

Benton Thompson said the saw mill was running when they came here in 1853, when he was a lad of 12 years.

Capt. Charles M. Link said of the burg: "The wood turning and furniture factory was built in 1853 by Charley Richards; then Mr. Nichols bought it out and put in the grist mill. This changed hands several times, Mr. Ederedge being the last owner. He operated the flour and feed mill until the dam washed out about 1880, and the mill was never started again."

In a letter to the *Fennville Herald*, January 1, 1910, Capt. Andrew Reid said: "In the year 1848, as given by one of our early settlers, Charles Richards came to Pier Cove, set up a building and started a wood turning shop. After running the shop a few years he sold out to Mr. Nichols, who put in a millstone and converted the shop into a grist mill about 1860."

H. H. Goodrich and William Sheffer had a fanning mill shop on the flat back of the saw mill between 1855 and 1860. This was not in the turning shop, as some say. About 1855 the turning shop was in the basement of the building. Possibly in 1850 the stone was put in the upper floor for making flour.

Mr. Goodrich and his sister attended school at Pier Cove in 1852. At the time his people lived on the farm on section 2, Ganges, one half mile south of where schoolhouse No. 1 now stands.

The above statements conflict only at to dates. I do not know who Mr. Reid's informant was, but it is safe to say the dam and turning shop were installed at some date between 1848 and 1853. Mr. Link said the turning shop was the first mill built here, and we have found that the saw mill was in operation by 1853.

Mr. Link said: "About 1853 Mr. Squires and another man built the saw mill at Pier Cove. It was an upright saw, being before the time of the circular saw. Later it was sold to Raymond & Abbott. They operated it for some time. It was a steam mill, and was moved to Fennville during the late sixties.

"The first post office established in the vicinity was at Pier Cove in 1854. Sam Thompson was the first postmaster. It was kept here until 1882, when Martin Pratt moved it to the present site at Ganges. In the early sixties there were four stores, a post office, one saloon, a hotel, a saw mill, repair shop and grist mill at Pier Cove.

"Two schooners have been loaded with cordwood alone in one day at the pier, besides lumber, shingles, and tanbark that went over it."

I learned from Stephen Atwater and John P. Wade that the Pier Cove steam saw mill was moved to Fennville by Fenn & Loomis in 1869 or 1870, and C. G. Abbott said his father, who owned the mill at Pier Cove, moved to Fennville in 1869. At the time the mill was moved Mr. Atwater operated a general store there, and Mr. Wade was bookkeeper for the mill company.

The traffic that passed over the pier can hardly be realized at the present time. The lumber cut at the Hoizington mill, two miles north of Fennville, previous to 1862 was drawn to Pier Cove. After Fennville was started in 1862, until 1871, when the railroad was established, the lumber and shingles from there went over this pier, besides the cut of the mill at the Cove. All this lumber and shingles added to the cordwood and tanbark and other local freight, made an immense traffic.

W. A. Woodworth of Saugatuck said in a talk at the Western Allegan County Pioneer Society, Oct. 6, 1917: "When I first came to Pier Cove, in 1864, the burg was noted for its sidewalks of cordwood. All along the streets, where sidewalks should have been were immense piles of this wood. I saw no steamboats at this time, but on one occasion I counted 28 sailing vessels from the pier, and four boats loaded at one time at the pier there."

Darius Billings, now of Akron, Iowa, but who lived here during those times, said at the meeting that the cordwood of 1864 and 1865 was a mere shadow of what it had been previously, when not only the streets and piers were piled high, but the woods were full of it.

16
Pier Cove Continued

The removal of the saw mill in 1879 was the beginning of the end of the old time Pier Cove. The cause of its removal was the saw timber within reach of this mill was gone and no further need for it existed. The cordwood and tanbark also has played out, and the surrounding country had been worked over into agricultural and fruit lines, which was getting a fair start as a branch of industry, but not sufficient as yet to demand the expense of maintaining a pier. And too, the railroad at Fennville having been put in operation in the spring of 1871. Fennville took on business proportions in a commercial and transportation way, which lessened the need of a lake outlet; so there was little to hold Pier Cove as a trading point. One by one the stores closed and were torn down or moved away. The blacksmith and repair shop was discontinued for want of patronage and the hotel ceased to operate. It was in about the early eighties that the church, post office and school were removed to their present locations. The pier had gone out by way of ice and the sea, and all that remained to represent the business of former years was the old red grist mill, which was being operated by the last owner, Joseph Eldridge, and this went out of operation by the washing out of the dam a little later. The picturesque old structure stood for years as a reminder of former activities, with its great water wheel sagging away from its original postiion. The mill foundation finally crumbled away and the whole structure began toppling over into the pond. It was torn down by the present owner of the land, O. C. Symmons of Chicago, about 1916.

Only a few years after the destruction of the pier there was a new cause for an outlet for freight by way of the Cove and the lake. This time it was for the marketing of the fruit from the young orchards in the vicinity. R. M. Moore & Co. of Saugatuck owned and operated a line of steamers between that place and Chicago, and we are told that a new stock company was formed and put out a pier in 1877. My impression is that it was later, or in the eighties. But however that may have been, it was taken over by the R. M. Moore Company, and their boats touched here for cargo.

About 1885 or '86 Rogers & Bird of Saugatuck, running a competing line of boats to Chicago, joined with William Corner and Capt. C. M. Link of Ganges and put out another pier a few

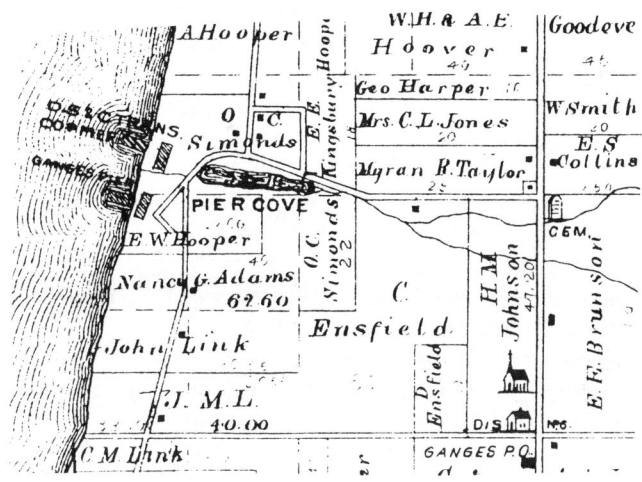

There were two piers at Pier Cove in 1895.

rods south of the creek, and they also took freight here. Each of these companies had two daily boats on the line during the busy season; also at times each had a daily boat to Milwaukee. These piers differed from the earlier sort in that they had commodious warehouses at the shore end of the pier, with steel tracks laid to the outer end, and were equipped with large cars, upon which the fruit was run out to the boat. Also at this time the Wells-Higman Fruit Package Company of St. Joseph had a sales warehouse 100 feet long, 200 feet wide, and two stories high, for the sale of packages. But what a change! No mills, no stores, not a church or school. Only a few families had their homes there, and their activities were not concerned with the traffic.

The freeze of 1899 killed the peach trees of the whole lake shore district, and the other freights were not sufficient to warrant a regular line of boats and maintenance of a first class pier, though there was a moderate amount of traffic in freight and passengers, which was taken care of by a small coasting steamer, the **John A. Aliber**, owned and operated by Capt. W. P. Wilson of Saugatuck, and which transferred to Chicago boats at South Haven. The Rogers & Bird line was dismantled and allowed to go down, while the traffic went over the other until the advent of the auto truck, which was put in operation by the Haile brothers, Fred and William, in 1916. They established a receiving station at Ganges, and delivered the freight to the Holland interurban road at Saugatuck, this being a more central point of delivery for the growers near Ganges, and by the trucks gathering the fruit along the road they took away the balance of patronage, so the boat service at Pier Cove was discontinued in August, 1917, when Capt. Wilson made his last trip with his new steamer, the **Anna C. Wilson**, and Pier Cove became a place of the past.

Mrs. S. G. Fiegert, who came to Ganges in 1855, said in that year Giles Rockwell built the first part of the hotel at the Cove. later he built another having a hall on the second floor. There is some difference of opinion as to the date the house was built. At any rate it was the only hotel in Ganges township, and for a time was a popular assembling place for elections and social gatherings. It was operated in turn by Messrs. Rockwell, Ballard, Scott and Charley Mack. Mr. Mack operated it a few years closing its doors in the late seventies. C. E. Ensfield bought the property and sold half of the building to the R. M. Moore & Co. who moved it over to their pier for a warehouse. The remainder was torn down. "On Christmas eve, 1871, 101 couples danced in the hotel hall, music being furnished by the Chase orchestra."

There was also a Mr. Cook who managed the place for we read, Oct. 23, 1869: "The dance at Pier Cove was quite well attended, and the participants seemed to enjoy themselves very much. We must say we believe Mr. Cook, the proprietor of the hotel, is well versed in keeping a public house."

Among those who engaged in the mercantile business during the life of the burg were Raymond, Walter Billings, J. S. Payne (who also owned the saloon), L. Weaver, A. C. Collins, and B. F. Hall.

Pier Cove was perhaps at the peak of its fruit shipping period in 1887, when there were 336,730 baskets of peaches sent over the pier during the season, in addition to the quantities of apples, and other freights though there were several years when the amount handled would equal or surpass the above, for which we do not have accurate data.

Commercial Record, February 27, 1925 -- In again taking up the work of compiling the history of Western Allegan county, which he began several years ago, the earlier articles being published in this paper at that time, Mr. H. H. Hutchins writes to *The Commercial Record* as follows:

"I have had in mind ever since I left off my history of Western Allegan county to finish, but have simply neglected to get at it. I an now starting in, and will try to have a section in each week until completed.

Today I am bringing the first settlers into the section between Allegan and Singapore, and plan to follow the line of settlement as to business, such as brick yards, schools, mills, and perhaps some about churches, etc., as they were introduced, and will finish with Fennville, which was the last town to be established in Western Allegan county. These will interlap of course, as to time, but as it is a jumpy affair no harm will come if we jump a little more. Pearl and Bravo came a little later, but I have no plan as to them -- that will work itself out some way, no doubt. There will be six or eight weeks of it. In completing this history I shall repeat from letters published in 1904 and 1910 in part, but shall add fresh history here and there, with some corrected matter where statements were incomplete. People who have copies of or remember the former letters will please bear with the repetition.

Taken as a continuance of the other, this article will be No. 17.

I am setting back somewhat, since I have already described much that happened after the first settlers, but it is done, so I will go on as though we did not know it."

17
Ganges Township

In the summer of 1836 Harrison Hutchins and his father, David Hutchins, went from Rochester, N. Y., to Buffalo by canal boat, from Buffalo to Detroit by schooner, and from Detroit to Allegan they followed Indian trails on foot, carrying their provisions and blankets and sleeping on the ground in the forest by night.

Upon arrival at Allegan they found Leander Prouty, who had arrived on June 6, 1834, and who was the first settler in that section. There were three or four other families here also in 1836, among whom was Mr. James McCormick and his family. At this time there were no settlers between Allegan and the lake shore, nor on the shore, except at the mouth of the Kalamazoo. As has been stated in earlier letters, there was a settlement there, begun by William G. Butler in 1830 or 1832.

In 1837 Mr. Hutchins walked back to Detroit on his way to Rochester to bring his sister, Mrs. Sophia Stillson, and her two children, Kate and Sam, and on his return he walked the same route for the third time.

In September of 1837 James McCormick, Harrison Hutchins, Cyrus Cole, Mr. Hayte, and possibly John Billings cut a wagon road from the Bailey mill, which had just been built west of Swan Creek, to the corner of the four towns -- Saugatuck, Ganges, Clyde and Manlius. Mr. McCormick took up a claim in the southwest corner of Manlius, and Mr. Hutchins on the northwest corner of Ganges, cornering to each other. They turned out to be the first settlement in the vicinity of what is now Fennville -- in fact the first between Allegan and Singapore.

Mr. McCormick built a log house where the old homestead now stands, and moved his family over from Allegan that same year (1837), but the logs were green and the house damp, and the folks had colds, so he moved back to Allegan for the winter, but in the spring of 1838 they came here for a permanent home, and were the first white settlers in the town of Manlius.

Mr. Hutchins also began on his land in 1837 by clearing off a small plot of ground and planting some crops among the burned logs. He, too, went away for the winter, but at that time the saw mill at Swan Creek was in course of construction and his father had a contract there, where he worked with him through the winter of 1837-38. During the season of 1838 he cleared more land and built his log house, and in December of the year he moved his sister there and began life on his own land, and was the first settler in Ganges.

The McCormick log home built in 1837

During the winter of 1839 James Wadsworth built a house on his land on the northeast quarter of the northwest quarter of section 2 in Ganges, and moved his family there in the following spring. This farm lies on the west side of the road running south from the school house of district No. 1. His was the second family to settle in Ganges. John Billings also moved onto his land in the spring of 1839 -- the place now owned by Verne Kenter. Levi Loomis moved from Singapore in the spring of 1840 to his land on section 11, Ganges, and his son Marion was born there soon after, being the first white child born in Ganges.

18
Allegan County Organization

It occurs to me now that we have been ahead of our story from the very beginning, and that the first point of importance is the organization of Allegan County. Let us take a hasty glance at the remote past, and continue more recent matters later.

From the *Michigan Tradesman*, January 10, 1908:

"The settling of western Michigan was progressing rapidly in the thirties, one county after another being organized, until by the time it became a state the counties from Detroit clear to the lake were well organized. On March 30, 1833, a law was passed that changed the county of Allegan to the township of Allegan and made it a part of Kalamazoo county, and on April 6, 1833, the first township meeting was held in the house of Samuel Foster in Otsego. In 1835 they petitioned the legislative council for a separate county organization, which was granted and became effective September 1, 1835.

"The following year an act was approved which divided the county into four townships, viz." Plainfield, Otsego, Newark and Allegan. Plainfield township embraced what is now Martin, Wayland, Gunplains and Leighton. Otsego embraced the present Otsego, Watson, Hopkins and Dorr. Newark embraced the present townships of Lee, Clyde, Manlius, Fillmore, Casco, Ganges, Saugatuck and Laketown. Allegan covered Trowbridge, Allegan, Monterey, Salem, Cheshire, Pine Plains (now Valley), Heath and Overisel. These four townships elected supervisors in April, 1836, and the board of supervisors met October 4 of that year. By 1861 the boundaries and names of the present 24 townships had been settled, and were as they are now."

The following is quoted from a letter prepared by Gen. Elisha Mix, and read by him before the Allegan County Pioneer Society in August, 1898. It had been written at times long before that date, the statistics being collected through several years of Mr. Mix's long life in Allegan county. The date of organization and name of first settlers and first supervisors is given for every one of the 24 townships. The paper was as follows:

"Allegan county, under territorial government, comprised four townships, as follows:

"Plainfield -- Range 11, towns 1, 2, 3 and 4.

"Otsego -- Range 12, towns 1, 2, 3, and 4.

"Allegan -- Ranges 13 and 14, towns 1, 2, 3, and 4.

"Newark -- Ranges 15 and 16, towns 1, 2, 3, and 4.

"The county seat was laid out by Oshea Wilder, Cyrus Lovel and Isaac E. Crary in 1834. The first election was held August 12, 1836. Elisha Ely and John Anderson were elected justices of the peace; Alexander L. Ely, clerk; J. L. Shearer, sheriff; Martin L. Barber, county surveyor, and Oka Town, judge of probate. Eber Sherwood, Joseph Fisk and Daniel A. Plummer were chosen a committee to carry a report of said election to the legislative council. Elisha Ely was chairman and J. L. Shearer secretary of the election. The above named were commissioned August 25, 1835, by the acting governor of the territory Stevens T. Mason. The same year Michigan passed to a state. Elisha Ely was elected the first representative from Allegan county to the state legislature March 23, 1836. Milo Winslow was elected treasurer, and Joseph Fisk register, thus making the first organization of Allegan county complete. The first supervisors elected by the four townships were as follows: Hull Sherwood for Otsego, Alexander Ely for Allegan, Daniel A. Plummer for Newark, and John Murphy for Plainfield. Hull Sherwood was elected chairman and Hovey K. Clark was chosen clerk and duly sworn in. Thus the county and townships were in full working order by officers duly elected by actual settlers of the county and towns of the county.

"The first settlement of Allegan county was at the mouth of the Kalamazoo river by William G. Butler in the fall of 1829. Organized in 1836. First supervisor, Daniel A. Plummer.

"The second settlement was at Otsego, by Giles Scott, Urial Baker and Sloan Eaton; in 1830. Organized in 1836. First supervisor, Hull Sherwood.

"The third settlement was in Gun Plain, by Dr. Sirenus Thompson, Calvin White, John Adams and Jonathan Russell, in 1830. Organized in 1836. John Murphy, first supervisor.

"The fourth settlement was in Allegan, in 1834, by Leander Prouty, Elisha Ely, Joseph Fisk, and Alonzo Weeks and his brother, Corydon Weeks. Organized in 1836. First supervisor was Alexander Ely.

"The fifth settlement was Trowbridge, in 1835, by Leander Prouty and his wife. Organized in 1842. First supervisor, John Ware.

"The sixth settlement was Wayland, by Lucius A. Barnes and Daniel Jackson. Organized in 1843. First supervisor, Joel Brownson.

"The seventh settlement was Martin, by Munford Eldred, in 1836. Organized in 1839. Cotton M. Kimball, first supervisor.

"The eighth settlement was Watson, by Daniel Leggett and William S. Miner and Wells Field, in 1836. Organized in 1842. First supervisor, Amos Dunning.

"The ninth settlement was Monterey, by Gil Blas Wilcox and John Sweezey, in 1836. Organized in 1847. First supervisor, John Chase.

"The tenth settlement was Manlius, by Ralph R. Mann, in 1836. He founded the city of New Richmond in 1836. Organized in 1839. First supervisor, John Allen.

"The eleventh settlement was in Clyde, by Jacob and Leonard Bailey, in 1837. Organized in 1859. First supervisor was Ralph Parrish.

"The twelfth settlement was Hopkins, by Jonathan O. Round. Organized in 1852. First supervisor, Jonathan O. Round.

"The thirteenth settlement was Pine Plains, by T. M. West and Daniel Ammerman in 1838.

Organized in 1850. First supervisor was Timothy Coates.

"The fourteenth settlement was Ganges, by Harrison Hutchins, Levi Loomis, John H. Billings and James Wadsworth, in 1837. Organized in 1847. First supervisor, A. H. Hale. [Hutchins came to Ganges in 1837, built and moved in in 1838. Wadsworth and Billings came in 1839, and Loomis in 1840.-H.H.H.]

"The fifteenth settlement was in Cheshire, by Simon Pike, Marcus Lane and Jonathan Hinkley, in 1839. Organized in 1851. First supervisor, James Lindsley.

"The sixteenth settlement was in Leighton, by Lucius A. Barnes and William Logan, in 1837. Organized in 1848. First supervisor, George W. Lewis.

"The seventeenth settlement was Fillmore, by Smith Shorno, also Isaac Fairbanks and Daniel Lamoreux. Organized in 1849. First supervisor, Isaac Fairbanks.

"The eighteenth settlement was Casco, by John Thayer and Timothy McDowell, in 1844. Organized in 1854. First supervisor, Timothy McDowell.

"The nineteenth settlement was Dorr, by Nathan Goodspeed and family, in 1845. Organized in 1847. The first supervisor was John Parsons.

"The twentieth settlement was in Laketown, by Arend Neerken and James Rutters, in 1847. Organized in 1859. First supervisor was John Rouse.

"The twenty-first settlement was Overisel, by Rev. Bolks and Gerrit Veldhuis, in 1848. Was organized in 1857. First supervisor was C. J. Voorhorst.

"The twenty-second settlement was Heath, by Simon Howe and John Sadler, in 1850. Was organized in 1851. First supervisor was James Heath.

"The twenty-third settlement was Salem, by Michael Strayer and John Teed, in 1850. Was organized in 1855. First supervisor was L. P. Brown.

"The twenty-fourth settlement was Lee, by Thomas Scott and Thomas Raplee. Scott came in 1844, but no regular settlement was made until 1858. First supervisor was Thomas Raplee.

The clipping from which the above is a copy is without date or name of paper, but no doubt is from an Allegan paper, and was in a report of the pioneer meeting.

Gen. Mix came from Connecticut to Allegan in 1852, and was elected county surveyor that same year. He was well and favorably know by all the old settlers, and his name is sufficient guarantee of a careful and reliable accounting for these early doings.

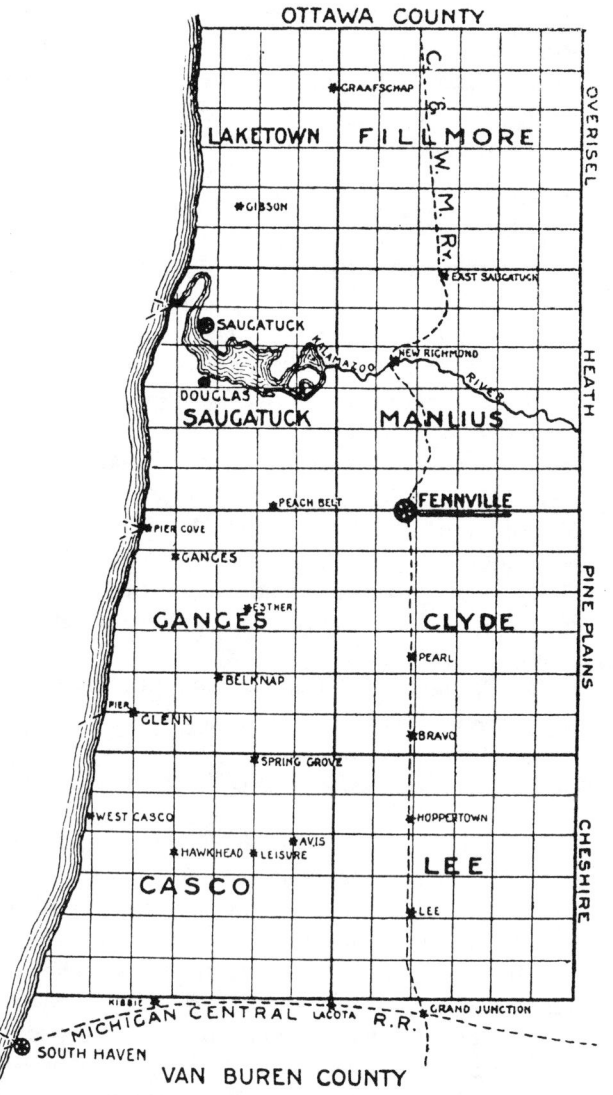

Eight townships were formed within the boundaries of the original large township called Newark.

14
Subdivision of Newark

Townships Formed from Newark

1 -- MANLIUS, 1838

Manlius, which was set off by itself in 1838, held its first town meeting at the house of R. R. Mann, April 1, 1839, with the following officers: John Allen, supervisor; James A. Poage, clerk; Samuel Town, Orrin Ball, John Allen, assessors; R. R. Mann, John Allen, Truman D. Austin, commissioners of highways; Orrin Ball, constable and collector; Samuel Town, Paul Shepard, Isaac Vredenberg, school inspectors; Paul Shepard, treasurer; R. R. Mann, Samuel Town, James A. Poage, J. W. Palmer, justices of the peace; R. R. Mann, Isaac Vredenberg, directors of the poor; John Allen, James McCormick, overseers of highways; Truman D. Austin, poundmaster. Only ten votes were cast in the town at the time.

2 -- GANGES, 1847

Ganges, taken from Newark in 1847, embracing the present Casco, held its first town meeting at the house of Orlando Weed, April 5, 1847, with the following results, 27 votes being cast in all: A. H. Hale, supervisor; S. H. Weaver, Clerk; Levi Loomis, treasurer; N. D. Plummer, G. F. Hughes, justices of the peace; Daniel Platt, A. H. Hale, school inspectors; J. W. Wadsworth, Nathan Slayton, directors of the poor; J. W. Wadsworth, L. B. Goodeve, assessors; Nathan Slayton, Roswell Dailey, J. B. Goodeve, commissioners of highways; John Lutz, Henry Baragar, S. H. Weaver, O. C. Thayer, constables; Henry Baragar, David Updyke, N. D. Plummer, O. C. Hamlin, Timothy McDowell, pathmaster.

3 -- FILLMORE, 1849

Fillmore was part of Manlius until 1849, and no doubt from 1841, when its area was attached to Manlius, until 1849, some of its residents served as officers in Manlius and voted at its town meetings. The first town meeting was held in Fillmore as a separate town in April, 1849, at which time Isaac Fairbanks was chosen supervisor; Benjamin Fairbanks, clerk; Anton Schorno, treasurer; Isaac Fairbanks, Anton Schorno, George N. Smith, George Harrington, justices of the peace.

The earliest record now in the hands of the town clerk is dated 1852, at which time there were 66 votes cast.

4 -- CASCO, 1854

Casco, taken from Ganges in 1854, completed its civil organization at the first town meeting, held in April, 1855, when Timothy McDowell was elected supervisor. The records of the meeting and early township affairs were destroyed by fire in 1869.

5 -- LAKETOWN, 1858

Laketown, set off from all that remained of the original Newark in October, 1858, held its first town meeting April 4, 1859, when the following officers were elected. The whole number of votes cast was 48. John Bouws was elected supervisor; Gerrit Rutgers, clerk; Arend J. Neerken, treasurer; Arend Neerken, John Bouws, school inspectors; Harm Bouws and Albert Klomparens, directors of the poor; Reinderd Poorenkamp, Gerrit Rutgers and John Lucas, commissioners of highways; Arend J. Neerken, Hendrik J. Brinkman, John Rutgers and Harm Klomparens, justices; Geert Heneveld, Berent J. Brinkman, Derk Ten Cate and Hendrik Bakker, constables; Gerrit Lubbers, Gabriel Rosbock and Harm Bouws, overseers. (Signed) Arend J. Neerken, Geert Rutgers, John Lucas, inspectors of election.

There were cast at this same meeting 45 votes against a tax for building a county jail, and one for the tax. It was voted to raise $75 for incidental expenses of the town, $10 for town books, and $75 for roads.

Voted the following by-laws: All horses shall be restrained from running at large. All persons violating the said law to pay the sum of $3. Voted to restrain all swine under 25 pounds from going at large. Persons violating said law to pay 25 cents fine.

6 -- CLYDE, 1859

Clyde, detached from Pine Plains in 1859, held its first town election April 2, 1860, there being thirteen votes present, who cast their ballots for Ralph Parrish, supervisor; George G. Smalley, clerk; E. H. Heath, treasurer; C. T. Billings, justices of the peace.

7 -- LEE, 1859

Lee, at first a portion of Newark, from 1841 to 1850 a part of Manlius, and then until 1859 a part of Pine Plains, contributed its township activities in various directions. At its first township meeting after organization, held April 4, 1859, the officers elected were: Thomas Raplee, supervisor; E. H. Heath, clerk; H. B. Rice, treasurer; H. B. Rice, Henry Davidson, Thomas Raplee, John Orr (subsequently declared to be an alien), justices of the peace; Michael Hoy, David W. Matthews, highway commissioners; Henry Davidson, school inspector; David W. Matthews, Michael Hoy, Winchester Jenkins, constables; H. B. Rice, Winchester Jenkins, Michael Hoy, overseers of highways.

The earliest record with the Lee town clerk now is 1864.

8 -- SAUGATUCK, 1861

Saugatuck, really the nucleus of the original

Newark, which name it retained until 1861, had a continuous civil history from 1836, but the early records were destroyed.

* * *

Horses, cattle, sheep and hogs were allowed to run at large until about 1880. Everybody fenced to keep random stock out of crops, instead of keeping his own in, as has been the case since then. When fields began to enlarge, and woods pastures grew less, the towns voted all stock out of the roads. During those days a lawful fence was, of necessity, horse high, pig tight, and bull strong. Wire fencing was unknown. The earliest fences were made of logs, followed closely by the rail fence. Then, while lumber remained at low cost and posts were to be had for the cutting, board fences were in order. Later wire crowded them out of use.

Horses and cattle learned to jump by getting around in the woods, where many times they had to jump over logs and creeks, so soon an ordinary fence was but little hindrance. Hogs likewise learned to root their way under logs and brush, and soon found a very easy way to get into crops in general, and it became very difficult to protect crops. It caused no little controversy and some harness when people had to keep their animals at home, but that soon wore away, and no one would have voted to go back to the old way.

20
Wildlife of the Forest

The earliest pioneers lived on "barter and trade" for a time, and until there was call for lumber, wood, bark, shingle bolts and other uses for timber their only way to get money with which to pay taxes was on road jobs, and they could turn the road orders in to the county in place of cash. This condition did not last long, as the milling business soon grew in. Good clear pine logs were worth $4 to $5 and whitewood $6 to $8 per thousand feet, delivered at the river or mill. Other timber values were on a parallel with logs as to selling value. It was not until after the civil war that a good quality of pine lumber would cost more than $10, and common lumber cost less in proportion to its quality.

The principle occupation from a financial point of view for perhaps twenty years after the timber market came in was in the woods output. Great quantities of choice beech, maple, hemlock, and the other varieties of timber were slashed and burned on the ground where it fell, to get it out of the way for crops. It was a terrible waste, as we see it now, but not so then. Choice whitewood and walnut was split into fence rails. Other timber would make rails, but it was harder to split and heavier to handle.

Back in the forties and early fifties Mr. H. E. Blackman, who lived about three miles out of Allegan on the Otsego road, fenced his farm with walnut. Fifty years later a furniture company came from Grand Rapids and took the rails away and refenced the farm with good cedar posts and woven wire on an even trade. All Mr. Blackman had to do was say, "Yes, go ahead."

* * *

Men's wages were 75 cents a day and girls' $1 a week. The day began as soon as we could see and ended at dark. In the fall we all husked corn in the barn until 10 at night. When we were little boys we were allowed to go to the house at 9. At perhaps 12 to 14 we were presumed to take our hand with the men.

The saw mills ran from 6 to 6 with one hour off for dinner.

As an example of what the poor boys just starting in the woods endured, I will note my father's beginning. In the fall of 1838 he built the body of his house, which was about 16 x 20 feet, sawed siding into shingles for the roof, put on the gable ends with rough green lumber, and the floors of the same. The first floor was laid on mud sills, and the attic floor placed on poles laid across the top of the log body. Not a window nor door, and the cracks between the logs were all open. The fire was built on the ground, where the floor boards were left out for the purpose, and the smoke passed off through a hole in the roof left for it.

He brought his sister and her three children there and did the best he could until he could finish the house. He made a rough door, with wooden latch and hinges, chinked the cracks, and used paper in the window holes until he could get windows, and made a large fireplace with mud and stick chimney. This is only one instance. They all had like conditions in one way or another. Few of them had money, and it was a case of "Get there, Johnny."

There were five in his own family and by the time the house was finished he took in John Billings with his wife and five children, his father David Hutchins, David Hall and Cyrus Cole, making it a household of 14 for the winter. Mr. McCormick had his wife and family and James Wadsworth and his wife and family and one or two others. If I remember correctly Walter Billings was there also, so he had 12 or 13 in the house for the winter. Help one another was the way of the pioneer.

* * *

Where there is deep forest there is also wild life. Perhaps a few tales of incidents in that line would be timely here. More about the people quoted, later. In letters No. 1 and 2 we gave a history of the pigeons of early days by Hall, Goodrich and Billings, and in No. 4 some experiences of Mr. W. A. Dressel with wild animals, which we omit here.

My cousin, W. W. Hutchins, on September 3, 1910, told as follows:

"My father (Alvin Hutchins) came out here from Rochester about 1841, stayed two years, and went back to New York. In 1845 he moved out with his family. They came by rail to the end of the M.C.R.R. and the rest of the way by wagon. He worked at Swan Creek while here at first with his father, David Hutchins, who was running the Swan Creek saw mill. The wolves were so thick it was not safe to go from the house to the barn after dark, for when they opened the door at night the wolves would scatter away only to return to lick up scraps from the kitchen waste as soon as the door was closed. At one time they heard wolves lapping and snarling at the hog trough, and John Billings finally became so enraged at this noise the he aimed his gun at the wolf noise and fired. he succeeded in wounding a wolf, and the dogs worried it about until daylight, when the men shot it.

"They had a dog that was bold enough to fight the wolves, and when he heard them outside he would tear around so they would have to let him out, and he would chase them off into the woods, but presently he would return with a heavy thud against the door, closely followed by a pack of wolves snarling at his heels, and the folks would let him in."

Wild animals were so plentiful during those times that the men finally organized hunting parties to kill off those kinds that were destructive to flocks and crops. When all were assembled they would elect two leaders. They separated and chose from those present first one and then the other, from the assemblage, until the hunters were all chosen. This done, they all started for the woods on the hunt. The side that got the least counts had to pay for the supper for the whole party. In this interview Wat said the rating or counts placed on each kind of animal was in proportion to its destructiveness, as the chipmunk counted 1, squirrel 2, owl 5, hedgehog 10, and so on -- he didn't remember them all. In the sixties there had been a hunt and the losing side put up the supper at the home of John P. Wade, and on the way home at night he and Will McCormick, with others saw a fire to the east, and when they reached the place they found the Fenn saw mill in flames. This was the first mill, but he did not remember the year.

My cousin Jack Hall told of an incident: "Uncle Alvin (Hutchins) had some pigs in a log stable at Swan Creek in the early forties, and one night a wolf, in trying to get the pigs jumped onto the roof and fell through. He was so frightened at finding himself imprisoned that he forgot the pigs entirely and did his best to get out again. but the pigs did not forget him and the resulting noise caused the folks to investigate with the result that they shot the wolf between the logs of the stable.

* * *

Mr. Benjamin Crawford, who came to Manlius township in 1852, told me that not long after he moved to his farm here he went after the cows one night, finding them over east by the creek. There were his own cows and those of neighbors, and he started them homeward; but presently they elevated their heads and tails and began to look around and run.

He looked in the direction that seemed to disturb them and saw that over the bank in the creek bottom there was something running out on the tree limbs and jumping from tree to tree, and making in his direction. Another look and he saw it was a panther, and he immediately got the same notion the cows seemed to have -- that it was high time he was getting home.

At another time, when Mr. Crawford had just got into his house, but had no door as yet, closing the doorway with a blanket, he heard some one calling, over east. Thinking some one was lost, and it was after dark, he held the curtain aside so the light from the fireplace would shine out until they could come in. He called, and they answered several times, but finally they stopped answering. He held the curtain, thinking they saw and would appear soon, so neither called further, Presently a very large animal leaped across the doorway within four feet from him, immediately followed by another of like proportions. He closed the curtain hurriedly and let the stranger go hang. It was two panthers.

My uncle, Henry Hudson, came to Allegan from Hudson, Ohio, in about 1847, and was staying with his cousin, James Blackman, on his farm southeast from Allegan. One night he heard some one calling and thinking it was some one lost, he answered. The call and answer were repeated a few times, when some one came hurriedly to him and asked what he was doing. He replied that there was a person lost in the swamp on the river bottom, and he was helping him in. His friend said: "You are calling a panther to you, and you had better get into the house as fast as you can." And he did.

* * *

In the early forties my father had been helping Mr. Levi Loomis, and was after dark in getting home. There were no roads then, and he was following a trail through the woods. It was a dark night anyway, and he was in the tall timber land, which made it so dark that all the way he could keep the path was by feeling it with a stick he carried. When he arrived abreast of the large elm that stands in front of Mr. Barron's house he heard some animal jump out of the path a few feet in front of him. Thinking it might be a deer, he though to frighten it further away, so he rapped on a tree and screamed. He was immediately answered with a much more fierce scream than he was capable of giving and not more than 15 feet to the side and slightly in front. He did not enjoy such defiance and his first impulse was to turn back and make his way to Mr. Loomis' again if he could, but upon reflection he thought it as safe to go ahead as back, so he did that. He heard nothing from the animal, so fearing it might be following him, he rapped another tree when he reached the swamp, and it answered immediately, but seemingly in the same spot. He was glad to hear it this time. It screamed once or twice more before he reached home, but did not follow. A council was held next day and it was decided the animal was a lynx.

Hedgehogs and coons were fond of green corn and would go into the field in the night for it. Their method was to climb the stalk, their weight breaking the stalk over so they could get the ear. The trained dog would not attack a hedgehog for fear of the quills, but an inexperienced dog would grab a mouthful of quills from the first one he attacked. The hunters all carried rifles with ball and cap at that time, and cast their balls in what were called "bullet molds," and these latter made good pliers with which to pull the quills from the dog's mouth. The quills are provided with barbs all over the point and will work in deeper all the time. It is very difficult to jerk them out, but the hunters held the unfortunate pup and got all they could find. After two or three experiences of this kind a dog became more particular about his adventures.

* * *

Sometimes the coon would get to the woods and climb a tree, and one would go up after him and knock him out, while those on the ground would, with the aid of the dog, get him. This was called "going cooning." If the coon went up a tree they could not climb, they cut the tree down. One time the hunters treed a coon and Jim Henderson went up. When he neared the top of the tree he could see better, and just as he was ready to hit the coon he discovered he was facing a wildcat, and that the wildcat was just ready to spring at him. He got in the first blow, however, and happened to strike the animal on the nose, which felled him to the ground. he gave the alarm, and the others did all they could, but if memory serves me correctly the cat got away.

All these things happened before I was old enough to take a hand in it, but with a boy's eagerness I drank them all in after I was old enough to comprehend what the older ones were talking about -- and that doesn't have to be very old.

Settlers rush to help a young Indian treed by wolves.

21
Bears and Indians

When he lived in his log house where he first settled, my father was a good deal troubled for lack of water. He tried digging a well, and when down 25 or 30 feet it caved in. It so happened that he had just come out, otherwise I would not be here to tell the story. He abandoned it, and as soon as he could he built another house about 80 rods back from the road and near the lake, where there was a good spring and it was to this house that he brought his bride in 1847, and here it was that the family of eight were all born. This house was made regular barn frame, and sided with planks, matched the same as flooring.

But I was telling in my last letter about wild animals and that is what I am coming to now.

When a very small boy our mother remarked one day that wolves were chasing a deer. We could not see them, and I wondered how she knew but she kept a close watch over towards the west shore of the lake. Presently we saw a deer come out of the woods onto the ice, and it was headed toward our landing. She ran in the house, got the long dinner horn, and began tooting it. The deer kept coming, and she was afraid it would bring the wolves near our barnyard and among the sheep, but finally it seemed to notice the sound and turned toward the point across on the east shore. We watched, and just before it reached the land two wolves came out on the ice where the deer had first appeared. They saw the deer and left the track (there was no track, for it was smooth ice and the deer slipped badly) and made directly for the spot where the deer left the ice. Mother was greatly relieved when it was over and they were all gone. I remember well seeing deer swim across the lake when chased by wolves or dogs. And men sometimes went out in boats and shot them for venison. Once they came too close, and the deer lunged onto the edge of the boat and spilled them all into the lake.

* * *

In a letter from Mrs. Flora (Loomis) Goodrich, under date of March 1, 1925, she says: "Father (Levi Loomis) had built his first little shanty, into which they first moved and after his brother Lyman brought his wife he, too, built a shanty. I remember by the way, of aunty telling me that, before it was finished one night she was so frightened by the wolves so near that she went on the roof and screamed there until uncle came home. He was at work with my father and your father, or not, I do not remember."

In a talk with Mrs. Alice (Squires) Kibby (Mrs. Will Kibby), Sept. 20, 1910, she said: "My father located the farm here while putting up the Pier Cove saw mill, in 1852 or '53, and about 1854 moved his family here. Father had to go to Allegan for grist milling, and mother was afraid to stay alone, as the wolves were howling around the house, so she took rails into the house to prop the door shut."

Well, perhaps this will do for wolf stories, but during my early recollection the general talk was of men making it a business to hunt and trap wolves. There was a man from Allegan -- a Mr. Streeter, if I recollect rightly -- who made a fine business of it. I think the bounty on wolves was $25, and the pelt was of value, but as the timber was cleared off they were driven into narrower regions, and by 1870 or thereabouts they were gone.

When small children we used to sit on the south "stoop" and count them by their howls. They had a difference in tone of voice for one thing, and then too, they were scattered in different directions in the woods.

There was occasionally a bear seen and sometimes killed. The last I remember of was perhaps in the eighties. N. W. Lewis and his two sons, Will and Charley, with E. B. Morse, found a mother bear and her two cubs in the swamp south of Hutchins lake. Anyway it was before that tract of muck land where Frank Crane, Gordon Spencer and the Todd ranches are, was cleared. They killed the three bears.

The bear was not nearly so much dreaded as wolves, and did not molest domestic animals so much, though they were fond of young pigs. But I have no recollection of any humans being injured by any of them, though many a fright was had.

Deer were quite plentiful as long as the timber lasted, and I have found them with the cattle in the woods when in search for the cows. But no sooner did they discover that I was near than they made off and away.

In the earlier pioneer days, and perhaps until 1870, hunters used dogs to chase the deer, and he would place himself on the runway so when the deer came along he could shoot it. A peculiar trait of wild animals is that when chased they run in a circle. It may be twenty miles across but follow him long enough and he will lead back to the starting point. They had what was called runways, and hunters knew where they were, so took advantage of it, and while the dog found and ran the deer he watched on the runway. Of course, that was not always done, but frequently. Finally some of the more thoughtful hunters saw that the tendency was to drive the deer out of the country, besides it was not the act of a true sportsman to take such advantage of the beast, and decided to call a halt on the dogs. There were no laws regarding any of these things, so the people had to settle it themselves. It was made known that dogs would be shot if found chasing deer and the threat was put in practice. Men would let the deer go by and shoot the dog when he came up. This caused much hardness, but no one knew who did it, and nothing could be done. Finally laws were passed to control such matters and no one presumed to use dogs.

Deer would jump the highest fence and pasture on the growing crops near the woods. They were especially fond of young wheat, and I have seen quite a strip along the edge of the woods where they had eaten it down. It was a graceful sight to see a flock of five or six running through a logging fallow after it was burned over and before it was logged and the heaps burned. They bounded so lightly over logs and through openings. I only saw a few occasions of the kind, but I did see it done.

Other wildlife dwindled with the forests, so that it has been a good many years since we have had other than a few red squirrels, skunk, rabbit, woodchuck and an occasional weasel.

* * *

Indians were quite plentiful from the first coming of the white man until my earlier recollection. It was their habit to go north in the spring and come back here in the fall for the winter hunting and trapping. For years they camped in our sugar bush every spring. My father was a great friend to the Indian. They never asked any privileges of him; and he never granted then any. They simply came and did as they liked, and nothing was said. I remember he had noted that whitewood timber was coming into value, so saved several trees in the woods. Finally some one discovered one fine large whitewood had a colony of bees in the top, and put a cross on it. (It was the practice that the first to discover a bee tree should chop a cross in the bark, and others were upon honor bound not to molest it,

and the finder would go at his leisure, fell the tree and secure the honey. Father did not care for the honey part of it, but he did value the tree, so he placed a notice on it forbidding its being felled. Soon after the Indians came he found the whitewood lying flat, and at a glance he saw too, that it was the work of the red men. He grumbled some about it, but said not a word to the tenants of his sugar bush. Next winter he cut it into logs and drew it to market.

When an Indian chops a tree down he cuts clear around it, so when it falls it goes where it leans or where the wind blows it, but a white man squares a notch ar right angles to the direction he wants it to fall, and thus directs its course. The Indian leaves the butt of the fallen trunk sharpened to nearly a point, while the white man, if he chopped it down, has it resembling a wedge, and if sawed down it is mostly square across the butt. (This explanation is not for old woodsmen -- to them it would seem silly.)

* * *

It was really an amusing sight to see a company of Indians migrating. The old one was in the lead, gun in hand and head erect. Then followed the lesser ones -- always in single file, no matter how wide the road. Squaws with big bundles lashed to their backs or papooses (babies) if need be. Squaws astride little ponies, with bundles before, and bundles behind. Ponies loaded almost out of sight; ponies with poles lashed to their sides, with the back ends dragging on the ground, and loaded both on their backs and on the poles with bundles. *Skinneglsh* (boys) with bow and arrow, running and shooting arrows at any wild bird, squirrel, or what not -- and they could shoot. Never stop the run, but let the arrow fly, and if they did not hit the mark they came very near doing so.

They made maple sugar, and brought it around to the white folks to "swap" for flour, or perhaps potatoes or cloth. But if taken, it was later melted and thoroughly renovated, as it was customary for the boys to swim in the trough in which the sap was stored until it could be boiled down. This was before the day of beet and cane sugar here. It was not until 1870 to '75 that we left off depending on maple sugar for our sweetening. By that time it was more profitable to buy sugar than to take the time in the spring to make maple, since we always had the rush of cutting summer wood and cleaning barn yards on at that time of the year, so as to have all clear for farm work as soon as frost was out and the ground settled.

But the Indian dwindled in numbers along with the other woods life, and now we see no more of the migratory sort. The few now in these parts are settled in communities and depend upon manual labor for a livelihood. And they are not bad citizens either.

22
Early Settlers

Those stalwart young men who first broke the trail into the wilds of Michigan soon became true sons of the forest -- lovers of its moods and ways and sounds, and an authority on its trees and plants, and of the kinds and habits of the wild life it sheltered. They became each an adept in woodcraft and, since "Necessity is the mother of invention," they devised ways and means to surmount all obstacles found in their way. Of necessity they all built log houses, as the only available construction material was the green standing timber, and many of them moved in as soon as the building could be put up in the rough, since they were out of reach of our habitations, and then the shanty could be chinked, doors and windows put in and fireplaces built. Those of us who have lived in the woods know full well that such a habitation is far more comfortable located in dense woods than out in the open where the wind can search us out. I have been in woods houses when the wind would be blowing over the tree tops so that it was dangerous to be out in the timber, but we felt none of it on the ground.

They all had to contend with predatory wild animals, rough and rootey roads winding and twisting their way through the forest and around hilly and swampy places. They were all hunters and trappers and fishermen to a greater or less degree according to their liking, for the surroundings were alike the country over. Besides, many had to depend on fish and game for much of their sustenance until land was cleared so crops could be grown.

Some were so fortunate as to own a yoke of oxen, but those not so provided could get team work done by changing work with a more favored neighbor, giving two days of his time for one of the man and team. Slow work, to be sure, but the only way until he could buy or raise them for himself.

* * *

The eight squares, known as towns, that lay stretched across the west end of Allegan county were all embraced in the one township of Newark, but as a matter of convenience we will hereafter designate them by their present names in introducing the first settlers.

John Allen seems to have been the first to start operations between Allegan and the mouth of the river, for in 1836 he came to where New Richmond now is, in Manlius township, and started a town, employing several helpers, among whom was Ralph R. Mann.

The town proposition at Richmond proved a failure, and later they settled near there. We do not know where Mr. Allen lived but "after the failure" Mr. Mann went about a mile south and built a water power saw mill on the creek. "This was the first practical milling enterprise in the township (really the first between Allegan and Singapore) and became the nucleus of a settlement that received the name of Manlius. A store was opened by Johnson Parsons and a tavern by John Roe. The place had some importance as long as the mill remained and before the railroad came, but it was abandoned in 1874.

At the first township election, held in April, 1839, both Allen and Mann were elected to township offices, so we may recognize them as settlers at that time. I am holding to the position that until a man gets a home and moves his family into it he is merely a transient.

We have no further records of either Allen or Mann, though as a boy I knew them both. By this time, however, Mr. Allen had gone to Allegan and had engaged in the sale of agricultural implements, and some time in the early sixties sold my father the first mowing machine brought into this section.

Whether any of the other helpers on the Richmond venture remained to become residents I never knew, nor do I know who they were. However, from my viewpoint, Jas. McCormick, who in 1837 built his cabin and moved his family thereto as a permanent home, became the first settler in the township of Manlius, or between Allegan and "the flats" as the section around the mouth of the Kalamazoo was called.

Allen and Mann were engaged in a venture, and it failed, and not until then did they settle in a definite home, as I understand it. In the meantime McCormick, though a year later in, had settled.

Be that as it may, the odds is the difference, and a like condition prevailed in Ganges. Hutchins moved into his house in December, 1838; Wadsworth in February, two months later; and Billings in the same month. The three were settled within two months, so the honor of being the first settler or the second is gained by a very small margin.

Copied from a letter written by John H. Billings, and dated March 2, 1839, to his brother-in-law, James R. Brown, New June, Niagara county, New York: "I bought 68 acres of S. Cole for 280 dollars. I have built a house on it, and moved in two weeks ago." He then tells about his payments, and goes on to say: "Hutchins moved onto his lot by McCormick. Wadsworth has moved onto his lot on the east side of Cole's. . . Wheat is 9 shillings, corn 6, potatoes 4, and oats 4 shillings a bushel at Allegan. . . They have built a flouring mill at Allegan and it is about ready to run. . . It is as hard times for money as it was when you was here. . . The twins grow well, but they cannot stand alone yet. We call them John Darius and Jonathan Hosias."

The above extracts were taken from a long letter that was shown me by "John Darius" October 7, 1917.

Though I was well acquainted with Mr. Cole in his later years, I knew nothing of his origin nor his migrations. I also knew his daughters, Mrs. Sarah Jane Adams and Mrs. Nettie Thorn, as well as his son Henry, who enlisted in the army in the civil war, and while at home on furlough was drowned while attempting to cross over on the dam at Allegan with some comrades. Mrs. Cole died, I should say, in the sixties, and he lived until in the eighties, as I remember. Mrs. Thorn is the only one of the family now living (1925).

* * *

John Henry Billings was born in Monroe county, New York, December 22, 1811, and was a son of John and Mary (Townsend) Billings. On December 30, 1830, he married Mary Baragar, daughter of Peter and Helen (Van Natten) Baragar. In 1837 they came to Allegan, Mich., where they remained until February, 1839, and then settled on their farm on Section 3, Ganges, as previously stated.

On July 23, 1841, he and his family, consisting of his wife and children -- James, Peter Henry, Mary E., Hannah M., John Darius and Jonathan Hosias -- ranging in age from 10 to 1 years old, and Mrs. McLaughlin and her two children, aged 4 and 6 years, started in an open sail boat from The Flats for Richmond for a visit to the Mann, Bowker and Meeker families who lived in Manlius. When nearing Richmond the boat struck a snag and capsized, and Mrs. Billings, James, Mary and Hannah, with Mrs. McLaughlin and one of her children, were drowned. This left him with three small children, who were cared for by an Indian woman until June 23, 1842, when he married Mrs. Miranda (Clark) Leonard who died on March 10, 1885. Mr. Billings died December 12, 1874. In 1842, he moved from Section 3, Ganges to Section 31, Manlius to the farm now owned by E. D. Wadsworth, one mile west of Fennville, having sold his Ganges property to Peter Baragar. This was his home until 1859, when they went over to Saugatuck and lived the remainder of their days.

Mr. Billings was active in many of the early transactions of this community. He drove the stage line from Saugatuck to Allegan for many years, carrying mail and passengers and took an interest in local politics. Three of his sons -- Peter Henry, John Darius and Charles C. -- were veterans of the civil war. Jonathan Hosias was drowned in Hutchins lake when about 12 years old. He was sent around the lake from their home in Manlius township to Mr. Platt's, who lived where Al Hoover now lives, and on returning he chanced the ice for a short cut, and broke through.

* * *

Mr. Wadsworth was a native of Connecticut, and his wife of Massachusetts. They went to Fulton county, New York, and from there came to Michigan in 1836. He bought his land here and settled as stated.

* * *

Levi Loomis was the next to come into the woods in this section. He was born in Madison county, New York, in 1810, and came to Allegan county and built the first saw mill at Pine Creek, then came to Singapore in 1835 (See letter No. 8 for his experience with the bank there.)

He was a son of Josiah and Rebecca S. Loomis. The father was born in Blanford, Connecticut. After their marriage the parents moved to New York, where they bought a farm in Halton county. Levi's sister Emily became the wife of William G. Butler. The senior Mr. Loomis fought in the war of 1812 and voted the Whig ticket. His father, Alexander Loomis, was a soldier in the war of the American revolution. Levi married Miss Sallie A. Skinner, born in 1808.

The Loomis cabin built in 1840

They moved onto their land on Section 11, Ganges, on January 9, 1840 (earlier we stated he came in the spring which was an error), and this was their home through the remainder of their days. They had seven children. She died in 1889, and he died in 1892.

He helped to organize the township of Ganges and all the school districts in the town, hired and paid the first teacher, also aided in building the first school house (District No. 1) in Ganges. He, with the aid of his wife, made out the first tax roll for what are now the townships of Lee, Casco, Ganges, Manlius, Saugatuck and Laketown. A carpenter by trade he made the coffins for deaths in the community free of charge, and was always ready to lend a helping hand in case of sickness or trouble. As has been stated, his son Marion was born on March 10, 1840, and was the first white child born in Ganges.

* * *

Arba N. Crawford was born in Madison county, New York, in 1807, and was the son of Joel and Jemima Crawford, the father being born in Massachusetts in 1767.

In 1835 A. N. migrated to Calhoun county, Michigan, and in 1836 married Miss Eunice Mack. In 1843 they came to Allegan county with an ox team and settled on Section 30, Ganges township. Levi Loomis was their nearest neighbor, and his home was eight miles away. St. Joseph and Kalamazoo were their nearest markets to the south, Allegan to the east, and Singapore to the north. Holland was not settled 'til 1847. They, like the rest, had their experiences with woods life and predatory wild animals.

* * *

In a talk with W. H. Collins on November 3, 1912, he said: "My grandfather Collins was a drum major in the English army in the war of the revolution, and was an Englishman by birth. He was taken prisoner by the colonists, heard their side of the controversy, and was used so well by the American soldiers that he became converted to their cause and joined the American army. where he served the remainder of the war." [I have the same tradition from other sources -- H.] "I don't know his given name, nor where he settled. My father, Joseph Collins, came here from Genessee county, New York, about six miles from Roanoke, in about 1847. My brother Sprague and John Goodeve came two or three years earlier. Father was a Baptist, and always a farmer." (Mrs. John B. Goodeve was Sarah Collins, sister to Sprague and Harley Collins.)

Sprague Collins and John Goodeve were also among our tall timber settlers, having settled on Section 4, Ganges, in about 1844. Mr. Collins' home was half a mile south of the town line on the northwest quarter of the section, and Mr. Goodeve occupied the northwest corner, but his house was to the east, just on top of the hill, Charles Goodeve came later and settled in Saugatuck, on the opposite side of the road from his brother John.

* * *

The following is taken from a letter written many years ago by my mother: "George Veeder, John Billings, Walter Billings, James McCormick and Harrison Hutchins were all whose dwellings were in view upon the road between the old Bailey mill place and the swamp where stands what we now know as Peach Belt. Charles Billings, Levi Loomis and Nathan Slayton were neighbors whose humble residences on their places were out of sight from the town line road. Beyond the place now called Peach Belt lived James Wadsworth, Cyrus Cole and Mr. Baragar, father of the Baragars so well known in this section. Farther on lived John Goodeve, near the lake shore. Beyond him and on the lake shore were James Haile and Banner Seymour. They were all the residents, as the writer remembers, on the direct road from the Bailey mill place to Saugatuck village, across the Kalamazoo. This scarcity of settlers is a fair specimen of the best portion of the lake shore country in 1849."

The Bailey mill stood about four miles southeast of where Fennville now is, and Peach Belt was at the corners where the school house of district No. 1 now stands. The only roads to Saugatuck were by the lake shore and ferry or by New Richmond.

23
Schools

The first physician to practice medicine in Western Allegan county was Dr. C. B. Goodrich. The Goodrich family trace back to the feudal times in England. They settled, one branch in Vermont and one in Connecticut. This arm of the family is from the Vermont settlement.

Dr. C. B. Goodrich was a son of Chauncey and Hannah Brayton Goodrich, and was born in Fowler, St. Lawrence county, New York. His father was born in Connecticut in 1786 and was raised on a farm.

He first came to Newark, Allegan county, Michigan, in 1843, and lived in the home of James C. Haile on the lakeshore in Saugatuck township. They lived there about two years, and then went to Saugatuck. Later they were in the home of Harrison Hutchins, and on the south shore of Hutchins lake for a short time, then in Manlius, and back to Saugatuck, and in 1855 settled on their land on section 8 in Ganges, where they remained to the end.

He traveled on foot and on horseback, and where roads would permit he drove with a buckboard -- but he went. I well remember his coming to our house on horseback, with his saddle bags attached to the saddle, and to those he went for his medicine. He was a kindly sympathetic man, and was respected and loved by all. His patients were scattered all over the eight towns of Newark, and his travels were very exacting. When completely exhausted he would shoulder his gun, along with a blanket, and tell his wife if any one called to tell them he had gone hunting. His hunt was for a friendly tree under which he could lie and rest until he felt strong enough to start off on his professional work again.

It was a sad day for the people of the Lake Shore when they had to lay the dear old doctor away in his last resting place. His work has been very ably carried on for the past fifty years by our own Dr. E. E. Brunson.

* * *

The first bridge built in Newark was at New Richmond -- no doubt in the thirties. The first in Ganges was at Pier Cove, over the mill creek. This was a small affair and hardly worth mention.

The Chicago and Michigan Lake Shore railroad was built during 1870, and its trains began on schedule early in 1871. Later it bore the name Chicago and West Michigan railroad, and finally the Pere Marquette.

There were no large industries established for perhaps twenty years, though small mills were brought in and operated at different places almost from the first. These will be mentioned later. From perhaps 1860 on, and until the pine was exhausted there were saw mills at Singapore, Saugatuck, Douglas and Fennville that employed quite a number of men. At Saugatuck, especially, there was more industry than elsewhere on account of the added number of mills. About 1880 the pine began to close out and the mills were taken out. Smaller mills took their place, and from 1890 there was not lumber sawing enough to be worthy of mention.

No large mills were established for the hardwood cut, the demand for that lumber being limited mostly to furniture and floors, and the small mills did that work. In fact, the demand for hardwood lumber did not develop until the pine was about gone.

Much of the hardwood was slashed and burned to clear the land for crops until about 1860, when there was a demand for cord wood in Chicago, and for railroad fuel after the road came, and from then on not much good wood was wasted.

About 1880 coal began to come into use for fuel and the demand for wood grew less on the market, but local demand for house fuel took up such as was yet for sale. And, too, the wood surplus was being exhausted. In some sections considerable wood was used in the manufacture of charcoal, but not here.

* * *

It was the custom to receive all comers with open arms, lodge and feed them until they could get a start. They were not only willing to do so, but were obliged to, for there was not place where strangers could stay. All were considered honorable until proven otherwise.

There were jolly times at barn raisings and logging bees, where everybody turned out, and they all worked with a will. No one was in good repute who lagged behind with the work and partook freely of the bountiful feeds put up on such occasions. A logging bee was for a day, usually, and men came with teams and drew together the timber that had already been cut down and the brush burned, piled into good sized heaps, and it was burned to clear the land ready for cropping.

Barn raising was for just the time necessary to place the heavy timber frame in position, which usually required half a day. Always a good meal at the finish, and a jolly time, as the ladies were as busy as the men were at their work.

Corn huskings were more of the nature of a social, where they all got together and had a good time, the same as paring bees and candy pulls. A boy and girl would sit at a shock of corn, one on either side, and if the boy found a red ear he was privileged to kiss the girl. That caused much merriment.

Sheep washing and soap making were individual affairs, as these were chores that did not require extra help. If a man needed help in these he hired it.

* * *

It was not until about 1880 that commercial sugar could be had at a price that warranted its purchase, so we all depended on making our own sugar. Maple trees were tapped, from the number of fifty to perhaps five hundred, in the spring. Large store troughs were made by digging out a white wood tree and placing it at the "boiling place," and the sap was gathered in a hogshead placed on a sled, drawn in and emptied into the trough. The boiling pan was kept busy all day, and if the sap was running too fast for the capacity of the pan by day only, they ran day and night. The sap was boiled down to a good table syrup in the pan, and if required as syrup it was stored in half barrel wooden tubs. The same was the case when soft sugar was the need, but when we wanted loaf sugar or cake sugar as it was sometimes called, the syrup was transferred to a large iron kettle, possible ten to twenty gallon capacity, and evaporated sufficiently for that condition, and that was called "sugaring off" or "boiling down," and when started we had to keep it boiling until done, which frequently took until midnight or after. That proved a fascinating occupation. Quite a crowd of young folks would gather at the "boiling place," off in the woods, and have the time of their lives. We usually had plenty of snow, and would keep testing the density of the sugar by turning a little onto some snow to cool -- and I never knew of it being put back into the kettle, whether done or not. Sometimes it would settle into a wax unless the maker understood the process of sugaring off. The wax was not every desirable.

* * *

We had our singing schools, and spelling matches, too, and dancing parties for amusement, though the early dance was nearly always interrupted by a rowdy element that knew no other way to makes themselves conspicuous than to start a fight. It was their habit to bring whiskey and get boozy as part of their preparation for the occasion. If they could muster up a sufficient element to break up the dance they considered they had made themselves famous. Perhaps they had. But as society became better established that element grew up and out of the race and the younger generation grew up more civilized and out of the woods, and such people came to have some respect for the law, the rough house gangs were eliminated and we had no more of it. In fact, we might say it vanished along with the woods and the lumbering crowd.

Sleigh rides were a popular pastime during the winter season, when a goodly amount of fresh straw was placed in the bottom of the sleigh box, blankets over that, and the young folks piled in. With robes (many of them genuine buffalo) spread out over the whole. The colts skipped and danced and the bells set up a merry jingle, while the merriment of the crowd joined in to make it a gala occasion. Occasionally two or more sleigh loads joined in to give some unsuspecting neighbor a "surprise party." Talk about fun! The auto and the movie of today are not in it. And we always had snow in season, for the good and sufficient reason that there was standing timber to afford a wind break, and the snow lay where it fell instead of being blown about and worn out in drifting.

* * *

In 1851 the Ganges M. E. church was organized by Rev. B. F. Doughty, and in 1860-61 the parsonage and church were built at the north edge of Pier Cove. In 1882 the church building was torn down and moved to its present location at Ganges corners. Mr. Mullen succeeded Mr. Doughty as pastor.

The Baptist church was organized on July 16, 1853, by Rev Harvey Munger. The first pastors were Rev. Austin Harmon, followed by Rev. Dr. C. P. Grovener. The church and parsonage were built at the present site, southwest corner of section 3, Ganges, in 1880. Church services were held in school houses until churches could be built.

* * *

The history of the first schools in western Allegan county was contained in earlier letters. (See sketch on Singapore.)

The first school between Allegan and Singapore was taught in the first shack built by Levi Loomis on his land in Ganges, 1842. Mrs. Lyman Loomis was the teacher. The next term was held in a log house owned by David Hutchins, back on the hill at the east end of the crossway at north line of section 1. Fred Lymon, teacher. The following year school was held at the same place: Abe Gidley, teacher.

Mary Elizabeth Peckham (Morrison) the first school teacher on the western side of Allegan County. She began near Singapore about 1836.

In 1845 a school house was built on the James Wadsworth place, on section 2, Ganges. It stood on top of the hill, south side of the town line road, west of the present location of the school house in district No. 1. I have not learned who taught the first term there. As a matter of history, as well as to settle a controversy as to what became of this first school house, I will produce here a letter from Mrs. Sarah Knox Grover, dated April 20, 1922:

"The little unpainted frame school house in district No. 1, township of Ganges where I was a teacher, was burned to the ground late in February, 1861. Disastrous to the school, for there was no room available for school, and for me, for I was paid in the wild cat bills which were the circulating medium at that time, when they might be good one day and good for nothing the next.

"There were three boys about 16 years old who kindly relieved me of the duty of building the morning fire, and that unlucky morning, when I had plodded over more than a mile through the snow, I found the house in flames. Below are the names of all the pupils that I recall, and Henry Mead is the only one living, I think: James, Eugene, Alfreda, Alzeda and Azella Billings, Sarah Jane and Henry Cowles, Addie, Sophia and Jay Smeed, Delos and Nellie Fuller, Abbie and Alicia Baragar, Tommy Braman, Judson Loveridge, James Henderson, and three temporary ones whose names I cannot recall." [I well remember the time the Billings school house burned. I was in my eighth year, and it was the first time I learned that a building could burn. -- H.]

There was another school house built on the same site right away, and this was used until the school year of 1867. The following extracts from the minutes of school meeting will show when this building was sold and the present one built, all in district No. 1, Ganges:

"Special school meeting, Sept 3, 1866. Voted to raise by tax $300 to be expended on a new school house.

"Voted John Wadsworth, Amos S. Braman and Nelson Smeed select a site for a school house."

"Sept. 22, 1866. Voted to purchase one acres of land of James W. Billings for the sum of $40, said land to be purchased for a school house site. The acres of land to be purchased is to be a site for a new school house, and is situated on the n. w. corner of the n. e. fr., 1/4, Sec. 2, town 2 north and range 16 west."

"Voted to sell the old school house, wood house and privy. Nelson Smeed was authorized to sell the old house for the sum of $32.25, to be paid for by January, 1867."

"At a special meeting held in school district No. 1 on Thursday, the 28th day of March, for the purpose of choosing a building committee. The voters of said district met at the school house site in said district, and was called to order by the moderator, and a committee of three was chosen -- Seth Loveridge, Jilett Spenser and Nelson Smeed."

"Voted to raise by tax $300.47 to pay Nelson Smeed for services on the new school house."

"Voted to raise $500 for finishing said school house."

Monies were voted for grading the grounds and building a fence, and Horace Fuller was given until the 1st day of May, 1868, to finish painting the school house.

"Nov. 8, 1898, paid John Shaeffer $400 for repairing the school house."

This last must have been when the siding was taken off and the building brick veneered.

* * *

The first school house, built in 1845, seems to have been the seat of learning for the next two years, and until the term of 1847, when there was another district established farther east, and what proved to be the first school in the Fennville district. The session was held in a little shanty Mr. McCormick had used to shave shingles in. It stood in the road right of way about ten rods east of the west line of the J. H. Wadsworth place, 3/4 of a mile west of Fennville. The teacher in this case was Miss Laura C. Hudson, who had come to the county the previous year from Hudson, Ohio. In June following she became the wife of Harrison Hutchins, and passed the remainder of her life in Ganges. She was a direct descendant from Henry Hudson, the navigator, who discovered the Hudson river in 1609, and Hudson Bay in 1610, which last became both his grave and his monument.

I will let cousin Jack Hall tell the next term of school in the Fennville district. In a talk of February 15, 1914, he said: "My first term of school was in a little log shanty, about 16 or 18 by 20 feet, shanty roof. Martha Lamoreaux was the teacher. She married Henry Baragar. Probably this was about 1848. The house stood on the southeast corner of the first crossroads west of Fennville. It had a loose board floor, slab seats made by sticking pegs into a slab, no back to the seats, and the roof leaked when it rained."

The first school house in the Fennville district was built on the southeast corner of what is now the E. D. Wadsworth place, about ten rods west of where the shingle shanty above mentioned stood, and the next term of school must have been held there, which would be the school of 1849. I have never been able to uncover any except the two terms mentioned, outside the "Veeder school house," as it was called. Miss Lucy Lonsbury of Allegan was one of the first teachers in the house, though I an not sure she was the first.

24
Building Roads

A. H. Stillson said: "The first road job let in this section was to Uncle Hat Hutchins, about 1840 or '41, and was for the building of a crossway over the swamp west of his house and in front of and west of Grandfather Hutchins' house. Previous to this time the road followed around to the south on top of the hill. Uncle Hat cut the logs, I hauled them in with old Pete and Larry, and grandfather laid them in the swamp.

"Uncle Harrison worked another road job in the fall of 1844, beginning at the four corners of sections 27, 28, 33, and 34, Ganges, and running south between sections 33 and 34 half a mile. At that time I was a lad of 15 years. He and I built a brush house, and I did the cooking while Uncle Hat did the chopping on the job. The road was cleared by falling the timber out either way from the center of the road line and chopping the body into logs ready to be hauled aside, and clearing off the brush.

"At this early date the scattering settlers transacted most of their business by barter and trade, about the only way of getting money being from the county by working road jobs, as there was no outlet to market such produce as they were able to raise. And frequently when the job was completed there was not enough money in the county road fund to pay the orders and they were either passed as currency or held until the money was collected by the county treasurer.

"All western Allegan county was in the one township of Newark at this time, so all the eight squares, except Manlius, were under the supervision of one set of officers, and in drawing town orders they were all supplied by the one commissioner. While uncle was doing the job mentioned above in the south part of what is now Ganges, another man (we will call him Jones, though that was not his name) was working another job over in Saugatuck. Each understood the situation as to payment of town orders, and each put forth his best efforts to complete his job first, and get his order, as it was known there was little money in the Newark road fund and both could not be paid at present.

"I never in my life saw timber fall as they did. As long as there was daylight the air swished, the chips flew, and the trees fell with crash after crash under the ax of the strong and experienced woodsman. Finally one day at about 10 a.m. the last tree on the contract fell and the job was finished, all but a few underbrush. This uncle left for me to finish while he went on foot for the road commissioner, eight or ten miles away. Towards night I had finished clearing off the remaining brush when they came. The job was accepted, but Jones was the commissioner, and claimed he could not make out the order, as he was out of blanks. He looked for them at any time, and would bring the order over as soon as he could. We packed our blankets and utensils, strapped them on our backs and started through the woods for home, where we arrived a midnight. One morning a few days later Mr. Jones with another man, drove up and gave uncle his order and went on east. Uncle suspected he was headed for Allegan, so he put his order in his pocket and followed behind on foot, just before reaching Swan Creek Uncle took an Indian trail that cut off about half a mile of the distance, and came in the road well ahead of Jones, the latter not suspecting what was on. He reached Allegan and got his order cashed, but before starting home asked the treasurer how much money there was left in the Newark road fund, and was informed that 75 cents covered the balance. When uncle came to the edge of town on his way home he met Jones going in.

The latter was much surprised and asked where they had passed. Uncle said it must have been at the Indian trail. We called it a good joke."

Yours Truly
Harrison Hutchins

The second white man to arrive at Singapore. This information has just come to light, and was not at hand for mention in earlier letters:

Elisha Weed came to Michigan from the state of Maine, when a boy in company with his parents, who established a home at Silver Creek, this county. In 1832, when 19 years old, he went from there to the mouth of the Kalamazoo, via Black river. At the mouth of Black river he found one small shack to represent the place where South Haven now is. The Indians pointed out a place where he could ford the river, which he did and came on. On arriving at his destination he found Mr. William G. Butler and two Frenchmen. One was called St. Pierre and the other One-Eyed John. Mr. Butler hired him to build a warehouse. Later he helped build nearly all the other buildings there -- the New York saw mill, the bank, etc. He frequently spoke of the early comers -- Stephen D. Nichols, J. P. Wade, S. A. Morrison and others.

Elisha Weed was born in Penobscot county, Maine, October 12, 1813, and was married April 3, 1841, to Sarah Bates of Portage, Kalamazoo county, Michigan, who was born in St. Lawrence county, New York, in 1813. Their children were Theodore, Ames (born in Saugatuck in 1844), Louisa, and Eoline (born in Ganges in 1851). We do not have the date of Mrs. Weed's death, but his second marriage was in 1856, when he married Myra Jane Burwell at New Haven, Indiana, bought a home at Plummerville, Ganges, and settled there. Here it was that their three sons were born and who now live -- Orlando and Frank at South Haven and Cephas at Douglas. He died at the home of his son Orlando in Casco in 1904, and his widow died in 1914. His brother Orlando also lived at Plummerville in 1847 when the first Ganges town meeting was held at his home. he went to California in 1849, and did not return.

* * *

Elisha Weed had three cousins here who also took their part in the early doings of the community. They were William, Lorenzo and Joshua Weed.

Joshua Weed came to Singapore in 1833, where he worked at the carpenter's trade. When 20 years old he walked through from Toledo, Ohio. He worked in several of the mills in Saugatuck, and built the first Jimmy Haile saw mill on the Lake Shore road before 1845. About 1860, when that mill was overhauled, Mr. Weed built in the new water wheel. Mr. C. M. Link said Dan Reamer rebuilt the mill in 1860, so no doubt Mr. Weed put in the new wheel at the same time. Mr. Weed also built the M. E. church at Pier Cove, and the old Newcomb house in Ganges, and worked at Plummerville for two years. He and his cousin Elisha were frequently on the same jobs. Perry, Elmer, George and Will are his sons. Perry and Elmer are still living.

The only knowledge at hand of Lorenzo Weed is that during the civil war his family were living at Pier Cove, and his wife was either a widow or a war widow. I knew of his children only, Arthur, Charley, Alice (Mrs. Cobb), Maria (Mrs. John Wilkinson of Casco), and Inez (Mrs. Wallace White). I have no record of the family of William Weed.

* * *

A bit of Douglas history has just come to light which seems worthy of mention. In raking over the dusty corners of my old cranium it occurred to me that the Weeds used to operate a basket factory in Douglas, but I could not satisfy myself from what I found there, so I wrote Frank Weed of South Haven for anything he might know, and following is his reply:

"About the year 1876 I began working in

the Douglas basket factory, then owned by Capt. Robert Reid. William Weed, coming from Iowa, together with Joshua Weed, bought the factory, then valued at three or four thousand dollars, and moved it to its present site, where they built the present factory after buying out Capt. Reid. I think about the year 1878 they gave the company the name William Weed & Co. Later E. E. Weed and others, taking over the interest of William and Joshua Weed, gave it the name of E. E. Weed & Co."

* * *

The Billings Family

I believe no other family, taken as a whole, had a greater hand in the early activities in this community than the three Billings brothers -- Charles T., Walter, and John H. Let's go back east, and bring them in.

James Billings was born in Stonington, Connecticut, October 11, 1751. In May, 1775, he enlisted at Stonington in the Colonial army, in Capt. James Eldridge's company, Co. L. H. Parsons' regiment, served his time, and received his discharge, re-enlisted, and repeated until he received his final discharge on February 6, 1780. He died in November, 1829, at the home of his son Walter at Clarkston, Monroe county, New York.

Charles Townsend Billings was born in Monroe county, New York, December 11, 1813, and was a son of James Billings (James, son of James) and Mary Townsend, his wife. On September 16, 1837, he married Rebecca Baragar, daughter of Peter and Helen (Van Natten) Baragar, of Monroe county, New York, who was born July 23, 1815. They came to Michigan in the summer of 1845, and stayed in Allegan until the summer of 1846 when they came to Clyde township and settled on the farm where they lived until October, 1884, when he died, followed by his wife in 1901. His daughter Mary was the first white child born in Clyde, and his daughter Helen the first bride when she married Stephen A. Atwater. He cleared his land, built his home, and took the part of a member of the community. Both were highly respected people, as are their children and grandchildren at the present time.

* * *

Walter Billings was born in Monroe county, New York, April 18, 1818. He came to Michigan in 1837 with the family of his sister Maria (Billings) McCormick, and married Sarah Wilson of East Allegan in 1838. He then returned to New York state and lived at Rochester. After about five years he came back to Michigan and bought the James Wadsworth place on section 2, Ganges, where they had their home until she died on April 6, 1881, and he followed, October 19, 1899.

In addition to his farming, Walter owned and operated a store in Pier Cove, during the peak of its prosperity, and too the position of a lawyer in settling court actions, and trafficked in various ways. He served as a soldier during the war of the rebellion, and underwent the suffering common to the southern military prisons, receiving his honorable discharge at the close of the war. His son James and sons-in-law, H. B. Hudson, who married Ann Billings, and Samuel Stillson, who married Maria, also were veterans of that conflict.

During his later years he owned a horse named Billy and a dog he called "Watchie, my son." The three drove to Iowa, Kansas and Nebraska several times from here, camping out nights the same as in soldier life. It was often remarked how the three of them understood each other and how faithful they were, each to his share of the combination.

Maria Billings was born March 23, 1816, and was married in August, 1830, to James McCormick of Monroe county, New York. He was born February 7, 1806. The history of their coming here and their after life has been given in earlier letters. Their great-grandson, George DuVal, now owns the old homestead, which has never been out of the possession of the family. And now what about the Jimmy Haile saw mill just mentioned?

It stood on the Lake Shore road, on a little creek that crossed section 29, Saugatuck township, about one and a half miles north of the Ganges line. I have not been successful in getting the exact year in which it was built, but it seems to have been the first saw mill in the lake shore section after Singapore. It was in operation during the summer of 1845, we know.

Captain C. M. Link said he was on board the schooner **Francis Mills** in 1845, when they took a load of tan bark from the Jimmy Haile place, "the lighter being made by digging out two logs, and planking them over. There was a flutter wheel saw mill on the site before I came here."

A. H. Stillson said it must have been built at some time in the forties. "I saw them digging the pond and putting in the dam."

Mr. Perry Weed said his father built this mill, and that about 1860 or 1862 put in the new water wheel.

For some reason this mill seems to have been rebuilt about 1860 and a new overshot wheel installed. Stillson said it would take two or three

44

days in ordinary weather to fill the pond, then they would run for a day or two. "The old lady would set the saw into a log, and go over across the road and take a smoke. When the board was cut off it would trip itself, and she would go back and set it into another cut." It served a needed purpose, however, as people could bring their own logs there and have them cut into lumber, where otherwise they could not afford the cost of buying ready-made boards.

Mr. A. D. Goodrich said the oldest saw mill here (after Singapore) was that of Mr. James Haile, on the bank of Lake Michigan, about two miles south of Douglas. "The mill stood on the top of the bank, which must be 60 or 70 feet high, and was operated by a 24 foot overshot water wheel that stood down the bank and was fed by a small creek. It was a sash saw mill, and as a sash saw mill ran more slowly than a muley, the capacity of the mill could not have been very large. The lumber was slid down the bank and scowed out to vessels for the Chicago market. I do not know the date the mill was built, but James C. Haile was living here as early as 1836 or 1837."

The "Jimmy Haile place" was not only noted for its having the first country saw mill, but the residence was a large rectangular frame house, the second floor of which was fitted out as a community hall, and here it was that gatherings of all sorts were assembled. It was the only place where public dances could be held for years before the main street of Fennville was more than a frog pond and a breeding place for mosquitos. It was a landmark, and distances and times were recorded from the "Jimmy Haile place."

James C. Haile and Amos A. Haile, the first supervisor of Ganges, were brothers and came from Niagara county, New York.

25
Early Steamboats

From *History of Allegan and Barry Counties*, published in 1880:

"The first flatboat of any size on the Kalamazoo was the **Pioneer**, built by James D. Bush of Allegan for Milo Winslow. This vessel carried 100 barrels of flour, and twelve men were necessary to pole it up and down the river. The **Great Western** employed ten men and the **Tippecanoe** eight. There were several others but these were the most important. These boats were in active operation on the river until the opening of the Michigan Central railroad in 1846 furnished a quicker and more convenient mode of transportation.

"About 1842 a flat bottomed steamboat named **C. C. Trowbridge** was built at Singapore by Porter & Co. for river service between Saugatuck and Allegan. It made but two trips, however, and was then transferred to lake service.

"The steamer **Adelaide** was built in the village of Allegan about the year 1847, the machinery being that previously used in the **Maid of the Mist** of Niagara Falls. Capt. Elliott was the commander. It ran from Allegan to Saugatuck one day and back the next for about two years, and was then sold at Chicago.

"J. D. Bush built the **Helen Mar** at Allegan about 1854, and subsequently ran it five or six years on the river. It was finally dismantled. All its machinery was built at Allegan except the boiler. Two barges were built at Allegan about the same time named **Adam** and **Eve**. They were intended for towing on the lake and were the first experiments of the kind.

"The schooner **Lavinda** was built at Allegan in 1861 and was used on the lake, running from Saugatuck to Chicago. (It was still in use in 1880.) The steamer **Aunt Betsey** was built for Ira Chaffee, George Stone and J. J. McMillan. It plied the river for about five years, and was sold to parties in St. Paul, Minnesota.

"In the year 1867 the propeller **Ira Chaffee** was built at Allegan for the lake trade. It was owned by Ira Chaffee, Frederick May, E. B. Costain and George Dutcher. The same year the schooner **White Oaks** was built at Allegan for the lake trade, and the next season the propeller **Dunbar** was built. In 1865 the barge **Utell** was built at Allegan. It ran on the river for a time, but was finally sold to parties in

Grand Rapids.

"Ship building has ceased at Allegan, but is still energetically carried on at Saugatuck. Numerous tugs and lumber barges have been built there, besides several large grain carrying vessels. The year 1879 was an extremely busy one for Saugatuck ship builders, and the business is still increasing there."

Ira Chaffee came to Allegan July 2, 1836, was foreman in the first saw mill at Allegan, assisted in the erection of the Stout mill on Swan Creek, where J. D. Bush built a mill years afterward. This mill was built by and under the supervision of Levi Loomis of Ganges. Mr. Chaffee was connected with the lumber business in Allegan many years, and also in railroading, and built the first pier at the mouth of the Kalamazoo river, and anything that would give employment to labor. He died August 18, 1889, aged 77 years.

J. P. Wade said: "The **Rossiter** was the first steamboat to enter the Kalamazoo river. It was owned and sailed by Capt. Robinson, a one armed man. I do not know the year, but it was after I came in 1844. She only made a few trips, then went away on account of low water at the mouth. The first line steamer that sailed between Saugatuck and Chicago was the **Ira Chaffee** -- E. B. Costain, captain; George Dutcher, engineer."

* * *

Mr. J. P. Wade, who has been quoted at times in these letters was born at Scituate Harbor, Massachusetts, December 15, 1822, and was a son of Snell and D. A. R. (Jacobs) Wade, both natives of Massachusetts and of English descent (a son of Issachar Wade, who was a sailor during the revolutionary war under the colonial government). He was given a good education, and in 1844 came to Singapore to serve as clerk in a general store. Later he operated a mercantile business on his own account, and in 1855 bought a block of 70 acres of land on section 11, Ganges, where he had his home during the remainder of his life. He filled town offices, was bookkeeper at Fenn's mill and for Brooks Hazelton at Clyde Center (now Pearl) in the O. R. Johnson lumber camps. On the farm he shifted gradually from agriculture to fruit, in which he won out and found himself in easy circumstances during his declining years. Like the rest, he started in the woods and conquered the forest, wrestled with logs and stumps and stone and oxen, but he pulled through and landed on top. We all liked J. P., with his New England soft "r."

In 1846 Mr. Wade married Miss Sarah Gilman who bore him one daughter, Lotta. Mrs. Wade died in 1849, and in 1851 Mr. Wade married Miss Sarah Barnes, and to them were born nine children. He died in January, 1913, aged 90 years. She died in February, 1911, aged 78 years. Thus closed the career of two of the outstanding characters who had a hand in establishing the community.

* * *

The Rockwell Saw Mill

Mr. Giles Rockwell and his brother William built a water power saw mill on the southeast quarter of section 6, Ganges, straight back of the house now owned by Mr. H. H. Schoo, on the south bank of the creek, in 1855. It was in operation two years. They sawed lumber for the old Dr. Goodrich house in Ganges, among others. William Rockwell sold his interest to Levi Loomis, and later died in the army during the civil war. After the two years the dam went out and was never repaired. Giles Rockwell came to Allegan in 1846 and moved to Ganges in 1850.

There was a steam power saw mill set in on the southeast quarter of section 11, Ganges, by William S. Phillips in the sixties to cut hardwood lumber for their chair and furniture factory in Chicago.

It was the first chair factory in that city. The lumber was hauled to the lake by wagon and shipped in sailing vessels from Pier Cove and Plummerville piers. It had a capacity of 10,000 to 12,000 feet a day. It was burned in October, 1871, at the time of the great Chicago fire, when all West Michigan was burned over, and was not rebuilt. This mill had a circular saw, an edger, and slab saw. James Gardner was foreman and Thomas Wilson engineer.

* * *

Henry Baragar started a brick yard in 1855 on his farm on section 3, Ganges. It was on the east side of the quarter line, about forty rods south from the town line road. Baragar owned on the east side of the quarter line on the northeast quarter, and S. W. Loveridge on the west side on the northwest quarter. Philetus Purdy and his brother Erastus were somewhat experienced in the art of brick making, so Mr. Baragar hired them to work for him. Also J. H. Barden was on the job. A little later in the season the three boys rented the plant of Mr. Baragar and ran it themselves. Mr. Loveridge cut the wood for them. They were hindered by having to burn green wood, but they had good clay and got out good brick. The community was new and the demand for brick was limited, so the business was not very satisfactory, and after one season the plant was abandoned. Some of their brick is still in use and in a very good state of preservation.

Mr. H. H. Goodrich put up a saw mill on the Plummerville creek about half a mile up from the lake. It was on the south end of the old Goodrich homestead, on section 8, Ganges. The plans were drawn by Jerry Mansfield, an old mill wright, and patterns for the water wheel were made by him also. It used what is called a Muley saw, a stiff saw that supports itself with just a guide at the top, and differs from the older sash saw, which was thin and ran in a frame to support both ends, and the frame went up and down with the saw. The capacity of the mill was about 15,000 feet of lumber a day.

* * *

Glenn Settled in 1843

The first to come to what is now the hamlet of Glenn was Mr. A. N. Crawford in 1845. Mr. George F. Hughes bought forty acres of land that took in the creek that runs half a mile to the west of the cross road there on January 1, 1846, of Mr. Crawford, and the following summer he set in a small water power saw mill on the same land, using the creek for power. Later the dam was carried away and the mill moved some by the flood, but he set it back and enlarged the structure, so he had quite a sizable mill. A sash saw was used in this mill, and it was in operation until 1880. Mr. Hughes was born in Hampshire, England. In 1830, when 15 years old, he came to New York state, and in 1845 moved on to Saugatuck, Michigan. Here he met Mr. Crawford. He was looking for a mill site, and Crawford had one, so he settled there.

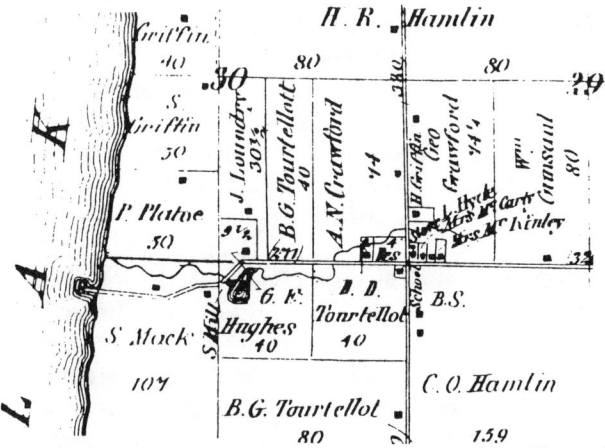

Glenn in 1873 showing a small pier and a mill pond for the Hughes sawmill.

In 1862 Mr. William Packard set up a steam power saw mill on the northwest corner of the cross roads at Glenn. This mill used a Muley saw and had a capacity of 15,000 board feet a day. This mill also operated until the available saw timber played out, and was then moved to Covert, Van Buren county.

These activities created a demand for convenient water transportation, and a pier was run out into the lake at the end of the road running west from the Glenn cross roads. Cord wood and tan bark also came in for shipment here, and the combination of freights made it a point of considerable importance. The Webster pier was later built about two miles north of this place for the shipment of wood and bark.

While the wood output was growing less, agricultural crops increased on the ground cleared, and gradually the fruit industry grew in and continued the life of the place, so the pier was held in active use until the completion of the West Michigan pike on November, 1921. The use of the auto truck had cut in on the pier trade for the previous few years to some extent, but the pike drew away so much that the pier was abandoned here as well as at Ganges, so in 1925 there is scarce a stub standing to show where the business of the community had been carried on.

* * *

A post office had been established here in 1876, and the place was first known as New Casco, and then as Packard's Corners, but in 1879 it was given the name of Glenn, which it has held ever since. I do not know who first operated a store here, but Mr. George T. Clapp was the only merchant for a long time. He was burned out by robber bandits and Mr. L. A. Seymour succeeded to the position and is still in business there. There are now in the place three stores, one meat market, blacksmith shop, package salesroom, school, M. E. church, garage, cider mill, a large community hall, and twelve resort hotels in and near by, besides several others farther away but tributary to Glenn. Autobuses running between South Haven and Saugatuck and taxis care for the passenger traffic and freight is carried by auto truck. It is estimated that 1,000 is about the summer population.

* * *

Thayer First in Casco

John Thayer was the first to come to Casco, in 1844, and moved his family onto section 2 in 1845. Mortimer McDowell and William B. Reynolds began in April, 1845, and settled on section 18, and began at once to make a clearing, so by June of that year Timothy McDowell, father of Mort, moved the rest of the family into the cabin the others had erected. Thayer had begun clearing first, but McDowell was moved in a month ahead. Orletus, one of the sons of John Thayer, was the first man to be married in Casco, when he married Clarissa, daughter of James W. Wadsworth of Ganges. Their daughter Eutheria was the first white child born in the township. And Mrs. Hayes, the mother of Mrs. John Thayer, was the first white person who died there.

The McDowells and Thayers were the only settlers in Casco until 1850, when others moved into the township. They were followed by the Sheffers, Mungers, Hollisters, M. F. Rose, E. H. McLouth, the Thomas brothers, D. H. Cady, the Reeds, Crosby Eaton, A. B. Avery, John Flint, the Buys, John Faben, Thomas Iddles, R. Bowles, W. Crates, the Hamlins, L. W. Osborn and Andrew Brown, all of who settled in the town between 1850 and 1860.

* * *

Thus far the settlements were along the lake shore mostly, and the eastern portion was not settled to any extent until after 1865.

Soon after the McDowells settled here a road was cut out along the shore to Saugatuck, but the lake beach was the only road to St. Joseph for some time.

A good sized dam was put across the north branch of Black River, in section 9 in Casco by an eastern company, and a water power saw mill and grist mill established, superintended by a Mr. Manning, who was sent here from the east for the purpose. It appears this was done in the early sixties. It ran a Muley saw and had a capacity of 8,000 or 10,000.

Mr. Ed Kenter set up a steam saw mill on the land of John Wilkinson, on the northwest quarter of section 4, Casco, which was in operation three or four years during the seventies. There also was a mill on section 16, Casco, owned by a Mr. Hawkhead, that operated from perhaps the early seventies until the timber supply was gone. That stood a short distance north from the Hawkhead post office as it is now.

Most of these later named mills were worked in beech and maple timber, though there were scattering amounts of other kinds, as oak, hemlock and some pine. The principal growth in this section was beech and maple.

26
The Plummers

One of the outstanding pioneers of Newark, Mr. Benjamin Plummer, has been mentioned earlier, and a short biographical sketch of his early life may be of interest. He was born in Maine on November 20, 1802, and was the oldest child of David and Hannah Ames Plummer, both natives of New Hampshire. They were in Pennsylvania for a brief time, then went to Waynes county, Ohio, where his father died in 1828. The mother accompanied her son to Michigan, where her death occurred in 1857.

In 1827 Mr. Plummer married Miss Elvira Andrews who was born in Onodaga county, New York, in 1805, her parents having been natives of Connecticut and pioneers in Ohio in 1824. In 1834 they came to Michigan and as there was no way open for travel further than Pine Creek, Mr. Plummer constructed a raft at the place and floated his family down the Kalamazoo to its mouth. They had some narrow escapes on the way down, but nothing serious happened. Their son Andrew was born in a shanty that stood on the corner of the Morrison lot, just south of the Leland block in Saugatuck in 1835, and was the first white child born in Saugatuck -- in fact the first in western Allegan county, since there were no settlements elsewhere at that time.

We have noted his mill at Wallinville ("Dingleville," as it is called on account of the cow bells to be heard in the vicinity at night), and his establishment of a mill at Plummerville, which still bears his name.

* * *

Daniel A. Plummer was born and raised on his father's farm in the state of Connecticut, and removed with his parents to Medina, Ohio, when that section was quite new. He was a veteran of the Black Hawk war, and settled in Kalamazoo county, Michigan, in 1830. Here he met and married Miss Jane Giddings. In 1834 they removed to Saugatuck where they were the third family to settle at the mouth of the Kalamazoo river, where he engaged in ship carpentering. At the first election of township officers he was elected supervisor for the township of Newark, and at the first meeting of that board in 1836 he was chosen as one of a committee of three to carry the report of the election to the legislative council. A few years later he operated the old Exchange Hotel and the Allegan House at Allegan.

In 1849 Daniel A. Plummer crossed the plains to California, in company with several others, they being six months on the road with oxen. He was quite successful and finally located in Oakland, where he died in 1888.

* * *

Nathaniel D. Plummer, who was elected justice of the peace at the first town meeting in Ganges in 1847, sold his holdings on section 9, Ganges, to Richard Mack in 1864, and started for California with a horse team. They ran away and he was injured, so gave up the trip, bought a farm in Cass county, near Cassopolis, and had his home there to the end. One of his daughters became Mrs. Lyman Davis, and another married James Keirnan. Mrs. Plummer and Mrs. Capt. A. A. Johnson were sisters.

* * *

There are three points of especial interest in Clyde Township. First, arranged by dates, the Bailey mill; second, the Pine Plains tavern; and third, Fennville.

Regarding the Bailey mill, some say Jacob Bailey and others say Leonard Bailey, while still others credit both as the builders of this historic little saw mill. We will therefore use the latter version, and say that in 1837 the Baileys came into section 10 of Clyde with a crew of men, and erected a steam saw mill for or in the interest of some New York state land owners known as Green, Mitchell & Co. (In a former letter I said Mann's mill, at Manlius, was the first between Allegan and the lake shore, but that was an error, for Swan Creek and Bailey's mills were in operation while Mr. Allen was establishing his plant at Richmond, and Mann built his mill after Allen had failed. Mann's mill was the first in Manlius.)

The Bailey's sawed lumber and cleared land industriously for two years, and then moved out with men and machinery in 1840. I well remember the sawdust pile still remaining in the sixties. Old settlers told me years ago that the cause of closing this mill was the difficulty in disposing of the lumber. They were in the heart of the virgin pine, and should have succeeded had it not been for the long haul over the sandy trails to Allegan or the Kalamazoo river. In either case there was the added cost of rafting to the mouth, since there was no local market of consequence at Allegan. This mill stood one-half mile west from the cemetery in the woods southeast of Fennville, and a few rods south of the Rosenaw corner there.

BENJAMIN PLUMMER.

There were two trails from Swan Creek to the lake shore during these early times. One was by way of the Bailey mill to Ganges, known as the Bailey mill road, and the other by way of the Pine Plains Tavern and the Richmond bridge to the mouth. These two points became landmarks by which routes and distances were calculated.

Mr. James Harris was a millwright working at the mouth, and in 1839 was called to repair the Bailey mill. After the failure of Green & Mitchell he built the tavern on section 1, Clyde township, on the Allegan-Singapore road. It was located on the east town line, half a mile south and directly east from Fennville. Mr. Harris operated the tavern nine years, and then traded it to Dr. Coates for land in Otsego. Coates ran it about two years and sold it to Mr. B. W. Phillips. Later it passed into the hands of George Smalley. It was the half-way house between Allegan and the mouth for a good many years, and the stage always halted there. Dancing parties were held there, and there was a bar in connection, so it did quite a thriving business until the railroad came and the stage was discontinued. From then on it was of doubtful importance as an enterprise, but was a landmark until it burned down, perhaps in the late eighties.

* * *

Mr. Boyd W. Phillips died in Allegan, March 8, 1892. He was born at Manlius, Onondaga county, New York, August 16, 1813; came to Michigan, then a territory, in 1836, settling in Cass county. In December, 1853, he came to Allegan, and soon after moved into the old Pine Plains House, which he kept many years and afterward for a short time kept hotel at Saugatuck. He was three times married -- first in Lockport, New York, to Miss Harriet A. Barton, who died in Cass county in 1846; second in Pine Plains to Mrs Pamela Cook; and third at Saugatuck to Mrs. Kate Sherwood who, with two sons, and a daughter, survived him. Mrs. Phillips was a Universalist in religion. He was well known by all the early settlers in Allegan county.

* * *

At about the time Mr. Harris built on section 1, Clyde, Mr. R. G. Winn came into section 6, and they were the only settlers in the town until the summer of 1846, when Charles T. Billings came in on section 6. About this time Mr. Winn moved to Saugatuck (still known as Newark), and Mr. Harrison Fry moved into the Winn shack. It stood on the southeast corner of the cross roads first west of Fennville, and this was the same shanty in which Miss Martha Lamoreaux taught the second term of school in the Fennville district in 1848, mentioned earlier.

* * *

David Walter built the first public hall in the Fennville district in 1867. It stood on the northeast corner of section 6, Clyde township, one-half mile west of Fennville, and was in the capacity of a community hall. Fennville at this time was merely a small saw mill, with a boarding house for the hands, post office in a small store, and blacksmith shop. The community, though scattering was more to the west. Here it was that political rallies were held. Dancing parties and socials were brought here, and it was the half-way hall between Pine Plains and the Jimmy Haile place. Mr. Walter used the first floor for a general store and lived in a wing placed on the west side, the hall occupying the whole of the second floor. by 1878 Fennville had become established and other halls were in use in the hamlet, so in that year Mr. Walter moved his building over to the east side of the railroad track, near where the oil tanks are, but near the street, and converted it into a hotel. In the spring of 1890 Ed Williams was operating the hotel that stood where the Stevens now stands and he bought the Walter house and joined it on his building, forming a south wing, where it stood until the old Fennville House burned.

David John Walter was born in Wurrtemberg, Germany on May 15, 1823, and died at Fennville, March 30, 1890. Caroline Augusta Junke (pronounced Yunke) was born in Hanover, Germany, December 13, 1815, and survived him by several years. About 1849 they sailed for America, and formed an acquaintance on board ship. They were married on reaching New York, and settled in Rochester. Here it was that William, Charles and Lizzetta (Mrs. Horace Hutchins) were born. In the summer of 1854 they came to Clyde township and settled on the southeast corner of section 6, where their land butted against Hutchins lake. Mr. Walter was a shoemaker by trade, and there it was that the footwear for this whole community was manufactured. People took choice calf hides to the Morrison tannery at Saugatuck for tanning and then to Mr. Walter for the making.

At this home Henry, Caroline and Julius were born. Will now lives in Fennville; Lizzetta died here November 27, 1922; Henry and Julius live at Deer Park, Washington; and Caroline, now Mrs. James Palmer, at Blanchard, Idaho. All are doing well in their western homes. Charles is a miner and owns mining property of value in Montana, and has his home with his nephew, Emery Hutchins, near by.

Mr. Walter took more than an ordinary interest in public affairs, and was accurate and punctual in all he undertook. He filled various offices in the township and school district, and while not one of the first to come to the community, he was here before his town was set off, and was an early member of that town.

We can never forget the boots he made us -- we did not have shoes until about 1880 -- with red tops and copper toes. They were the pride of all the youngsters at school, and there was some difference of opinion as to which was the preferred color, red or blue, Mr. Walter supplied either color on request.

* * *

An amusing incident occurred at the Walter place by the lake about 1857 or 1858. A friend of the family named Charles Hahn came from Rochester, New York, to visit them, and had expressed the wish to hear the howl of a wolf. He did not want to return home without that experience. One still evening the folks told him if he would step outside the house he would realize his wish. He stood there a few moments, and sure enough there they were, just off to the east a way. The sound came nearer until it sounded like it was coming right into the house. Hahn rushed in and up the ladder into the attic to escape. His curiosity was fully satisfied right then, and he wanted no more.

The fact was there was a runway that came from off the pine woods to the east and ran just south of Walter's house and on toward the west by south. The wolves had found a deer and were chasing it along that path, making their usual fiendish howl while on the chase. A pack of wolves were intelligent animals and when after a deer one would run on either side, off at a short distance, while others would follow behind. A deer could outrun a wolf, but would be so frightened that it would tire out and they could overtake it after a long run.

On another occasion Mrs. Walter and some of the children were in the yard waiting for Mr. Walter to return from away, when they heard a disturbance at the brush fence in front of the house. Presently a large bear ambled over the fence and came toward the house. It turned and went out the gate where Mr. Walter was expected to come in. This frightened them terribly, and they were relieved when he returned safely, as he carried nothing for defense. John Billings shot the bear a little later. Their son Will, now living in Fennville, well remembers these incidents, and more, as he was a witness to both mentioned. Their home was at the north edge of the big swamp, which abounded in bear, wolves, deer and rattlesnakes.

* * *

Such was Clyde during the middle of the 19th century, but what a change! The valuable forests of the eastern portion of the town all were stripped away by the lumber barons, and most of it is now just a waste section of sand. On the western portion the swamp was long ago cleared and drained. Valuable mint and vegetable lands, some in large blocks, lie where the wild life above mentioned prevailed. Some of the most valuable muck farms in the state now lie where fifty years ago it was hardly safe for humans to cross. Thus we see such tremendous reversals of condition within the span of many now living here.

Next week we will let Mr. E. A. Fenn tell of the foundation upon which Fennville was when he first visited the locality in 1851.

27
Address by E. A. Fenn

[Mr. Fenn's address, in part, as given at the County Pioneer Society in Allegan, August 27, 1890.]

First of all, let me say I am glad to meet and participate with you in the exercises and festivities of this annual pioneer meeting. I notice, however, that this is not exclusively a meeting of the early pioneers of Allegan county. I do not count myself as one; I know practically but little of the experiences of the early pioneers. They were here when I came, and had provided homes of comfort for themselves, and the newcomer was invited to share in the comforts of their homes and their large hearted hospitality until the log cabin or shanty could be prepared for their use -- and in those preparations, with willing heart and skillful hands, assisted in preparing the logs and placing them in position, and soon the first home of the newcomer was ready for occupancy. And then, again those early pioneers sometimes found it exceedingly difficult to obtain provisions for themselves and their families, and were often obliged to make long weary pilgrimages in order to do it. When we came they were producing enough for themselves and some to spare, so that we had no difficulty in obtaining enough of such things as were needful for us at our own doors. And so I say that we who came in '52 knew but little of the experiences of those who came in '32, where there were none before them, and they were obliged to construct, with poles and bark and boughs of trees, a dwelling place which would protect them, partially at least, from storms and from the numerous and not very desirable inhabitants of the forest -- for I am told that in the early day the howling of wolves, roaring bears and festive hedgehogs were quite numerous and that the subtle, venomous massauger was abroad in the land; and I was told by an old pioneer (he is dead now) that the long, shiny blackeyed racer would often follow the traveler on his way in very close proximity, whether on foot or on horseback. he did not say whether the traveler or the racer was on horseback, but I suppose it was the traveler, for he said that when turned upon and pursued he would rapidly glide out of reach of harm -- evidently meaning the serpent -- but when the traveler turned to pursue his journey the racer would turn and pursue him, insisting upon very intimate companionship for a long distance.

* * *

Now, my friends, I have had no experience in the blue racer business (perhaps some of you have had), but I do remember one time my wife sending our little five or six year old daughter to pick up a garment which had fallen from the line upon the ground. She gathered it up in her arms, brought it into the shanty and laid it on a low chest near where I sat reading. I immediately heard a noise that was not at all familiar to my ear, and said to my wife, "What is that?" at the same time looking in the direction from which the noise proceeded, and there I saw, protruding from the folds of that garment the head and about a foot of the body of a monstrous massager, and unless that snake was crosseyed, he was looking directly at me. I lost no time in reaching for a broom that stood near by, and I pressed the handle of the broom down upon his body about as near the biting end as I could get, for, judging from appearance, attention to that end was of more immediate importance than to the noisy end. I gave the broom handle about all the pressure it would handle until some member of the family procured an instrument of destruction, and he was dispatched.

Now the point I want to make is this: That if the old pioneers were gnashed upon by the prowling wolf, and menaced by the roving bear, and pierced by the quills of the festive porcupine, and daily listed to the rattlings of the massager about their dwellings, and were obliged to submit to the companionship of the blue racer, with fever and ague thrown in if you please, it was nothing compared to those ever present, ever remember ten thousand times ten thousand tiny songsters of the forest. They were exceedingly familiar, tame and intrusive, and were quite numerous at the time of my coming, and even a few years after. I remember meeting a gentleman here in Allegan, from the east, who had no experience with these tiny inhabitants of Michigan. We started one warm summer morning, after a night of warm rain, for what is now known as Fennville, through an almost unbroken wilderness. We had not proceeded far before I noticed my friend was becoming uneasy and restless, and after a little seemed to be quite nervous, but when we reached Swan Creek he was just frantic, and his hands and arms were moving about in a very energetic and careless manner. I was sitting as composed as possible by his side in the wagon, watching the movements and taking in the situation. I noticed that his raiment was better calculated for hot weather than for protection against mosquitos. I expected every moment to hear him vehemently remark, for he had been speechless for quite a while. I concluded finally that he was too busy to talk, or too full for utterance, or perhaps not sufficiently familiar with those words which would fully express his feelings. he might, however, be turning them over in his mind -- and he might, for aught I knew, be saying his prayers.

But I wanted to know what his thoughts were, and said to him: "You seem to be a little uneasy; are you cold, or what is the matter?" "Matter!" he exclaimed. "I should think if you had any eyes you could see, or any feelings you could feel." "Oh," I said, "do the mosquitos trouble you?" And again he was speechless and his whole mind seemed to be intensely occupied with his business. But I tried to comfort him with the assurance that it was only a mild introduction into pioneer life -- that it seemed necessary that all bad blood should be extracted from the newcomer before he was properly prepared for pioneer life. But he refused to be comforted, and declared in most positive terms that he would not stay in this godforsaken mosquito hole twenty-four hours if we would give him the whole state of Michigan. But, my friends, he is here yet. He doesn't own half the state, either, but seems to be well satisfied with one of those beautiful peach farms at Fennville. What makes it doubly valuable at the present time, however, is the fact that it has a gas well upon it. [The gentleman mentioned above was Stephen A. Atwater. H. H.]

* * *

We often speak of the hardships and privations of the early pioneers. True, but don't let us fool ourselves for a moment with the thought that they had no enjoyment, for I have come to believe, from my own observation and experience, that there was more real enjoyment in the anticipation of what would follow as they result of those labors and privations than has ever been experienced by the most fortunate of the later ones. The clearing of the first acre -- the first production from the garden -- the first blossoms from the fruit trees -- with what interest they are watched as they develop into mature fruit; and even the first chickens, and the various little promises of production and ample returns for all those labors. And then, again, those good old fashioned gatherings -- no caste, no inviting a select few to the feast that was often prepared in some one of the homes, and neglecting the others. Whole families would come together from miles around upon the long winter evenings, first in one home and then another, until every family had been visited within a radius of -- taking Fennville as a center -- McDowell's in Casco, Benjamin Plummer's in Ganges, James C. Haile's and William G. Butler's in Saugatuck, Thomas Lamoreaux and Ralph R. Mann's in Manlius, and Timothy S. Coates' and B.

W. Phillips' in Pine Plains. Chicken pie, roast pig, luscious venison, hot biscuit, wild honey, and such other good things as were to be had were lavishly provided and eagerly disposed of by a crowd of guests with keen appetites and unrestricted manifestations of real pleasure and enjoyment. Yes, there was much of pleasure in those early days.

* * *

But I find I am getting away from my first thought. I said I did not count myself as one of the old pioneers. I am forcibly impressed with the thought today that, if I am not now I soon will be standing with the very oldest. Those early fathers of our country are fast going into silence, and I may be one of the mediums to perpetuate their memory and deeds to those who shall come after me in these pioneer ranks. It is not likely that any new names of old 1836 pioneers will ever be added to our list. As I said before, they are rapidly passing away, and I hope that the records of this society will hand down for many generations the names of those heroic first comers. Surely those shall be remembered with reverence and gratitude who commenced the conversion of this county into one of the most beautiful counties of the great state of Michigan.

But while the pioneers of my time cannot be remembered as veterans who have faced the hardest of the battle, yet we have done our work earnestly and passing well. Since my coming nearly all these forests have been subdued. Blazed trees and quarter post stakes, upon which was written their location, and which have often afforded valuable information to the weary traveler, and which many of us have eagerly sought, especially near the evening hour, when we were not certain as to our whereabouts, have been removed, and the broad, open, well worked highways now follow their lines.

The long sections of floating causeway logs have also disappeared, and their whereabouts are hardly known. I remember during my first visit to Michigan in June, 1851, crossing one of them in company with our venerable pioneer friend, S. A. Morrison of Saugatuck, and Gen. E. Mix, who was my companion in travel. (He was not a general then, however.) We were on horseback. Practiced horses they were, or they never could have kept on top of those rolling sinking logs. But we did cross safely over.

About the middle of the causeway, however, there was a little rise of ground, or a little island where the causeway logs had been omitted. It was just about large enough for our three horses to stand upon. And there, in the midst of the overhanging briars, cattails, brakes, brush and fallen logs, we stopped our horses that they might recover somewhat from their sea-sickness, before making another plunge. While we were on that island Mr. Morrison took occasion to remark: "Here is some good land. And that was what we were looking for." I supposed he meant the little island we were upon, as it was the only land in sight, but he went on to say that "Whoever lives a few years will see right here some of the most valuable and productive land in Allegan county." I looked earnestly to see whether he had become delirious by his horseback swim, or what was the matter. I knew he was not drunk, for he had been in our company all day, and had steadily refused to take anything when -- I will say Mix, as he is not here to deny it -- offered it to him. But here was a dilemma -- a man of his recognized judgment and business ability who seemed to have lost his mind; his reason had departed. We thought it an urgent case that demanded immediate treatment. The only remedies we had at hand were one or two half pint bottles of ague medication. (I guess, to be honest about it, there was not much ague in it.) However that may be, we insisted upon his taking a dose. I don't think he would have done it if he had been in his right mind. As it was he did it under protest, declaring that when a man was dry there was nothing that tasted as good as water, and when he wasn't dry he didn't need any drink -- another evidence of insanity. Mr. Morrison has recently assured me that that was the last drop of anything of the kind that has touched his lips.

HON. ELAM A. FENN.

Fennville, located by myself, now occupies that exact spot of which I am speaking, and nearly every store and business place is located upon the line of that causeway and those causeway logs lie deep buried beneath the principal street of the village, and there, where cattle were often mired beyond their power to extricate themselves, is now located our race course, and deep wells are necessary for the obtaining of water. Had I been absent from there from that time to the present, and returned, it would have taken strong evidence to convince me that that was the place of which the prophet spoke.

And so I say that we, the second crop of pioneers, have put our shoulders to the wheel and done something in moving forward the work commenced by the early fathers. No only have the fields been made to contribute to the ease and comfort of the husbandman, but education and religious attainments have been advanced with the school houses and churches witness to the energy and enterprise of the inhabitants. I like to see men coming to mill driving a splendid pair of horses of their own whom I have seen in other days wearily wending their way along the little footpath to their habitation with perhaps fifty pounds of flour or a bushel of potatoes on their backs. I love to see those beautiful homes and witness the independence of those who knew so well how they were obtained. But these homes are fast changing hands. Soon the last old pioneer will be gone. Well, if their life's mission is performed, if their work is well done, if they come down to the end as a shock of corn fully ripe, let them fall asleep hoping they will all awake into a higher better life. We will revere their memory, but need not be sad and sorrowful, for the inevitable has written: "The old must die."

* * *

Let us for a moment turn our thoughts from the consideration of things past and present to those which are to come. I see before me today young people who are soon to take our places. Permit me in closing to say a words to you. You will not be called upon to take the places of the departed pioneers in the true sense of the word. They have done their work. You commence where we leave off, and are to prosecute the work to a more perfect finish. There will be much for you to do. See to it then, that the moral atmosphere of your youthful lives is such as will prepare you to do even nobler work than we have done. See to it that not only the beautiful homes prepared for you by your fathers are kept green and productive, but that the lives of the dwellers therein are productive of good, remembering that every life touches some other life, and it should be our aim to leave a healthy impress upon all about us, and thereby make our lives richer and better.

To all I say, perpetuate these gatherings. Make it a point not only to be present, but contribute to the enjoyment of each other. Compare notes, make it an occasion of real pleasure and enjoyment. Let cordial greetings and heartfelt friendship be manifest and we shall come to feel more than ever that it is good to meet once a year at least as one great family of Allegan county.

28
Fennville

In 1852 Mr. Solomon Hoisington came from Akron, Ohio, and bought five acres of land on the northwest quarter of section 29, Manlius township, and built a small steam saw mill there. This location is just two miles due north of the present location of Fennville. He brought two Thair brothers from his home town -- one a son-in-law and the other a millwright -- to help install the mill. In the fall of 1856 John Gilbert Lamoreaux bought the mill on a contract, and sold it back again the next year. Then Hoisington sold the property to E. A. Fenn and Elisha Mix, and Mix sold his interest in the fall of 1860 to Levi Loomis. Fenn and Loomis operated the mill there two years. The late Mr. D. D. Tourtellotte told me he drew lumber from that mill to Pier Cove for shipment to Chicago, using two yoke of oxen as a team -- and O, what roads! In the meantime --

Stephen A. Atwater came from Plymouth, Litchfield county, Connecticut, to where Fennville is in November, 1859, and bought 260 acres of land, part in Clyde and part in Manlius. It ran from the quarter line by the M. E. church east one-half mile to Abbott's corner.

Mr. Atwater was much in need of a mill to cut his timber, and in order to induce Mr. Fenn to move his mill over to the Atwater holdings he deeded Mr. Fenn 50 acres on the west side of his lands in Clyde. The plan was to locate the mill on the east side of the swamp, on the high land near where the Baptist church stands, but then all the lumber would have to pass over the long corduroy in hauling it to Pier Cove or Mack's Landing on the Kalamazoo river for shipment to the Chicago market.

Mr. Fenn bought 25 acres of Henry Bushnell joining his fifty on the west and in the fall of 1863 located his mill on the west side of the swamp and about in the road running south by the blacksmith shop now owned by Mr. Teed. The corduroy road was made of small logs, nine or ten feet long and laid close together in the mud, and with no covering over them. The saw logs were mostly delivered to the mill during the winter, when this was covered with snow, and banked on the east side of what is now the school house hill. It was not graded down then, and made a good rollway. But the sawing was largely done in summer, when the corduroy was bare, and when ships were sailing and could dispose of the lumber.

Jack Hall, who worked in the mill before it was moved said it was a small steam mill, with one upright saw and one edger. It had a quick working engine, with direct connection, the saw being attached to the engine shaft, and the speed of the saw was controlled by the sawyer, who gauged the steam power used by means of a lever.

Fenn and Loomis began sawing in the new location early in 1863, and continued during the two following years, until in 1865 it burned down. Mr. Loomis having lost near $3,000 according to his son Marion, dropped out of the firm and a new and larger mill was soon built in its place. Mr. Emerson of Rockford, Illinois, taking over the Loomis interest, the firm became Fenn & Emerson. Later still Mr. Henry Fisher came into the firm, and the business prospered.

* * *

About 1868 Sherwood & Griswold of Allegan started the first store in the place, with I. P. Griswold in charge, and during the following year Stephen Atwater bought an interest in the stock. In 1866 a post office was established, with E. A. Fenn as postmaster, and the office was named Fenn's Mill. The building used for a store was originally built for a dwelling house, and consisted of a story and a half upright and a one story wing, and stood to the south and west of the mill. How well we remember the genial figure of Mr. J. P. Wade as he sat at his desk busily unraveling the mysteries of the general office!

In 1871 the firm built a new store out on the main road on the lot where the M. E. church now stands, and put in a stock of goods. A church had been built on the lot where the union school now stands, and a boarding house for the mill hands on the opposite side of the road, and several dwellings had been built, as well as a repair and blacksmith shop. The latter was owned by W. W. Hutchins, and Mr. Lacomby, father of Mrs. F. W. Robinson, was blacksmith. Also in 1871 the village was platted, and during the same year the Chicago and Michigan Lake Shore railroad was completed through the place and easy transportation provided close at hand. This rendered Fennville a marketing center and a place of more than ordinary importance to the community. In 1869 the Raymond & Abbott steam saw mill was moved over here from Pier Cove and converted into a shingle mill and placed a few rods south of the saw mill.

In the fall of 1871, while the mills were crowding the manufacture of lumber, lath and shingles, and the store and shops were full of business, came the "big fire of 1871," also known as the "great Chicago fire," and the entire hamlet was burned down except the little church and the boarding house opposite.

* * *

When the railroad time tables and other printed matter came we were all surprised that Fenn's Mill did not appear, but instead we found "Fennville," and for a short time the town had two names -- Fenn's Mill for the post office and Fennville for the station. But finally the name of the office was changed to correspond to that of the station and so it remains.

Will Sieber was the first station agent, and was highly appreciated. He was succeeded in a few years by John Supple, also one of the best agents in charge here, though a mere boy of 18 when he came.

Immediately after the fire of 1871 Bush & Dutcher erected the largest saw mill Fennville ever had. In fact it was built to cut lumber for the new Chicago. So great was the demand for lumber that they ran the mill nearly all the winter of 1871-72 without siding or roof to protect the men, and part of the time it was in operation night and day. During the three busiest years it cut over seven million feet of lumber.

At this time the road was new -- and rough -- and short of rolling stock, and mills all along the line were howling for cars. Mr. Dutcher had two cars loaded with special bill stuff which was to be delivered at a special time or the order would be forfeited. He had notified the agent they were ready, and they were billed out, but the train could not take on more by the time they reached Fennville. The time came when if the night train did not take them out the sale would be lost, and as it was out of the regular dimensions it would cause a big loss. Mr. Dutcher knew that mill men were cursing the train men and complaining to headquarters about lack of service. So, instead of complaining, he had his wife make up the best oyster stew possible, which he took over to the depot, set it on the stove, and told the agent to call in the freight crew and give it to them when they pulled in at midnight. Mr. Sieber did as told. The conductor sent a brakeman ahead to call the head end crew back, and they came swearing about being called out to wade in the deep snow, but no sooner had they begun their lunch than all was well in Fennville. When nearly done the conductor asked who was back of this. He was told that Mr. Dutcher, the mill man, said it was a cold, stormy night, and he thought it would be acceptable. The conductor said, "Hasn't he got some cars to go?" When told yes, and that if they did not go that night the sale would be lost, the conductor asked the train crew if there were not a couple of cars with hot boxes or something. And there were, so two cars were cut out of the train and Dutcher's two were taken.

* * *

Bush & Dutcher continued the manufacture of lumber until the desirable timber had all been cut off, and in 1876 took their mill farther north. A smaller mill was set in to cut out the pickup timber -- stuff that had been culled out by those who had cut down the forests.

During the time the pine was being slaughtered the hardwood lands had been in the process of clearing, and the community became more thickly settled, so by the time Bush & Dutcher moved the mill away there was considerable local demand for lumber, lath, shingles, and the old slashings were hunted over for anything that would make a four by four stick. And too, the price began to rise on lumber, so small mills came in for that work. If memory serves me correctly, Mr. Hulse set in the mill to replace the B. & D. J. L. Reed followed Hulse, and about 1893 George Huff bought the lots from Reed and cleared off the last vestige of the milling business at the old stand. Side tracks ran west from the depot south of the street back to the mill, and lumber piles were stacked along it from the mill to the railroad, and on both sides of the track, during the peak of the milling business here.

About 1879 J. G. Lamoreaux placed a small mill at the east of the railroad and north of the street, which he operated for four or five years, and the John Sherman mill cut the last lingering scrapings of the woods.

* * *

Gradually, as the woods were being stripped of the last vestige of saw timber, lumber began coming back from the north, and the local demand has been supplied by imported goods for the past forty years or more.

What a shame, that a few men with money should be allowed to take over large tracts of that commodity nature had placed within reach of all and for a mere pittance, and snatch it away from the local public. They produced nothing. They grabbed immense fortunes from nature and pocketed the lucre, leaving nothing but the stumps and brush as a thank offering for their gain. Not a park was donated, nor a cent for good roads or other public improvements. There were exceptions, of course, but in a general way that was the result.

No doubt we would any of us do the same thing under similar circumstances, but just the same it is all wrong. Our government should have prevented the acquirement of more of nature's resources than was reasonable for personal welfare. True, there are instances where large capital is required to develop industries, but where the base material is of nature's production, and the manufacturer has had nothing to do with its creation, the balance left, after a reasonable profit, should revert to the general public. And, too, the amount taken should be under strict government

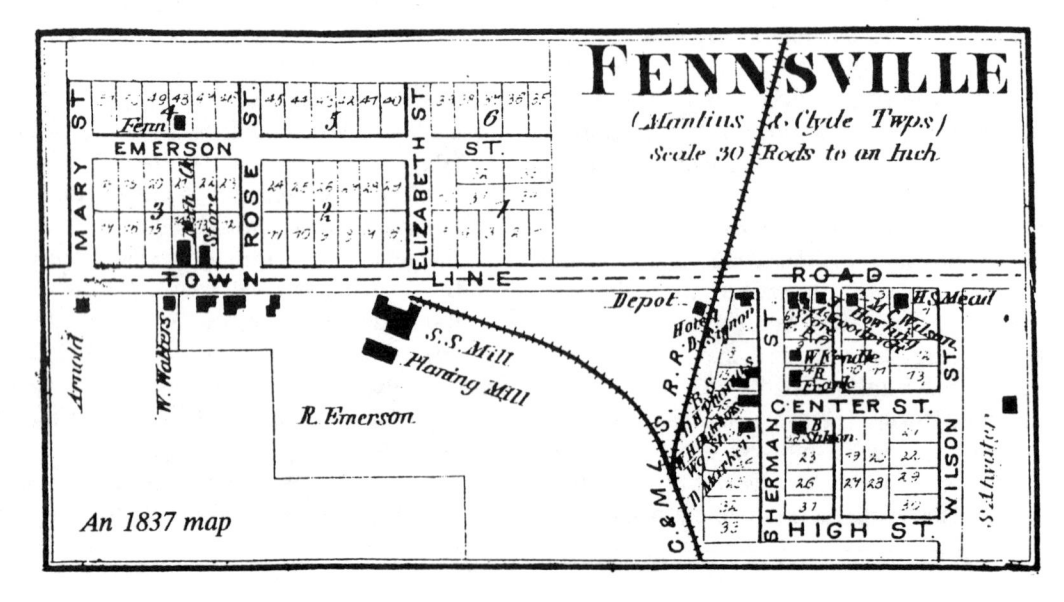

An 1837 map

control, so as to conserve our natural resources in the interest of those who are to follow. Much credit is due Roosevelt, Ballinger, and Pinchot for turning the tide of confiscation of natural resources. Men who used their gain later in local industry are not in this criticism. They remained and helped develop the community, and left their fortunes here to revolve in the business of the neighborhood. But it refers to those who came like a hawk, grabbed all they could, and sailed away. It is they whom I condemn. Direct election of senators and a general leaning toward control are the result, and may the good work go on.

* * *

But I digress. By 1855 our desirable timber had been stripped off, and the community had turned during the process to agricultural pursuits, and Fennville came to be one of the heaviest fruit shipping points along the lake shore.

The Fennville of today can boast of not one vestige of its first nine years' construction -- meaning the village as it was before the fire of 1871 -- except the first mill boarding house. The little church burned down about 1885, and the boarding house was moved over east of the railroad. It was later brought back, and now formed the upright to the residence of Clifford Atwater, on lot 29, Wilson's addition.

Fennville was platted in 1871 by Emerson & Co. Elisha Mix was the surveyor. It became an incorporated village in 1882.

Henry Blakesley, who married Irene Fenn, was the first to settle within the limits of the original village. He began on the east side of where the railroad now lies in 1860, made a small clearing, and in 1861 enlisted in the army under Lincoln's call, and was killed in action later. Dan Thomas was the first blacksmith; I. P. Griswold, the first merchant; Dr. Asa Goodrich, the first resident physician and druggist; W. W. Hutchins operated the first general repair shop; E. A. Fenn was the first postmaster as stated; Will Sieber, the first station agent; and Laura C. Hudson taught the first term of school in the district. All this before the fire. In 1895 Ira Hutchins built and owned the first electric light plant here.

29
Fennville Continued

Until about 1860 winter traffic was carried on with long sleds. A tree was located that had a natural crook that would form the front bend of the runner. This was taken to the mill and sawed into three-inch plank, with the crook crosswise, and these made a runner about ten feet long. Rolls and beams were put on and wooden shoes attached, and the sled was complete. It was a clumsy affair at best, for it would rise up over a root or hummock and balance over with a heavy bump when the front came down, and it was hard to turn around with it in the snow. When I was a small lad I remember the folks saying some one had made two short sleds and hitched them together like the front and rear gears to a wagon, and there was some speculation as to how it would work out. In a short time, however, the "bobs" were all the go and the old long sled was out of date.

* * *

In the season of 1862, while the road where Fennville's main street now is was yet bare corduroy, logs and brush, briars and cattails abounded on either side. Mr. Atwater, who lived on the hill east of the swamp, took his young wife, with his ox team, to visit her parents, Mr. and Mrs. Charles Billings, and were after dark in returning home. All went well until they were well out on the crossway, when they met two emigrant wagons. The road was darkened by the shade of the trees during the day and at night was very dark. Mr. Atwater thought he knew the bottom at this place, but seems to have missed his calculation for when he unhitched and started to drive the oxen around the wagon one got off into the mud, and that pulled the other off also. There was nothing to do then but get in himself and unyoke the oxen. This done, he and the men with the other teams got the oxen out of the swamp and drew the wagon back to solid ground. The emigrants went by and the Atwaters proceeded homeward. This occurred near or a little west of where the M. E. church now stands. While passing down that road today, with its paved surface, cement walks and fine buildings, one can hardly realize that such was the condition here but 60 short years ago. Still it is well remembered now by several of the town's inhabitants.

* * *

In 1871, right after the fire, David Signor, with Charles Ewing as head carpenter, erected the nucleus of what was known as the Fennville House. Fennville then was a typical sawmill town, and a rough element was ever present, though many of the people were of finer stuff. Perhaps a more correct explanation would be that the resident portion were fine people, but there was a transient population who were not so refined. What is now the main portion of the village was then a swamp, mostly mud and water, while the business section was located on higher ground on either side. Signor built on the ground where the Stevens now stands, and he managed the hotel according to the times. he was a sturdy frontiersman and knew his customers, so ran the business according to his own ideas. If his patrons did not like his ways they were free to go elsewhere. In fact it was a typical lumber town hotel. The main waiting room was simply a saloon, and patrons were compelled to witness the carousing whether they liked it or not -- but that was the usual way.

Ed Williams succeeded Signor, and added the Walter building, as stated recently, and later proprietors added improvements until it became a commodious and comfortable place. Williams was succeeded by Frost, Beals and others, and the last was F. L. Stevens, under whose management it became a first class hostelry. It came to be the headquarters for fruit buyers and traveling men in general, and was well and favorably known.

This structure was burned on May 30, 1910, and the new Stevens was erected in its stead, and from that time Fennville has had no occasion to criticize their hotel accommodations and management, but are warranted in boasting of the good qualities of both.

* * *

In viewing Fennville 53 years ago -- October, 1871 -- we found a new railroad line on the east, a long uncovered corduroy road across a swamp, and, on the west side of the swamp, there were a few ash heaps. On the higher ground to the west there stood the mill boarding house on the south side of the road and the little M. E. church that Mr. Fenn had built standing near the road on the present school house lot. Right here we let our voice fall.

Now, at the beginning of 1925, we find a large cider mill and vinegar factory, Sanocide spray works, flouring mill, canning factory, co-operative fruit exchange, general repair shop, a number of garages and automobile salesrooms, two hardware stores, one of the finest banks in western Michigan, two drug stores, two dry goods stores, express office, two clothing stores, post office, two baker's shops, shoe repair shop, millinery store, filling station, hotel, tailor shop, restaurant, furniture store and undertaking parlor, dentist, physician, lawyer, Baptist, Methodist and Christian Science churches, with a Seventh Day Adventist church now under construction, a $100,000 school building, $3,500 Woman's Club building, jewelry store, etc.

The fraternal societies are: Masons, Odd Fellows, Rebekahs, Eastern Stars, Boy Scouts, Camp Fire Girls, Rubinstein Music Club, Fennville Woman's Club, Business Men's Association, Parent Teacher Association. Also there is a Farm Bureau Co-operative Association with their various lines of supplies including feed and coal, and the Steffin coal yards. The 1920 census gave Fennville a population of 547.

Bravo

Alonzo Sherman and Ezra L. Davis came to section 32, Clyde township in 1867 and erected a saw mill, employing about twenty men and called the place Sherman. They also opened a store, and a post office was established. While we do not have the official records, parties who lived in the place at the time say the post office was first called Sherman, but there was another office of the same name in the state, causing confusion in the mails, so it was found necessary to change the name of this office. The name Bravo was sent in to Washington and accepted by the department and it has held that name ever since. Chandler Eaton was the first postmaster, and he told me how they came to choose that name. It was a long time ago, but if memory serves me rightly there was some discussion as to the new name, and he suggested Bravo, and it passed more as a joke than from any serious consideration. It seems to have been a joking compromise suggestion, and went that way. Eugene D. Nash succeeded Eaton as postmaster, and held the office for a number of years. Henry Mactraw was the first station agent but was transferred to Holland, and Mr. Nash took his place as agent, which position he held a long time and had the post office at the depot.

* * *

The following list of persons operated mills at Bravo, but we can only approximate the dates, as we have nothing but memory to go by:

Davis was not in company with Sherman in 1872, but Sherman operated the saw mill until about 1885. It did not do much business, however. His habit was to get logs enough for a carload of lumber and then saw it out. There was a shingle mill there before the railroad came, but we forget who ran it. Also Hyde & Eaton had a mill there before 1872. Hull & Collins had a portable mill there in 1871 and later. Blackmer bought out Hull & Collins in the early seventies, ran the mill a short time, and moved away. Welch & Crawford put in a portable mill after Blackmer left. Walters & Sprague had a mill also, and this was peculiar from the fact that they had two engines -- a stationary and a traction engine -- hitched to the same saw. They also had a steam skidder in the woods and drew the logs to the skidways by long cables and a traction engine. They were logging off from swampy ground where it was difficult to work oxen. Also they had a railroad, built with poles for track, and cars were drawn by team. They logged off a 40 acre lot for George Oliver of Allegan. It was mostly ash and swamp woods, and they were operating in 1877. Another mill that was run by a traction engine was there in the late eighties. The last milling business was a crate factory run by George Whiting and another man about 1908, before and after, but it burned, and was renewed in Pullman.

Bravo had been an important shipping point for the surrounding country ever since the railroad came. E. D. Nash operated a general merchandise store here for a long time, followed by his son, Will, and the store is now owned and operated by Will's son D. Nash.

30
Pearl

O. R. Johnson & Co. secured large tracts of land in Clyde and to the east, and in 1872, as soon as the railroad was completed, they caused a large saw mill to be erected on the line, and called the place Clyde Center. Their timber was mostly white pine. At the time the road was being built there was a general feeling that the Johnson company had considerable influence in its location so far to the east of the center of the agricultural lands. The first surveys were near the lake shore, and contributions were signed for a Ganges and Saugatuck route, but for some mysterious cause that was abandoned.

Brooks Hazleton and a Mr. Eggleston were interested in the mill, and Hazleton was in full charge of the whole works. Several houses and a large boarding house were built, and a depot and post office were established, both bearing the name Clyde Center. There were about 75 men employed there during the life of the place, and a large and rushing business was carried on, but by 1877 the saw timber was gone and the place became a thing of the past. The station, however, remained of considerable importance as a shipping outlet for the farming section tributary, and a store has been maintained ever since. Also the hall on the second floor of the mill boarding house has been used as a community and general public gathering place ever since.

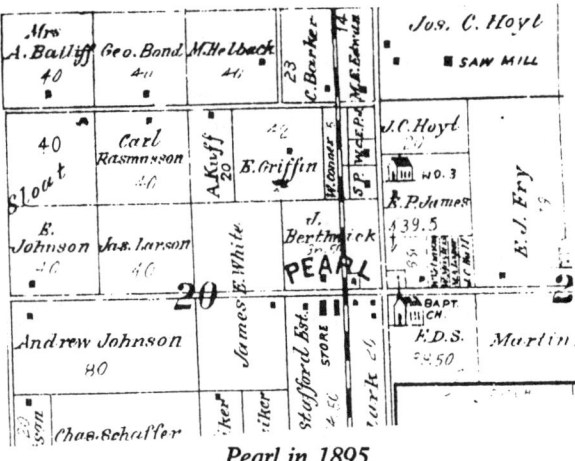

Pearl in 1895.

In 1881 the name of the post office was to be changed, I know not why, and the name Pearl was sent in to the department in honor of a distinguished resident of the township, Mr. Simeon O. Peorl. This was accepted, and the name is still held both by the post office and railroad station.

There was a saw mill set up about a mile east of the station by Joseph Piles, and another a mile east of that by Shelby Nash, both in the eighties. These were the usual "pickup" mills that worked up the timber culled out by the first slaughterers.

* * *

Pullman

Messrs. Hopper & Bennett owned land on section 9, Lee township, upon which two Clement brothers set up a saw mill in 1870. Holden & Loney took the contract to clear this land and bought the mill. In 1871 Bonfoey & Hulbut erected a shingle mill and Sweet & Ferguson a saw mill. In 1872 Hyatt & Anderson put in a saw mill. Twenty-three families, or about 215 people, comprised the town population by this time, and depended on the mill business for a livelihood. By 1876 the milling business ended the saw mills shut down, and but two families remained. In the following winter Snell & Cobb started a shingle mill, and by 1880 two saw mills were again in operation. A post office was established in 1876 and Ransom Snell was appointed postmaster. The change in name from Hoppertown to Pullman was made January 15, 1902.

New Richmond

From *Allegan County History* we quote: "The little village known as Richmond, at which is located the post office of New Richmond, was created by the completion of the Chicago and West Michigan road, being chosen as a station because of its easy access by river from Saugatuck. H. F. Marsh, who owned land in the neighborhood, laid out the village, called it Richmond, built a saw mill, and soon afterward a few people came in and put up residences. Mr. Marsh then opened a store and erected a commodious tavern known as the Western Hotel. B. F. Wheelock opened a hotel called the Richmond House."

One is led by this to presume that nothing was done there until 1871, but we happen to know Mr. Marsh had his mill in operation as early as 1868 or 1869, for father drew logs to the Marsh mill during that time and in the course of construction of the railroad we drew logs to the Marsh mill to be cut into timbers for the construction of the railroad bridge. This is of small consequence, however, the object of these letters being to approximate where exact data is not at hand.

The Marsh mill sawed quantities of lumber during the time there were repair shops and a saloon in operation, in addition to the enterprises mentioned. Mail was received here for Saugatuck and Douglas and taken by stage. Also it was the passenger and freight station for the whole county to the lake until the interurban came to Saugatuck.

* * *

The first post office in Manlius was established at Richmond in 1837. That was the John Allen venture that failed. Jonathan Stratton, a surveyor in the employ of Allen, was the first postmaster. Ralph R. Mann was successor to Stratton in 1838. In 1843 he resigned on account of lack of business, and the office was discontinued. In 1846 a post office was established at Manlius village and Randall Curtis was appointed postmaster. Mr. Curtis had built a tannery there. Those filling the position later were William C. Meeker, Ralph R. Mann, T. S. Coates, David Signor, Norman Bowker and James W. Sackett. In 1872 this office was discontinued and one established at New Richmond. This name was given as there was another Richmond in the state. J. G. Lamoreaux was the first postmaster in this office. He held the position until 1878, and was succeeded by William Delvin.

The data regarding all the earliest settlers in and around the location of New Richmond is not at hand, though a few may be mentioned. There seems to have been quite a gathering in that neighborhood in the early forties, though not in the compactness of a hamlet, since they nearly all took up tracts of land and settled on it. Those for whom we have dates are: Asa and Norman Bowker and W. C. Meeker came in 1841; John S. Gidley brought his family in 1842, and his son A. P. Gidley was a youngster at the time. Jonathan Wade came in 1844, also Thomas Lamoreaux with his family including his sons, J. Gilbert and Isaac, and his brother Daniel with his family, Ebenezer, Isaac H. and Mrs. James Smeed were his children. Mrs. E. J. Stow and Mrs. Henry Baragar also were Lamoreaux girls. George Veeder and family came in 1845 and settled on the southeast quarter of section 31. Mrs. Veeder was one of the Baragar family mentioned earlier. R. R. Mann, J. H. Billings and David Signor, with others mentioned earlier, came into the township in the early forties or earlier, but we do not have the years of their arrival

-----

(Note -- This finishes the history of settlements. I aim next to give a short history of the experiences in fruit disasters in connection with insects and fungus troubles during the discoveries of remedies and treatments and their application. It will be interesting to those now in orchard work. And finally a history of the telephone company to finish. -- H.)

31
Fruit Industry

People began setting fruit trees to supply home needs as soon as they had a clearing. A very convenient and out of the way place was in the corners of the rail fence around the garden. The peaches were of the seedling sort, but they were fruit, and filled an important place on the table. Apples, pears and cherries were brought in, and were of standard varieties as such were known then.

There was an Indian peach orchard on the south bank of the Kalamazoo about a mile east of Douglas, when the whites first came and the locality was known as "the Peach Orchard" until in the sixties. I never heard of the fruit, but presume it was seedlings. The trees had disappeared by the time of my first recollection of the place.

I find in my notes that the first peach trees brought to the lake shore by the whites was in 1839 by Harrison Hutchins. At the time of my first recollections, in the late fifties, they all had a variety of tree and bush fruits sufficient for home use, and nearly all the first comers had fifty to a hundred apple trees in bearing. There was no foreign market, and we peddled our fruits in "The Flats" (Saugatuck), to the mill hands. About this time or a little later an occasional coasting hooker would come to Saugatuck and buy a load to take to the coast towns along the lake. They also bought potatoes and anything eatable. My understanding is that they supplied lumber towns usually. Along in the seventies buyers began coming and bought our fruit and potatoes to ship away. I remember once in the late sixties Mr. Dressel, who lived north of Pier Cove, bought our peaches (all seedlings) and made containers of lath to ship them in. There may have been twenty bushels, but I doubt it. No one depended on their fruit as a commercial crop, so paid little or no attention to it. Such orchards as there were usually were used as pasture ground, and the only pruning was just sufficient to keep the trees in form, and hardly that. We knew nothing of spraying. In fact, there seemed no cause for it. There were some wormy apples, but not many and as the soil was of the virgin sort the trees grew vigorously and bore well.

* * *

As early as 1870 the peach industry at St. Joe had gained some headway, and I think it was in 1871 that McCormick and Hutchins and Loomis went to that section to investigate. They came back well pleased with the prospect, and the following year each set 1,000 trees. Half of them were of the Crawford varieties and the others were standard varieties -- Old Mixon freestone, Stun the World and Smock. My recollection is that this was the first starting of the peach here with a commercial aim in mind at the time of the setting.

These men took passing care of the trees from then on, and soon began getting good crops and good prices. Early in the marketing of this fruit it was sold to buyers, who bought it on the trees and harvested it themselves. Prices ran at around one dollar a peck, net, on the Chicago market. Growers soon began shipping to commission houses, and we were pestered to death with their solicitors. These prices stimulated the setting of peach orchards, and in a few years thousands of acres were set to that fruit in western Allegan county. Special fruit trains were run to take care of the output. Ten to fifteen cars a day was about the average from Fennville, though as many as thirty in a rush, besides cars from New Richmond and Bravo. At the same time steamboat lines were in operation from Saugatuck. During the rush there were boats from two piers at Pier Cove, and each had a boat to Chicago and one to Milwaukee, making four daily boats there, and Glenn pier had a daily boat, besides those from South Haven.

* * *

I should say it was in the early eighties that a new variety of peach was discovered. It developed on one branch of the tree, and the fruit swelled and matured about two weeks ahead of the fruit on the balance of the tree. It had a bright red cheek and red streaks ran from the pit out to the skin, and showed a red dot on the surface. At the same time sprouts sprang from the limb, that had small leaves of a light yellow color, and a stalk of spindling, almost sickly growth. In short, it was not a new variety at all, as was at first supposed, but the government pathologists named it the "peach yellows." No one could find out where it came from, nor a cure, so the only treatment at hand was the ax. The trees had to be taken away, root and branch. Large openings were caused in many orchards and in some cases whole orchards were cut out. The government sent pathologists from Washington to study the disease, and locally the towns appointed yellows commissioners with orders to mark all affected trees, and if the owner would not destroy the trees the commission was to do so, and the cost was charge in the taxes.

Just when the yellows was in its worst stages another disease attacked the trees, and this was the reverse of the yellows. It was called "little peach," as the fruit would remain very small and did not ripen. No cure for this was ever found, and eradication of the trees was the only remedy. Both these diseases seemed to have run their race and were on the decline when the big freeze came in 1899. More of that later. In either case the fruit was not found to be injurious to those eating it, but the trees died in a year or two.

Like all fruits, the peach was not a sure crop. About one crop in two or three years was the average. As the production increased, the selling price lowered, until in case of a general crop the season failed to pay its costs. Also in panic years there was no market at a living price. Perhaps the season of 1896 was the worst when there was an excellent crop but prices ran so low that we had to shake thousands of bushels of fruit on the ground to save the trees. (A peach rotting on a twig will kill the twig from the peach out if left where it grew, thus reducing the bearing surface as though the twigs were cut off.) It so happened that the season of 1899 was a complete failure of the peach crop also. This condition cast a damper on our ardor, and in fact we did not get very satisfactory results in after years until the big freeze of October 10, 1906, which killed every peach tree from the Indiana line to the Straits of Mackinaw. There was a severe freeze in the very early eighties that injured the trees to some extent. Some cut out their orchards, but others did not, and those left bore crops for several years following.

* * *

The disaster of 1906 threw some of the growers into bankruptcy. It left them without a dollar, and they had to vacate their farms. Others were left badly in debt, some of whom have regained their standing, but others are still paying interest on debts contracted before the freeze.

As an example of panic years and seasons where there was an oversupply, I might state that in 1896 my place ran behind $600 with 10,000 bushels of peaches on the trees. That year we had both panic and oversupply. True, we made money in favorable years, but it all goes to show the error of depending on any one crop.

The yellows and little peach seem to have been completely killed out by the big freeze, for I do not remember of hearing of either since that time. Some have set small peach orchards since, but that fruit has not taken much attention of late years. The peach is not so dependable a tree as the apple, pear and cherry as to hardiness.

* * *

A condition amusing to us now, but tragic then, was the discovery that after a peach orchard was taken out the soil would not produce vigorous farm crops as it did before setting to the peach. A natural result was that we all concluded peach trees killed the soil. We had practiced perfectly clean culture in our orchards, and some bragged that you could not find a weed in their orchards -- which was true from end to end of the season. Later we learned that we had ruined our land by this intensive culture, as we had worked all the humus, or vegetable matter out of the soil and left the bare earth, having added nothing to keep up the vegetable mould in the soil. Had we used cover crops, or allowed weeds to grow, or in any manner put back something into the ground, we would have retained the fertility of the soil. I have orchards in mind now, here on the lake shore, where they are doing the same thing, and I am wondering if those men know what they are doing. Chemical fertilizers won't do it.

The real case of such heavy setting of peach trees at the first was the difficulty in getting apple and pear crops. A discussion of that experience will call for a follow-up letter on the subject next week.

32
Apples and Pears

On a guess I would say that it was in the early eighties that we began to note what was called the "June drop." Apples would grow to about the size of a hickory nut, and in June drop off, but no one suspected the cause. Late in the eighties our apples left on the trees after the drop, in addition to having a dark blotch, were wormy also, and not saleable. People became very much discouraged, and considered apple trees only an incumbrance and to no profit. Some cut out sections of their orchards, with the idea of clearing off all the trees later. One man now living on the lake shore cut out a 20 acre orchard of 15 year old trees, all good varieties and in a thrifty condition. No doubt there would not have been an apple tree in this section in a short time had not the Agricultural College set to work in the interest of the apple industry.

The Agricultural department came out with the information that it was the codling moth that caused the wormy apples, and recommended spraying the trees with paris green to poison the moth and its larvae. This was in the late eighties, and Frank Morley of Benton Harbor, who owned a large orchard a half mile east of Fennville, was the first to begin systematic spraying. A few others followed Morley, and the experiment was watched -- and ridiculed -- but as results were favorable others followed, so in a few years spraying became more general. At this time the hand pump on a barrel, with one man lunging at the pump handle and another with a hose supplied with a nozzle, tied to a stick to hold it up, was the only method known of applying the spray. Improvements came slowly, but they came.

* * *

When it became a settled fact that worms in apples could be controlled the growers began to discuss the idea of power sprayers. In 1902 or '03 Edward Hutchins bought a little stationary steam engine and rigged it behind the rear axle to the wagon and hitched it to a pump, and thus had steam power instead of man power with which to do his spraying.

At about the same time, and perhaps the same year, the Wadsworth brothers (Dwight and

Leon) rigged up a gasoline power arrangement, so we had these as the first power sprayers in the community. Power sprayers were not yet on the market. However, there was some contrast between them and the machine we saw a few days ago which put on a demonstration of pressure at 200, then 400, followed with 600, then 800 pounds, and the demonstrator, said he could show 1,000 pounds which we did not doubt.

* * *

At the time of the first sprayers we were using paris green for coddling moth, but at about this time we were told the cause of the "June drop," and were instructed to use Bordeaux mixture to prevent that. It was the apple scab, a fungus disease, and the new growth must be covered to destroy the spores, so we mixed paris green and bordeaux and sprayed for both moth and scab at the same application.

This treatment served the purpose for worms and scab, but in a year or two the San Jose scale made its appearance and was killing the trees. Again the college came to the rescue and this time with lime-sulphur. The home made was used at that time and boiling plants were put up on most of the larger farms, so we all used that for scale. It came out that the latter preparation would prevent scab as well as scale, and bordeaux was in the discard, except for special purposes.

Shothole fungus in the cherries and plums made its appearance. I should say, about 1910, and pear psylla a little later, all of which call for special sprays. I forget when the peach curl leaf first appeared, but it must have been in the early nineties.

* * *

The pear was not set to any extent as a commercial fruit until perhaps 1886, and then not so extensively as apples and peaches had been, though there are quite extensive orchards growing here now. One thing that held the pear back was fear of the blight.

For perhaps fifteen years, and until a control was found for their enemies, apples and pears were at a standstill. No one dared to set new orchards of either fruit, and as we had not yet run the race with the peach, and did not know its drawbacks, we plunged into that fruit, only to be let down as told in the last letter.

Early in the game, when fruit was mentioned we all though of apples. Later it came to be peaches, but now when fruit is mentioned we think of apples and pears. Cherries, plums, currants and quinces have been grown here for a long time, but never to the extent that apples, pears and peaches have. Strawberries are a short term plant. They come and go as the notion strikes the grower, so are not classed with the others.

The foregoing concerns what happened here, but these fruit enemies originated elsewhere and were some time in reaching us.

In 1892 the pear blight was being discussed in the State Horticultural Society, but its cause was not then known. Also apple scab was under observation, but nothing is said in their reports about spraying for scab.

In the report of the State Horticultural Society for 1898 it is stated that there were four orchards in the state that had scale. In 1905-06 we find lime-sulphur recommended in combating scale.

A Correction

In letter No. 31 I stated that the freeze of the morning of October 10, 1906, killed every - peach tree from the Indiana line to the straits of Mackinaw. This statement had brought out some raking over of the dusty corners of memory, and as a result of statements from men who were in the peach business here at that time it may be best and nearer to the facts to say that 90 per cent of the trees were killed. There were a few small favored spots where the trees escaped and some of them bore fruit the next season. I believe it is safe to say that as a result of the freeze those trees went into decline and did not live for long afterwards. On the morning in question the mercury went to 6 degrees above zero, and it had to be a very favored location that would save trees, yet full of sap, from destruction.

33
Local Phone Company

In the late eighties and very early nineties we in the fruit belt found ourselves very much in need of telephone communication. Whole farms were set to fruit, and in harvest time we would get loads to the piers only to learn later in the day that the boat could not land. Again we started loads to Fennville, a much longer drive, and when too late the boat would whistle for the piers.

As is always the case in a hurried time, we needed telephones, so I wrote to the Bell company to find at what rental we could get a pair for our own use. They stated that they did not care to rent them in an out of the way place like this, but would accommodate us at a rental of $75 a year for each instrument. We could not see $150 in it, so did not order the phones, but about 1894 the Harrison Electric Company won their suit with the Bell, and the next year we stood a good chance to buy phones from them.

* * *

In July, 1894, during the time between cultivation and harvest, I went to the swamp and got out cedar poles to run a line from my place to the Ganges pier. During the same period in 1895 I set the pole line, but as yet had made no arrangements for phones. Dr. Brunson came along and asked what was on. When told, he said he wanted an interest in it. Captain Charles McVea did the same. Mr. Link at the pier said the same, as did also George Barber, who was in the Grange store. In fact, the idea struck the whole community at once.

During this time I was at Saugatuck and C. E. Bird proposed a line from Saugatuck to Ganges pier, so they also could learn if the sea would let boats land. He said the Rogers & Bird company would give $40 as a starter. I called on Capt. R. C. Brittain, and he said the R. M. Moore company would match the other offer. Both companies had boat lines running from Saugatuck to Ganges and Chicago. Everybody worked for the enterprise, and Fred Wade, who was publisher of *The Commercial*, did all he could in the columns of his paper and it all helped. I took subscriptions, and soon we were ready to begin in earnest.

* * *

A meeting of subscribers was called at Douglas on July 31, 1895, to consider the construction of a telephone line from Saugatuck to Douglas, thence to Ganges post office, and thence to Grange Hall. Fred Wade was chosen chairman and H. H. Hutchins secretary. At this meeting it was voted to elect a board of five directors. Those elected were: Dr. E. E. Brunson, Henry Bird Jr., Fred Wade, H. H. Hutchins and Charles E. Bird. It was voted that the company be known as the Saugatuck and Ganges Telephone Company.

The board of directors met at the home of Dr. Brunson on August 2, 1895, at which Dr. Brunson was elected president, Charles E. Bird, vice president; H. H. Hutchins, secretary and treasurer; and Henry Bird Jr. superintendent of construction, under direction of the board. It was decided that Mr. Bird proceed at once to have the line measured and staked, and arrange a contract for setting poles.

* * *

At a meeting of the board of directors held at the office of Fred Wade on August 8, 1895, it was decided that H. H. Hutchins proceed at once to get out poles for the proposed line the same to be 25 feet long and not less than three inches top diameter.

At a meeting of the board held at the office of Fred Wade on August 10 Fred Wade was directed to take counsel on forms for the transaction of business and for incorporation of the company.

On November 23, 1895, the stockholders adopted the bylaws of the company.

We were incorporated for $1,000 in the fall of 1895, and two years later re-incorporated for $2,000. On April 15 we re-incorporated for the same amount of stock, but changed the name to Western Allegan County Telephone Company.

The line connecting Saugatuck, Douglas and Ganges was run in the fall of 1895, and switchboards installed. The next spring we ran on to Glenn, and in the spring of 1897, a line was run from Ganges to Fennville. Switchboards were installed at the last named places also.

* * *

At the beginning none of us knew a thing about telephones, and very few had ever talked over one. We thought putting a phone in the house was like furniture -- that was the end of it; that the folks at the centrals would be glad to attend switchboards for the fun of it, and there would be no expense. By 1897 we had quite a number of subscribers and each paid cost of materials and installation.

I think it was in September, 1898, that a small cyclone visited Saugatuck, and tin roofs were blown into our wires and twisted around them like a rope. Lightning burned out the telephone coils, and our system was completely knocked out. Being manager at the time, it fell to me to straighten things out. I could connect a phone to the line now, but that was the extent of my knowledge, so I went to Chicago for information. The boat companies gave transportation and I gave my time and expenses. It took about two weeks to get in order again. This method of getting information was repeated on occasions of trouble for some time, but gradually we became more self-reliant. All this time we held the notion that this would be the last trouble, and that all would be well with the telephone hereafter. But we finally learned that roses did not grow on telephones, and that we could not donate our time to the service. The switch attendants were voted 50 cents a day, and I got $1.50 for my time and horse.

* * *

At the end of three years the expense figured up at $9 per phone for the three years. This was considered outrageous and some threatened to withdraw. The cost soon ran to $5, then $6, and finally $9 a year, and the fact that it costs money to operate a telephone system finally became understood.

The company is now under good management, and we have 810 telephones. Our resources and liabilities balance in our favor, and all goes well in 1925.

I have been told by some of the foremost telephone men in western Michigan that ours is the first rural co-operative telephone company in the state, and, in their belief, the first in the United States. This came about by our having lines ready for the phones when the independent companies first started their manufacture. In fact the Bell patents did not fully expire until after our first instruments were installed.

34
Pioneering

My earliest memory carries me back to the late fifties and sixties, and as I compare the ways of the household now with those of a short 70 years ago and note the wide contrast, it does not seem possible, so a short outline of those days may be timely as a closing line to these historical sketches.

For instance, father sheared the wool from off the sheep, mother and grandma carded it, and spun it into yarn with the old-fashioned spinning wheel, then knit it into mitts and socks for the family. (Later they took the wool to Allegan and had it carded by machinery.) The sewing machine was not known as yet, nor any ready made clothing, so wearing apparel was all made by hand in the home.

About 1870 an agent came here and sold our folks the first sewing machine I ever saw or heard of. It was a little affair that sat on the table where it was held by means of a clamp. It operated by a hand crank, and made a chain stitch. Care had to be taken to secure the end of the thread, or the children would get hold of it and undo the whole seam. But it did its work well and was a great help.

Mother made pants for us boys out of the grain sacks common at the time. They were heavy and stiff, but they surely did wear well. Knee pants for boys were not known then, and men and boys wore boots. Shoes for men and boys were not introduced until in the seventies.

* * *

During the week we all tucked our pants into our boot tops, but on "the sabbath" we pulled them over the boot tops on the outside. I really don't see now what difference that made, but it was the rule. In winter we wore a felt hat, but in summer mother braided straw and made our hats.

At this time also the cooking was all done in the pots that were hung on the chimney crane and swung in over the coals in the great fireplace and the baking was all done in the brick oven. I well remember the first stove, but have no recollection as to the time it was bought. It was on legs about a foot high in front and eighteen inches at the back. The oven was back of the griddles and above the tops of them. Of course the top was level, but the firebox dropped down below the after part of the stove, which caused the short legs in front. The brick oven was in use until after I was old enough to put the fire in it. We put live coals in -- I should say a half-bushel -- and when one could hold the hand inside the door just long enough to count ten it was ready for baking. We must have used it until 1865. "Box stoves" (what we know as a range) did not appear for quite a while -- no doubt not before 1875.

The art of canning fruit was not known, and we dried such eatables for winter use. Berries were dried on tins; apples were quartered and pumpkins were sliced, strung on a string by means of a darning needle, and hung from the ceiling over the fire to dry. The string was about a yard long, and both ends were tied to nails above. Later we made trays of lath and spread the fruit on them and put them in the sun to dry, or secured them above the stove after we got a stove. Patent dryers were sold later. They were an inclosure with racks having wire netting for bottom. Some put them over the stove with a slow fire, and some used lamp heat.

* * *

Our night light was the tallow candle, but when there were no more candles at hand they made what was called a "slutt." That was a saucer of tallow, with a strip of cloth laid in it, with one end resting up over the edge of the saucer for a wick. The lantern was about the size and shape of a gallon kerosene can, perforated with fine holes, and a small candle secured in the bottom. As I remember, it gave about as much light as a lightning bug, though it was more constant and more scattered.

For tallow they killed a beef and tried out all the tallow possible. Our folks had a candle mold -- I have it now -- with pipes for eight candles. The wick was secured in the center of the tube, and the set was run full of hot tallow and set aside to cool.

But when making them in quantities this method was too slow. They placed two strips of wood about eight feet long on two chairs, with a space of about a foot between them. A set of candle sticks was at hand -- wooden rods 15 inches long by a half-inch in diameter -- and it was supplied with about ten wicks. The wicks were dipped in a kettle of lukewarm tallow and raised out slowly, so they would hold all the tallow that would adhere to them, and the stick was placed across the two strips of wood, with the wicks hanging down. Boards on the floor caught the drip tallow. Another set of wicks was treated in the same way, and so on until the length of the strips was filled. Then we went over the whole again and again, until the candles were full diameter. No doubt 500 candles were made at one operation. The tallow was kept warm by turning in warm water, which went to the bottom and left the tallow on top to make the candle.

* * *

No factory soap was known, and we made soft soap by leaching our hardwood ashes and boiling it in combination with grease fats. A barrel each spring was about the amount required for a year.

It must have been about 1870 when the first top buggies were introduced. Previous to that time we had "shell skein" light wagons. Springs for wagons were not known until some time after that. The first springs were for the seat only, and finally they were used under the box.

There was no protection against flies, mosquitos and bugs coming into the house. There were swarms of them

-----

Quite a long time ago as I saw the first settlers here passing on, it came to me that some one should take notes of their experiences and the dates of happenings in this community. There are county histories, but they are more of a general class and lack much detail that would be of interest to the distant future. I saw no move in that direction, so without any plan in mind, I began interviewing them. No one has appeared on the scene to use my notes, and I am no longer in the juvenile class, and what to do I didn't know. It is entirely out of my line, and if I was equal to the task of writing it up I had no time for the work. But in my desperation I plunged in, without plan or method, at odd times, and in a pure hit and miss fashion. The result is disconnected and rough, but the facts are noted down and ready for some capable person to hunt out and use when wanted. I have received a number of very complimentary letters, and wish to thank those people for them. If no particular good has been done, I am sure there is no harm.

Very truly,
H. H. HUTCHINS

35
Pioneer Cooperative Work

[Mr. Hutchins writes: "I am again sending you a "last" letter. Some of the old time fruit growers took me to task for omitting these happenings, so I had to take time to work it out. I really think this is the final "last" one.]

The Fruit Shippers' Association

The first co-operative venture in this section was introduced in the fall of 1888, and was brought about by the excessive freight rates we were obliged to pay between Fennville and Chicago. The American Express Co. was carrying our peaches, and their rates by the 100 equaled six cents for a fifth-bushel basket of peaches. Several growers got together and evolved the idea of handling it themselves, in the interest of the growers. Arrangements were made with a Mr. Goodrich of Chicago, who was engaged in unloading fruit there, to handle that end of the business.

The growers were organized under the name of "The Fruit Shippers' Association," though not incorporated, and closed a contract with the railroad company whereby they were to take over the entire charge of loading and unloading the fruit cars. Mr. Harvey J. Kingsley was elected president and John H. Crane, secretary. They really stepped into the shoes of the express company, assumed all responsibility, and paid the railroad a hauling rate that amounted to less than two and three-fourths cents per fifth basket. They began the season of 1889 with a charge to the shipper of three and a half cents a basket but soon found they could pay all expenses with a three cent charge, and there was a balance left in the treasury, thereby gaining a 50 per cent cut in charges.

While the express company was charging six cents a basket the boats were charging five cents, which rate was soon cut to meet the new rail charge.

The growers carried on the business for 20 years, and until after the freeze of 1906, which killed the peach trees and removed the necessity of the association's further existence.

Much credit for the success of this enterprise is due to the capable management of A. L. Whitbeck in loading the cars and manifesting the shipments.

In one year the saving in freight to the growers of this section amounted to $180,000 and it was carefully figured by Mr. Crane and Edward Hutchins that the total saving during the life of the association amounted to over $1,000,000. J. R. Goodrich shipped 40,000 baskets one year, and his savings in freight was about $1,200.

Good Roads Movement

In addition to this savings to the shippers there was still a neat little balance, amounting to from $500 to $1,200 per year, left in the treasury, which was used from year to year to improve the roads west from Fennville. Bad grades were reduced and gravel applied, the result of which we know so well, and before the end of this work the town line was in good condition for about four miles west, as well as some of the north and south roads. The association did not take over the road work, as is done by the state now, but put their work on as an addition to the regular highway work.

An interesting discovery was that when the surveyors came to lay out the grade for the present M-89 state road they found nearly all the leveling and grading done by the growers was perfect, so they made very little change. Some grading was done by the state to get dirt for widening the crossway along section 1, Ganges. The growers had no survey but left the supervision work to John T. Dickinson, who leveled it "by the eye."

Pioneer Cooperative Marketing

The first cooperative marketing here was in 1897 when two companies were organized, with perhaps a dozen members each -- the Fennville Fruit Company, with Ed Hawley president, C. B. Welch secretary, and James Wark manager, and the Fruitgrowers Company, Ltd., with Edward Hutchins president, H. H. Hutchins secretary, J. E. Hutchinson treasurer, and J. H. Crane and L. D. Wadsworth directors. Besides the officers named W. H. Owen was its first manager. Both companies built large packing houses, that put up by the Fennville Fruit Company now being occupied by the Fennville Fruit Exchange, and the one by the Fruitgrowers company having been torn down and the Fennville Canning Company now occupying the site.

Both of these associations enjoyed two seasons of successful operation, when the severe freeze of 1899 and the ravages of the yellows and little peach so injured the orchards that the members of neither had sufficient fruit to continue the enterprises.

I have been unable to obtain statistics of the amount of business done by the Fennville Fruit Company, but from a statement of the Fruitgrowers Company it appears that in 1898 there were 65 cars sold, mostly peaches, for which $18,783 was received, and sales in less than car lots brought the total receipts to $19,321.81. The sales made by the other company were probably about the same. I have no hesitancy in saying that if these organizations had been established so as to have handled the crops of 1896 the output of each would have been considerably in excess of 100,000 bushels.

To give an idea of the extent of the peach industry in this section, I may say I was sales manager for Wells-Higman Basket Manufacturing Company during the five years from 1887 to 1892, and in our banner year we sold, at our three warehouses in Fennville, Pier Cove and Glenn, over 400,000 bushels -- the total amounting to over $20,000. At the same time Weed & Co. were working this whole territory, and J. F. Barron and Fred Hall had salesrooms in Fennville and George Clapp in Glenn. At that, there was a shortage of packages that year.

* * *

The Present Fruit Exchanges

At the present time the Fennville Fruit Exchange and the Saugatuck Fruit Exchange have been in active operation for several years, so that they success is assured beyond question. During the years of those earlier co-operative ventures spraying operations had hardly started, and peaches were practically the only fruit handled, while today the enemies of apples and pears have been brought under such complete control that these fruits constitute the bulk of those put up, and peaches are but a minor part.

[Enjoying the role of area historian H. H. Hutchins continued to write for the newspapers whenever interesting topics were brought to mind, or artifacts with a story were given to him. Most were published in *The Commercial Record* in Saugatuck. Dates accompany the articles if they are known. Continuing the numbering this would be No. 36.]

36
Saugatuck's Other Names

For a Time it was Indiscriminately Called Kalamazoo, Newark or Saugatuck

In files of bills of lading accumulated by Mr. A. G. Spencer, dated during the years 1856, 1857, and 1858, of freight passing over his dock, it is interesting to note that there was no special name for the place. Some bills are headed Kalamazoo, some Kalamazoo Harbor, while more are given at Newark. Two orders written by J. P. Wade dated April 11, 1856, and May 5, 1857, for sash were addressed Saugatuck. Business letters from near by places were sent to Newark and Saugatuck. Nothing from away came to Saugatuck. Of the items of freight during those years were 5038 bedsteads, 171,230 staves and headings sent to Chicago. There were smaller amounts of sash, doors, leather, hair, etc., also ten barrels of bed pins July 14, 1857. For the benefit of the younger generation it may be well to say the bed pins went with the old style cord bed. Only once or twice were slats noted. 255 barrels flour on April 21, 1858.

All the boats were schooners. Not one steamboat was mentioned. There was the **Mager Curba**, captain not named; **Sea Star**, Capt. Horace Ames; **Tempest**. Capt. Richard Fountain; **Frank Miller**, Capt. L. B. Coates; **Josephine Dresden**, Capt. Wm. R. Wilcox; **Industry**, Capt. R. Carver; **Three Sisters**, Wm. Richardson; **Storm**, James Jones; **Alpha**, John Gwynn; **Hinsdale**, William Watts; **Gem**, T. Williams; **D. B. Holt**, Capt. Oleson; **Mount Vernon**, Henry Smith; **R. Darling**, Capt. S. R. Schovel. Two rafts were named in bills from Allegan, upon which all freight from Allegan was floated down the river, the Nichols & Sweet raft which transferred most if it, and the Ira Chaffee raft.

"Too Much Kalamazoo"

There seems to have been two places by the name of Kalamazoo at this time, as the following bill of lading shows. Namely:
"Kalamazoo. Nov. 5, 1856. Mr. G. Spencer, Newark, To Michigan Central Railroad, Dr. Ann Arbor, 25 bbls. apples $35.00. Railroad charges $10.85, Postage .03." The bedsteads were from Oliver & Co. Allegan. The flour from Kalamazoo. All bills from upriver were to S. G. Spencer, for transfer to lake boats bound for Chicago. A raft of those times was a boat with one deck and no motive power, but was propelled by men on each side who shoved the boat ahead by means of poles. they went to the forward end, stuck the pole into the bottom of the river and walked the boat ahead. Long sweeps were attached to the forward and after end of the boat or scow, by which its course could be governed.

The Captain "Beats It"

An interesting story is handed down of Capt. Henry Smith, and no doubt there is some foundation for it. It seems the schooner **Mount Vernon** was tied up in Chicago for the winter and towards spring Capt. Smith began fitting her out. Some one there held an account against Mr. Smith and planned to attach his boat when all ready for sailing. The ice was broken up, but not sufficiently for safe navigation when Mr. Smith got wise to the scheme, so one night he let loose from the dock, floated out into the lake and headed for Michigan. His crew consisted of himself and a boy. He lashed the boy to the mast so he could not get washed overboard, but with room to help handle the sails, took the helm himself and made the mouth of the Kalamazoo without mishap. Such nerve, if true was worthy of a pioneer.
[1922]   H. H. HUTCHINS

37
Kalamazoo Then Saugatuck

H. H. Hutchins writes as follows of some historic documents recently shown him by a friend:
Two deeds transferring title to property in what is now Saugatuck, 68 years ago, were handed

me by Gordon Spencer recently and no doubt will be of interest to your readers. The first is dated October 7, 1854, and reads in part as follows:

"These two tracts or parcels of land known and described as village lots No. one hundred sixty-nine (169) and one hundred seventy (170) in the village of Kalamazoo, in Newark, Allegan County, as per plot of said village laid out and recorded by William G. Butler in the records of Kalamazoo County."

This transfer was by M. B. Spencer to his brother A. G. Spencer, father of Gordon, and are the lots where the pavilion now stands. The consideration was $200. There was a small dock and slaughter house there at time of the transfer.

The other deed is dated Oct. 29, 1855, and shows transfer of title to lot 141 to A. G. Spencer by S. D. Nichols as follows:

"It being lot No. one hundred forty-one (141) in the village of Kalamazoo, in Newark, Allegan County as per plot of said village laid out and recorded by William G. Butler in the records of Kalamazoo county." The purchase price of this lot was $30. There were no buildings on this lot at the time of this sale but Mr. Spencer built and operated a store there after he took possession and this is the lot where Hotel Saugatuck now stands.
[1922]

38
One More Chapter About Singapore

In 1848 my father was working a lumber job at the Red Banks, on the north banks of the Kalamazoo about two miles west of the present New Richmond, for Stockbridge & Carter of Singapore. Mother chose to accompany him and serve as housekeeper in the camp. In the fall they went to Singapore and kept the mess hall in the "big house" for the mill hands.

In 1905 she wrote a history of their experiences there, and I will select sketches from their camp life and then pass on to a more complete detail of their life in the "big house."

Extracts from Mrs. Hutchins' Letter

"It came about one day (while in camp) that Messrs. Carter and Stockbridge required board for their crew of about a dozen men who were detailed to get out the timbers for a new steam sawmill they designed to build in the place of the mill recently burned beside the Kalamazoo at Singapore. There was no refusing as there was no one else to board the mill hands." (That sets the date one of the mills there was rebuilt.)

"I was standing beside the rude little work table in the kitchen one day about half past ten, perhaps, alone as I supposed, absorbed in my own contemplations, my hands busied with some household affairs, when suddenly a slight sound at the door behind me attracted my attention. Turning I was shocked to behold on each side of the door, peering curiously at me, the snapping black eyes and faces of two Indian boys with nearly nude bodies partly concealed by the door frame. They might have been anywhere between ten and fourteen years old. Each had in one hand what I first took to be a snake, but a moment's observation showed me a long string of lean mean. It was *sucsee weas*, venison. (*Sucsee*, deer; *weas*, meat.) They wanted *quashegun*, bread. "Swap?" Of course I would. The meat was prepared with all due care and I surprised my boarders with a savory venison steak. It was the Indian custom to carefully divide from the ribs the muscles alongside the backbone, as these young brothers had done. They came later, sometimes bringing a fine duck, etc., to "swap." Two widowed squaws, widows of a deceased chief it was said, were "resorting" that summer in their wigwams at Mack's landing. These boys were sons of the deceased chief; they might have been twins. Whether own or half brothers I do not know. Later these ex-queens of the forest favored me with a call, sufficiently formal, since we could not converse much, but a pleasant diversion in a lonely cabin. During the long five months at long intervals several ladies called. Most were my relatives and came miles to see me. One spent several weeks visiting. It all served to relieve somewhat the monotony.

"Nature is not partial and malaria, so all-prevalent in a new country, specially near the vast marsh, insinuated its poison, and Harrison with his robust constitution, and bilious fever claimed him for a victim. The doctor came; only a few hours and the inevitable chill would be due and another season of the dreaded fever would follow. Doctor thought deeply and long. Finally presuming upon the robust constitution of his patient, he prepared all three of the usual specific drugs -- blue mass, dover's powders and quinine combined in as many immense pills, and soon was on his way. The directions were faithfully followed and the effect was as doctor desired. The disease was broken before another paroxysm occurred.

"Time jogged along at its wonted pace. Summer wanted gracefully and blended into autumn. Autumn days shortened and cooled. Its rainy days required wood and warmth. Its evenings lengthened and when upon occasion my husband returned late from his business trip to Allegan, and I was aware I was alone beside the dark rolling river, in the rude shanty, the owls resting on the tall tree beside it and hooting and screeching at the sparks that rose from the low stovepipe and seemed to resent our intrusions, it was not fear -- no, my judgment said there was no cause -- but there was a sense of loneliness crept over me. I had formerly been used to companionship at home and I was indeed glad to welcome my husband; glad later when he accepted Mr. Artemas Carter's offer, to leave the lonely place and we would move to Singapore and keep boarders. Arrangements were made and we were to start tomorrow to take our abode for the winter in the "big house" at Singapore.

The "Big House" at Singapore

"That night there fell the first early snow. Weakened by ill-health and wearied by the labor consequent on the packing and moving, it seemed a little more than was desirable when, seated forward of the little load of goods and furniture, the lines were put into my hands to drive the gray ponies. Doll and Nell were gentle and would follow the road with scarce a care from the driver, and someone must follow after to keep the cows from straying. The damp snow lay heavy upon the bushes close beside the way and bent them low with the burden of fall leaves covered with the moist snow. They would often brush my head and fill my face with the chilly mass and cover wraps and drench gloves with the melting.

"There was no alternative but to patiently proceed. We passed the tannery and residence of Mr. Wells, well known in that day, father-in-law of Mrs. O. R. Johnson and father of Ed Wells, then a child of about three years and in later years in Saugatuck a merchant. There were one or two other residences at Wellsville (later known as Wallinville and Dingleville). A little later we passed the tiny Singapore schoolhouse. Then the road ran for a fourth of a mile perhaps on the dugway alongside a steep hill, until we came in full view of the site of the "Wild Cat" city of Singapore.

"Thus we bade a cheerful adieu of our late romantic resort at the Red Banks of the Kalamazoo. A few rods further and we were at the foot of the flight of steps that led up above the basement to the back porch of the noted "big house" that now lies buried beneath the drifting sands.

"Mosquitos! Oh, the great, black, savage, giant, musical mosquitoes; the tiny midgets of today bear little comparison to the monsters along the borders of the big marsh in 1848. Mosquito bar was expensive. Not everyone could afford a corner fenced off for a sewing room where the last offender could be singed by a burning candle, as was needful at retiring for the night, beneath the mosquito bar canopy. It was not quite convenient to curl up tailor fashion on the bed for hours to sew; but sewing must be done by one who was, perforce, both tailoress and dressmaker. She must contrive. Fashion? Yes, only six breadths of ordinary "print" was sufficient for a lady's skirt. O how ridiculously skimpy the gored skirts of their great-grandmothers! Have a nice full skirt while about it. Then a skirt of finer fabric could be turned inside out and bottom side up and back and front, when best to make economically presentable.

"Imagine now the seamstress of the resort sitting upon a low stool (those mosquitoes could invade the ankles between the meshes of hosiery), her sun bonnet with wide cape over the shoulders, pinned closely about her throat and ears, sleeves pinned tightly at the wrists. As she drew her needle a sharp jerk with each hand is needful to ward off the intruders. A quick brush occasionally before the face affords the needful protection. This is not a painted picture, but a fact. It is with such labors and patient perseverance that the pioneers laid the foundation for fortunes -- often for their heirs to quarrel over and squander.

The "Big House"

Our arrival in Singapore was surely very matter of fact. The tedious ride where the snow-laden bushes occasionally emptied their burden over my head, face, and wraps and saturated gloves with the moisture, ended at length. Those restless cows! They must be stabled before they should stray off -- perhaps attempt a premature home trip. Then Doll and Nell were quickly cared for. Meanwhile I climbed the flight of steps that led up above the brick basement to the wide porch of that gray unpainted structure, "the big house" at Singapore, and entered the kitchen-dining room to meet only a cold welcome from the immense cooking stove at the farther end of the room, and wait damp and cold.

"It seemed so lonely. Perhaps the dismal though distant roar of the waves on lake Michigan increased the sensation of loneliness unconscious to myself. A sensation that continued to haunt me as long as I remained in that house, and it was only relieved by companionship.

"I had not long to wait alone. Soon my husband arrived on the scene with material for a fire. Alas! the stove was a problem, but patience and perseverance sometimes accomplish great things and the great empty room began to warm with the glow of that obdurate cooker. Mrs. Fish, in her apartment in the basement, became aware of our advent, came up and kindly invited us to tea. Accepting her hospitable offer we left the stove to do its work and found comfort in the home of our newly acquired friend, to renew our preparations for housekeeping later. The few articles of furniture were easily arranged and we slept soundly that first night in our new home.

"My husband soon built a low partition between the kitchen-dining room and improvised a rude door between, and the place assumed a more homelike appearance. A capacious hallway and staircase divided the main building, leaving the parlor on the east side and "bar room" on the west, fronting the Kalamazoo south. Back of these were sitting rooms, each of these four rooms furnished with a nice brick fireplace.

"The chamber and basement duplicated the room on the first floor. A broad flight of steps led up to a wide platform in front of the hall. Beneath was the entrance to the basement. The long kitchen-dining room was an added ell behind the main building. This ell was entered through a wide porch on the east side which also connected with the hall to the upright. Then there was a pantry and store room and a wide back entry which opened out all east of the dining room, partitioned off from the dining room in front, facing east. Above in the "ell" chamber were two suites of sleeping apartments, divided by a narrow entry way that connected with the hall in the chamber of the upright and was reached only by the one flight of stairs.

"The space beneath the ell, corresponding to the brick basement to the upright, was open on the east most of the way, and the basement hall opened into the vacant space, which answered for woodshed and "catch all." Only the floor to the kitchen and dining room divided from this open space and as the wild winds and frost had full sway below that floor, it was terribly cold to the feet that trod upon it day by day.

"The Singapore flat was a barren like Sahara, dotted by an occasional juniper bush in the sterile waste. The western sand hills that hid from view the restless, roaring waves of lake Michigan, were also dotted with these. It was a dismal contrast to the verdant banks of the Kalamazoo in summer, to gaze all winter from my window upon the inhospitable waste. Now we are told that winds of over half a century have moved these hills and swept the sand around and over this big house with all else of the Singapore of 1848-1849, beneath the surface. If in my endeavor to pair a word picture of that buried structure so long known as the "big house," I have failed, it is caused for regret.

Boarders

"We were glad to welcome, as one of our Singapore boarders, Patrick Shawnsy, one of our last summer's boarders at the Red Banks. For some reason his stay had been prolonged a while after the others left and we seemed acquainted. Patrick was a devout Catholic. He made little show of religion. Evidently he did not desire to be singular. He never swore. Amid the usual profanity of rude lumbermen, Patrick would say, when a thing under discussion and rough words interspersed, "Well I'll not be damned if it is so." It was so glibly said that few would notice any language unusual with such company. He doubtless feared to draw down curses upon his soul. A fear of "purgatory" restrained him from the usual phraseology. Patrick was ever a true friend and gentleman. We shall have more to say of him later. His brother John too was his companion; very quiet was he. Doubtless a good Catholic mother had well-instructed as was in her power, for we heard no semblance of profanity from John.

"Our other two, of the first four boarders were two young men from Prince Edward's isle. John Rossiter was also very quiet and fond of books, history, etc. The name of his friend I fail to recall; very pleasant fellows all. Later Mr. Carter desired and we accepted two brothers, ship carpenters. The ship **Octavia** was being built at Singapore that winter, so Baptiste St. Germain and his brother Joseph came from Trowbridge, I think, as their families were there. Possibly some of them may remember these names.

"Only the **Ark** sailed on lake Michigan until late that fall or early winter. late one bleak afternoon a family of foreigners came into the east sitting room of the above named house. They built a fire in the fireplace and arranged their furniture. It was a Norwegian family. Mrs. Johnson told me her husband's name was 'Oolee Pee-ter Yohnson.' They had just arrived on the **Ark** from Chicago. Ola Peter Johnson was a skilled blacksmith. Mrs. Johnson came timidly to ask some favor. Learning they needed bread for their evening meal and could not yet get their stove and cooking utensils, I simply, as I ought, remembered the golden rule and helped her out in her extremity. A stranger in a strange land, in a cold house, on a cold day, her heart warmed wonderfully to the stranger sister who could sympathize. She was a fine woman of good intelligence and good breeding in her native Norway. We became fast friends. She proved very reliable.

The Hollanders

"The Hollanders under the guidance of their pastor, VanRaalte, had been coming into "de Colony" for over a year. They were reliable and usually honest. John Lukes brought his wife and occupied the room in the basement beneath our sitting room. He boarded the Hollanders. Sunday they had worship together there and their prayers and songs of praise were interesting to a person of serious mind, though in an unknown tongue. Occasionally I would call upon Mrs. Lukes. It seemed quaint of an evening to see an old man playing the needles upon his long hosiery. The men could knit as well as their *vrows*.

"Mr. Fish occupied the two front rooms of the basement; John Lukes, the Hollander, boarded the Hollanders in the northwest basement room; Harrison Hutchins and Ola Peter Johnson, the Norwegian blacksmith, with his wife and two children were on the first floor above the basement. Later John Weed with his young wife Elnora began housekeeping in the parlors opposite "the bar room." Later Washington Slayton, wife and two children, found a home in the chamber above the bar-room.

"'One house is seldom big enough for two families,' is the ancient truism, but the 'big house' at Singapore the winter of 1848-49 was a remarkable exception. I do not remember even one discordant occurrence worth the mention, while six families found ample room within its walls. However, there were only three of these with children. Arthur Fish, a boy of ten or twelve years, found entertainment elsewhere, about the store or among the mill hands. The other families had children too young and peaceable to make trouble.

"Mr. Carter's private room was the southeast chamber. Stockbridge & Carter were the business firm there at that day. Joseph St. Germain occupied the northeast chamber for his business as a caulker. In this great human beehive there was in the basement one room used by all, where to bestow a bag of potatoes or other vegetables. Alas! Jack Frost intruded; hence frozen potatoes were in order. Cooked while frozen they did very well. Alas, for the hands that (pre)pared them.

A Trip on the Ark

"The only boat that ran until late was a small flat-bottomed affair called the **Ark**. Captain Clawson persevered until late. An ignoramus can tell very little about the old craft. Sometimes called, too, 'the Old Scow.' Meanwhile we give a leaf from the notes of Mrs. Ole Peter Johnson, when with her husband and their little Maria of three years and babe of four months they crossed lake Michigan from Chicago to the mouth of the Kalamazoo, late in the fall of 1848, in the only boat then running -- the **Ark**.

"It had a small cabin heated by a stove. A storm coming on the **Ark** was tumbled and tossed about. Capt. Clawson did his best. For several days, amid zero temperature, Mrs. Johnson cared for herself and little Maria and her baby sister, each in their wraps, as best she could, while tossed about in the howling storm. Stove, pipe and everything crashed about until secured. Only imagine how little could be done for their comfort. Imagine the joy once more to tread terra firma, to find home and warmth, and comfort and friends in a foreign land.

"We engaged to board four men. Mr. Carter had distributed his men to board in the several families that resided in the little pioneer burgh. From time to time he increased his force, asking us to board another and another until we counted seven men around our board.

"Peter Shawnessy had also cultivated the friendship of our Norwegian neighbors and to them they related the circumstances as follows: Our last new boarder had been one of the roughs that had annoyed a former tenant, even robbing the cupboard one night. Since dinner chanced to be delayed he proposed they raid the pantry and help themselves. Securing accomplices they proceeded despite protests of Patrick, Baptise St. Germain and others who united in testifying that this was the first occasion and soon the cook would come and a good dinner would be served as usual. Had there been angry complaints the raiders doubtless would have thought it a cunning ruse and worth repeating since 'grievous words stir up anger.' One, in particular, drawn thoughtlessly into the raid, expressed to the Norwegian friends his shame and bitter regrets. It was the first and last occurrence of helping themselves to dainties.

The lumber job on the Red Banks was yet unfinished. In his absence for weeks to complete that job, Mr. H. employed a Holland boy to fetch water, milk cows and do chores generally. There were timbers lying between the boarding house and store and other buildings, laid to answer for walks, when Singapore, upon occasion would be all afloat with surface water. At the Red Banks was a well; at Singapore the river water was used. One evening *de vrow* gave John a pail, remarking, 'Hurry up now, the Kalamazoo is running out into lake Michigan as fast as ever it can. Get me a pail of water quick, before it has all run out.' John took the pail with a look of alarm, but returned smiling at the joke, with a full pail.

"As the family of boarders increased, John Lukes procured to assist in the housework Hilika. Dear, good Hilika -- only seventeen, but conscientious, industrious and true. Later Mr. Carter asked board for himself and nephew, as Mrs. Fish preferred not to keep boarders longer. With the advent of these, the help of Hendrika Lukes was in demand. Soon after board was asked for all hands, as, for some reason, all of the others declined to keep them longer. This was overwhelming but seemed a necessity from which we could not well escape. The aid of our two Holland girls was invaluable. Hendrika was younger but her work compared well with that of her companion. Pity the world is not filled with such.

Home Again

"The dreaded illness made sure to come the ensuing autumn, and we were glad the sick were in the quiet of our home instead of being surrounded by the heat, confusion and noise of the big house. Many a life has doubtless paid the forfeit of persistent homesickness. We cross the Kalamazoo at the old rickety draw-bridge (above the present ferry that later dropped to the surface of the river with a wagon and oxen and two ladies, floated gracefully along until the driver (who chanced to be on the body of the bridge) could hastily summon aid to the rescue. However, we passed with no suspicion of danger imminent and rode past the sand-hill, up the center hill and along the sandy road of the lake shore.

"The first house after leaving behind the Kenter home was a low house where the present residence of Capt. Reid is now located. It had been built by Mr. Sprague Collins. he later removed to his present home near what has since become the Taylor cemetery.

"The ponies pranced and danced along the sandy road with spirits in keeping with the beautiful day. Past the Banner Seymour cottage, where is now the Taylor mansion; past the Stephens shanty, where Dr. Goodrich began on the lake shore; past the unfinished house reared by Dr. Coates, who, by the way, was said to have given the name Ganges to that town when set off from Newark. Being our representative in the legislature at Detroit, the petition to receive the name adopted by another town in the county was put in his hands. Dr. Coates felt constrained to submit to another name, and deciding Ganges was quite suitable, he christened the town by that appellation.

"At the time we write of, Mr. T. Coates had just built the house since known as the Orr place. Fronting this a promontory point extended quite a bit into the lake which, with the tiny grocery upon it, has long since been among the things that were. It used sometimes to be remarked that if the Indians really did pay the price of firewater for pure water seasoned therewith, it doubtless was for their best interest seeing their money would soon go for drink at all events, and pure water was better for their well-being than the *scoo-ta-wau-bish* they craved. (*Schoota* meaning fire, and *bish*, water.)

"At that date -- 1849 -- there were only some half dozen small residences in Saugatuck, no Douglas known, and only one straight road running along the lake shore. All else was forest and morass. Mr. James Haile had a small cabin and sawmill beside the lake. The tiny bed of his pond to the right of the bridge is now filled with a growth of brush and weeds. The mill has long since vanished, though useful when the acres were covered with timber. It and the cabin too long since gave place to the mansion with the ball room above which was the attraction so long ago to the young people who loved to 'trip the light fantastic' or as grandfather Rogers used to say 'had allowed their brains to descend into the heels, causing them (the heels) to become light and giddy.'

"We pass no more buildings until we reach the log cabin of John Goodeve. There was one at the Baragar place, and Cyrus Cole had a cabin home. James Wadsworth's home was a log house with a frame house combined. He had, too, a frame barn. A tiny school house surmounted the hill east of this, and these were all the residences between our house and Saugatuck."

August 26, 1905   L. C. HUTCHINS

I was born down on the bank of Hutchins lake one and a half miles west of the present Fennville in 1853, seventeen years after the starting of commercial Singapore. All my life I was associated with those who had taken part in the early activities there or had lived close by and were familiar with the early doings there, so its early history was common knowledge among us.

Just why such an out-of-the-way place should be chosen for a beginning is a question but it would seem the idea must have been access to lake Michigan as all commerce on the lake was carried on in sailing ships and the difficulty in working their way up the stream from the original mouth would be somewhat excessive.

There were two periods in the life of the place during the forty years of its commercial activity -- 1835-1875. During the first twenty years it was the only commercial center for the surrounding community, but about 1855 Saugatuck began to spread out and became the trading point as soon as stores were opened, it being much more easy of access than Singapore. The sawmill continued there however, and about 1863 O. R. Johnson & Co., set in a mill capable of cutting 60,000 to 70,000 feet per day. The first twenty years formed the first period, but the following twenty years it shrank to just a mill site with nothing else to attract attention. When we speak or write about Singapore we have in mind the time when it was the only business center.

Counting the Mills

From statements of M. B. Spencer, J. P. Wade and Fred Plummer I condense the following: The first mill was in operation a few years and the company went bankrupt. In 1842 another mill was built upstream perhaps a half mile near the upper bend. It ran a couple of years and burned. In 1844 it was rebuilt and in perhaps two years it burned. In the meantime the first mill was started again and again failed. Later it burned. We find in my mother's letter above that in 1848 Stockbridge & Carter got out the timber at the Red Banks for a mill to replace the one recently burned at Singapore, so this must have been the upper mill.

W. G. Plummer said: "When I was sawyer in the O. R. Johnson mill at Singapore they had two saws, one circular and one muley, capacity about 6,000 feet per day. That was in the late forties and early fifties."

J. P. Wade said the mill and boarding house were built at the same time and were owned and operated by the same company. He also said the highest price for clear stuff body lumber was $5 per 1,000 feet and slow sale at that, for lack of demand, and the price did not pay cost of production, so the company failed.

There were never more than two mills standing there at one time, and seldom more than one in operation.

The bank was established there in 1836 and failed in 1838. It was said, "Of the $5,000 loaned, all but $4,998 was paid in."

The lower bend of the river, as it formerly was, has entirely disappeared since the new channel was cut through in 1906 and the old channel that turned at the point where the first mill stood and ran south for perhaps a half mile and then turned out into the lake has all disappeared and is filled with the drifting sand.

Fanciful Touches

In 1926 I received a newspaper clipping by mail which gave a glowing description of Singapore in the early days. This was published in 1875, right after the last mill there had been taken up to St. Ignace. Some of the statements I knew to be true and others I knew equally well to be exaggerations. That story was so fascinating that I sent a copy for republication, thinking the embellishments would be noted and passed by, but to my surprise it has been taken for fact and printed as such. The object of these comments is to counteract that understanding and leave for posterity a plain statement of actual facts without fanciful touches. In the article the writer says: "The mill was the finest one erected this side of Allegan." The fact is there was no Allegan at the time when the first mill and the "big house" or "boarding house" as it was known were built in 1835 at Singapore.

When my father came to Allegan in July, 1836 (he was a lad of 21 years then), he found five or six log houses and shanties just built or under construction and it can be said the town was started that year, but there was no milling industry there until later. Such lumber as was needed at the time was rafted down river from points farther back. And again, a mill that would cut 10,000 feet per day in 1835 was a wonderful machine, but thirty years later it was a very small affair in comparison to one cutting 70,000 feet. But this larger mill was not of the time when Singapore was the only settlement in the county, or in the western portion of it. That town had vanished and was replaced by another condition that was not of the original pioneers, so is not the Singapore of which we write.

The Astor House

In the clipping it was stated: "In the same year (1837) the "Astor house" was built. The building was 40 x 60 feet and three stories high. It was considered one of the finest hotels in the state of Michigan and many are the high old times the early settlers in the vicinity had tripping the light fantastic toe in its commodious ball room."

Now listed: that "Astor house" was purely a myth. No such structure was ever located in Singapore. It was created for a newspaper writeup as an eyecatcher and that only.

The foundation for the story was there in the form of the mill company boarding house with apartment rooms for the families of the mill hands and board accommodation for single men. It was built at the same time as the mill of rough lumber, and was never painted inside nor out. The "commodious ballroom" was the dining room of the structure and, with no settlers at first in the surrounding woods and but few for some time after, taken with the fact that there was a strong religious element among the arrivals it must have been rather a slim attendance at those early gatherings.

Singapore was just large enough to operate a sawmill capable of cutting 10,000 to 12,000 feet of lumber per day. The mill company shop did what little repair work occasion called for and the company store furnished the trade. Nothing more was needed. We must remember this entire region was in the wild for some time after 1835. The little burg at the start was simply an oasis in the woods, isolated and concentrated within itself. It was located in a wet hole subject to overflow during high water so they had to lay timbers between buildings for walks, like the "stepping stones" of old. It was a frontier settlement with no pretensions as to the finer conditions of life.

In 1873, two years before Singapore was abandoned, an atlas of Allegan county was published showing plots of all the villages in the county. In those plots the locations of all the buildings are indicated. The plot of Pier Cove has 27, Saugatuck has 209, and Singapore has 23, all told, including mills, store, shop, residences, etc. We may presume most of the residences were small, not more than sufficient for two or three, so that was just the size of the burg right when the greatest activity was going on there, and the mill was cutting its 70,000 feet per day, seven times the amount cut during the first half of its life as a community. It is a logical conclusion that there were more dwellings there than there were at the start, so the first half would be even smaller than that indicated on the map.

Now let us use a little common sense. Back in 1835 when the first start in this whole region was made, a mill with housing accommodations for the company's workmen was set up. Grand Haven was the nearest settlement to the north, St. Joseph the nearest to the south, and Kalamazoo the nearest worthy of mention inland, and they were all in their infancy. What sort of financial ability would a man have to invest good money in a mammoth palace hotel, finest in the state, away off in the woods fifty miles from the nearest settlement and with no means of approach except by following Indian trails, or by water, and no harbor?

Let's forget the "Astor house" and those other embellishments and remember Singapore in its true history as a frontier start, working out its destiny under trying conditions -- the first blow of civilized man in this wild regions, that and no more.

April, 1926   H. H. HUTCHINS

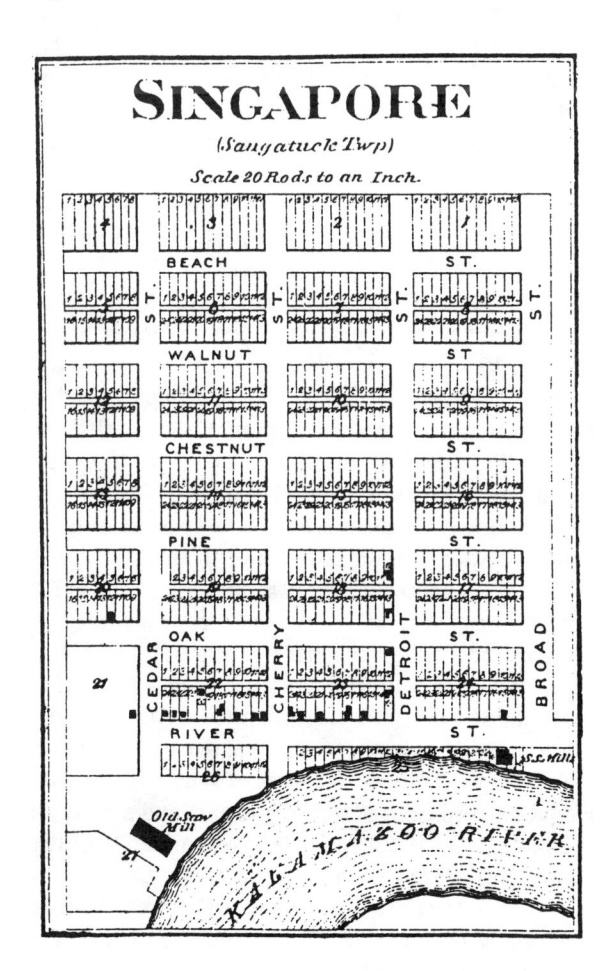

Singapore as shown in the 1873 atlas.

39
Oshea Wilder
Founder of Singapore

The following sketch of the life of Oshea Wilder, with a glimpse at some of his business activities, and especially his founding of the now vanished town of Singapore, at the mouth of the Kalamazoo river, is founded on correspondence with Mrs. Cornelia Lepper Kirby of Covert, Van Buren Co., Michigan, a granddaughter, and Mrs. Carrie Newark Wilder of Allegan, wife of a grandson. We gather from the correspondence that he was in business in New York City, then Rochester, New York. Thence to Marshall, Michigan; thence to Singapore and back to Marshall where he remained until death.   H. H. Hutchins

-----

Letter from Mrs. Kirby, dated April 26, 1926:

"Oshea Wilder, son of Elijah Wilder, came from Rochester, New York, to settle in Michigan about 1831. His wife was Cornelia Anthony and she and their children came on in 1832. They had nine children, two girls and seven boys, but John and Cornelia died in infancy. Those living to grow up being Daniel S., Dewitt C., William N., Isaac W., and Lewis C., and one girl, Sarah A., afterwards Mrs. S. V. R. Lepper, of Marshall, Mich.

"Before coming to Michigan, Mr. Wilder spent two or three years in London and Paris, about 1821 to 1823.

"Mr. Wilder came west in company with a Mr. Ketchum, who had previously settled in Marshall, then a small place with but few inhabitants. Previously to his coming cholera had carried off a great many of the people. Oshea Wilder, with a friend, started out to find a place to locate. They soon found a considerable patch which the Indians, very numerous in that locality, had burned and cleared of under brush and which had grown up to a beautiful flower garden. Mr. Wilder went about four miles southeast from Marshall and found a small stream of water and decided to locate, and purchased some 700 acres of land with timber. He had a dam built across the stream and a race. At the end of the latter he built a saw mill. This little stream has always been called Wilder's Creek.

"A township was formed which was named Eckford in honor of his friend, Henry Eckford, and is now a part of Calhoun county.

"A few years after Mr. Wilder settled in Eckford; together with eastern men he formed a company which bought considerable land at the mouth of the Kalamazoo in Allegan county and erected a saw mill running three saws at once. The settlement was named Singapore. After a time the company built a small steamer to run between Singapore and the then village of Allegan. Mr. Wilder contended the steamer could cross the lake and as evidence of his confidence sent his wife and oldest son, Daniel, and his little daughter Sarah, with the captain and crew for the trial trip. The boat put out from St. Joseph at sundown, but a storm came up and they were obliged to go ashore, running into a small quiet bay near New Buffalo. A Mr. Whitaker of that place had built fires about the entrance and was surprised to find that small boat, thinking it was a down lake steamer. After slight repairs they tried again and arrived safely in Chicago, returning later to Singapore.

"The name is spelled 'Oshea' in my mother's hand writing, and he came to Michigan in 1831, from Rochester, N. Y., but I do not think he was born there. It might have been New York City. He was born in 1786 and died in 1847 on the farm near Marshall, Mich., and was buried there where his wife and some of his children are also.

"Grandfather was a surveyor and I have always been told that he helped to survey the Michigan Central Railroad. We have in the family the chain and compass that he used. I cannot find anything as to why they named that place 'Singapore.'"

* * *

Extracts from Mrs. Carrie Newark Wilder's letters. January 25, 1926.

"Being fond of any kind of history, I used often to engage my husband's mother in conversation, and listen with keen interest and attention to all she had to tell. As she lived with the elder Wilders after her marriage she was well acquainted with all the family.

"This I do remember hearing, that he lived (whether born, I do not remember) in the city of New York, was married there, where all his children were born, several sons and one daughter, the late Mrs. Sarah Wilder Lepper of Marshall, Mich., being the youngest of the family.

"He was engaged in the crockery business in New York and when he sold, or went out of business he gave each one of his sons a set of dishes. I still have a piece of a set which he gave to my husband's father, Wm. N. Wilder.

"Whether he came direct to Saugatuck or vicinity from New York I cannot say positively, but my impression is that he first located near Marshall,

Mich., going from there to Singapore. I knew he spent the last days of his life at Marshall, or on a farm near there, and I think he was buried at Marshall.

"You may have gone at some time from Allegan to Toledo over the old road called the C. J. & M. If so, you passed through a little station just beyond Marshall called Wilderville, later shortened to Wilders, named after Oshea Wilder. He owned acres and acres of land at that place.

"He was a wealthy man at one time, and Mrs. Kirby has many valuable heirlooms -- pieces of furniture, silver, pictures, etc., which belonged to the family.

"He was a surveyor, but whether he platted Allegan or not I do not know."

Mr. Wilder's part in the founding of the now "vanished Singapore" was told in this paper two weeks ago. How he platted the town, built the mill, started the bank and store, etc., 1834 to 1838.
June 11, 1926   H. H. H.

40
Founders of the Village of Fennville

When these people from New England came to west Allegan county in the early 1850's they brought with them that sterling, puritanic integrity that had been instilled into their makeup from infancy. At home many of their kin had been in various positions in church affairs -- some ministers, some deacons and some lay members. There were variations, of course, no people were or are exactly alike, but they were all good honorable citizens. Most of them came before my time but I well remember them in later years. There were the families of E. A. Fenn, S. A. Atwater, Elisha Mix, Benjamin Crawford, Justice and Willis Barker, Henry L. Blakesley that I know came from Connecticut. Other equally good people came and settled among them but of their origin I am not informed. And perhaps it is not necessary to enumerate them all if I could, since the object of this narrative is to outline those most prominent in establishing the village of Fennville.

The Fenn Family

The first we discover in the Fenn family is Thomas Fenn, who was born in 1707 and died April 25, 1769, and his wife, Christian died May 1, 1768. Both were buried at Thomaston, Litchfield County, Connecticut.

Ten children are listed in this family, of which Jason was the fourth, and, being in line down to our subject we omit the others and follow him. Jason grew up among the home surroundings in Litchfield County and when the call to arms was sounded he gave his services, for we find "Jason Fenn, Sergeant 8th Co. 1st Reg. discharged Nov. 25, 1775." (Enlistment roll of company missing.) "Col. David Wooster, also Major or General. Captain, Phineas Porter."

Omitting much detail in the record, we find the regiment was raised on the first call for troops by the Legislature April-May 1775, recruited in New Haven, Connecticut, marched to New York in June. They were here and on Long Island until September, when the regiment marched to the northern department and took part in operations along Lakes George and Champlain. Assisted in the reduction of St. Johns in October and afterwards was stationed in part at Montreal.

We now drop down to the closing of the record and find "Among the minute men and volunteers of 1776" is this: "A number of the inhabitants of Northbury, in Waterbury, have formed themselves into a military company and have chosen officers -- July 4, 1776." In this list, 30 in number is the name of Jason Fenn.

On April 1, 1784, he bought a home in the outskirts of Plymouth, Connecticut, which was still held in the family at the beginning of the present century.

Jason Fenn, son of Thomas was b-Nov. 19, 1751: d-Mar.18, 1919, and his wife, Martha Potter, b-Mar.16, 1754, and d-June 21, 1827, m-Jan.15, 1778, buried at Plymouth.

Nine children were listed in this family, of which Elam was next to the last. He was b-June 26, 1797, d-Aug. 24, 1884, and his wife, Lydia Atwater, b-June 17, 1779, d-Feb. 3, 1873, m-Feb. 15, 1816, buried in Plymouth. He resided in the paternal home at Plymouth during life and here it was his family grew to maturity. There were ten in this family of which ELAM ATWATER FENN was the second.

Elam Atwater Fenn, son of Elam, was b-Mar. 2, 1821, d-Dec. 19, 1898, and his wife, Mary J. Barker b-Aug. 13, 1821, d-May 5, 1905, m-Oct. 15, 1842. Buried at Allegan, Michigan.

Elam A. Fenn was born in the ancestral home in Plymouth, Connecticut, and after receiving such education as was common there at the time he learned the trade of clockmaker in the factory of Eli Terry at Terryville, about two miles from his home. This clock was brought out in 1814, and was among the first shelf clocks invented, taking the place of the ponderous cabinets that stood on the floor. In 1841 he went to New York where he became superintendent of a large manufacturing business owned by two uncles. In 1842 he was united in marriage to Miss Mary J. Barker of Bristol, Connecticut. He held his position in New York for eleven years, and in 1852 resigned his position and migrated to Michigan, and settled on a tract of wild land on section 28, Manlius township, Allegan County, about two miles north and east from the present Fennville.

Arrival in Michigan

Ten years later, or in 1862, only 66 short years ago the entire locality where Fennville now stands lay in its primeval solitude and wildness. Not a blow had been struck to disturb the loneliness of the forest and the wild life it sheltered, yet there are those of the younger generation born and raised here who have no idea who planted the colony, how it happened, nor from whence he came. Generations yet unborn will, in time to come be delving in musty newspaper files and old books shelved in the attic dust of years agone for exactly what is to follow in the next paragraphs, so why not clip it out and preserve it.

Elisha Mix and Benjamin Crawford with their wives came west with the Fenns and settled on adjoining lands. Each year brought in its quota of new comers so that there grew up some local demand for lumber and building material, too, the new Chicago was using more each year so that market was growing. Fenn and Mix finally decided to branch off into the milling business. As a starter they bought the small steam sawmill Solomon Hoisington had built about a mile west of them on section 29. It was perhaps 1858 when they bought, but in 1860 Mix sold to Levi Loomis. Stephen Atwater arrived here from Plymouth, Connecticut, in November 1859 and bought 260 acres of wild land located in both Manlius and Clyde, extending from the quarter line at the M. E. church corner east to the section line between sections 32 and 33, Manlius, one half mile. As an inducement to Fenn and Loomis to bring their mill to his land he deeded them 50 acres on the west portion of his holdings in Clyde. The plan was to place the mill east of where the railroad lies now, but as the lumber would have to go west over the long corduroy road over the swamp they bought additional lands of Henry Bushnell joining to their 50 acres on the west and placed the mill on the west side of the swamp. By this plan the logs from the east could be brought in over the corduroy in the winter, on snow and the lumber taken to the lake in summer when the boats were in operation. There was no thought of a railroad here as yet.

In order to follow Mr. Fenn it has been necessary to repeat somewhat from my historical sketches published in May 1915. However, we will touch the high spots in local history and hold to our theme mostly. H.H.

Mr. Fenn erected a dwelling, both for a home for his family and in which to provide room and board for such of his helpers as had not yet built homes of their own and moved in during April 1862. The mill seems to have been held in operation at the old stand two miles north during 1862, and the following is our foundation for the statement.

While hunting for data regarding when the mill was first in operation I fell into a conversation with F. W. Robinson (by my notes I see this was on September 3, 1910) and he said he passed over the long crossway on August 4, 1862, and there was no move on the mill site at that time. He bought land and on November 19 of the same year he brought his family over the same road and noted that a few trees had been cut and a small pile of brick lay on the ground where the mill was later built. Therefore I feel warranted in saying that the "old boarding house" was built in 1862 but the mill was not in operation until the following year.

Should this vary slightly from my earlier statements it is because I have uncovered positive evidence to substantiate the above.

41
Founders of Fennville Continued

The mill boarding house stood on the south side of the road and opposite where the high school now stands, and the first church -- the one that burned down in 1891, stood on the school lot. The mill was located at the south east corner of the first cross street east. It was a small affair at best, but sufficient for the requirements of the time.

This mill burned down in 1865 and Loomis dropped out of the firm, Mr. Emerson, of Rockford, Illinois, taking his place. In 1869 the Raymond-Abbot mill was brought over from Pier Cove and set up just south of the saw mill and was used for the manufacture of shingles. But the great fire in the fall of 1871 -- "the Chicago fire" that burned mostly over this entire section, including Holland, took everything except the boarding house and the church.

Mr. Fenn had been the leading spirit of the place during these nine years, and had an accumulation of lumber, shingles and lath added to his mill property but practically all that was combustible was destroyed and he gave up in despair, gathered what he could from the wreck and as soon as arrangements could be made moved over to Allegan.

Not long after his removal to Allegan we find the firm of Fenn and Perkins in the factory down on the island where they were manufacturing fanning mills, milk safes, feed cutters and other useful articles and operating a planing mill.

Mr. Fenn was elected president of the village by a good majority in 1883, and re-elected again the following year. Ten years later he was elected on the republican ticket to the office of township clerk, which position he occupied at the time of his death, having been re-elected each successive year by large majority. Tho an active christian worker, he was not a political worker, and the nearly unanimous elections were largely due to the confidence the voters reposed in him and the general respect an upright man commands. He united with the congregational church in Allegan in 1877 and two years later was chosen a deacon, which office he held until death.

The present M. E. Church in Fennville has a memorial window with this inscription: "In loving tribute to Elam A. Fenn."

Mr. Fenn having been a member of Allegan Chapter # 111, F. & A. M. his burial rites were conducted by the brothers of that order.

The Fenns were kindly, sympathetic people. Their hands were ever ready to aid the needy, and in sickness or death their sympathy was expressed by word and deed alike. They never were known to use the misfortunes of others to their own material gain. It is good that the trend of events so shaped themselves as to leave so worthy a name indelibly stamped on the history of their principle endeavors in the community, and may we never forget the origin of our Fennville.

The foregoing has been built up from family records, obituaries and personal acquaintance and is true to life, and conditions instrumental in the planting of the town.

Five Children were born to the Fenns

1 -- Albert H. b-Aug. 8, 1843, d-Sept. 29, 1882, and his wife, Katie Bailey, d-May 2, 1924. He served in the army of the civil war, took up law as an occupation and became one of the foremost attorneys of the county during his time.

2 -- Irene, b. Nov. 24, 1844, d-Jan. 2, 1926., m. Henry L. Blakesley, Apr. 2, 1861. He enlisted in the army of the civil war in August 1862 and was killed in action in Kentucky on March 6, 1863. He was of one of the prominent families of Plymouth, Connecticut, among whom there were ministers, lawyers, legislators and high official soldiers, intimate friends of the Fenn families there. The Blakesley line traces back in direct line nine generations, including Henry Blakesley's daughter (granddaughter of E. A. Fenn) to 1707. Hattie E. Blakesley (now Mrs. J. H. Crane) was born in the "old mill boarding house" June 20, 1862 and thus became the first white child born within what later proved to be the original corporate limits of fennville. Henry L. Blakesley came to Michigan from Plymouth in company with Stephen A. Atwater in November, 1859.

On October 2, 1868, Irene married James Reeve. They resided at Fennville several years, where he was engineer in the mills much of the time.

We all knew "Jim Reeve" of course we did, but who of us knew of his military life? I take from his obituary cut from a Grand Rapids paper in March 1921, (where they had moved): "James Reeves, one of the last survivors of Admiral Farragut's fleet, which won the memorable victory at Mobile Bay, during the civil war, died Tuesday morning at his home 530 Lafayette Ave., N. E. His age was 88 years.

"Reeves enlisted July 20, 1863, at New York City as a second class fireman. He was assigned to the sloop **Seminole**, which was one of the 15 ships in Farragut's fleet. It was on the morning of August 5, 1864, that they proceeded down the bay. The

The Fenn window from the old Methodist Church, now at Crane's Pie Pantry, Fennville.

boats were lashed together in pairs, so that if one ship became disabled, the other could tow her out of danger. Two of the boats struck a mine and were sunk, drowning 120 men.

"In speaking of the battle, Reeves often related to his friends: 'We moved on down the bay under a heavy fire from the forts. Our vessels were badly splintered up before we got out of the range of the forts. We anchored and were just preparing for dinner when that old ram, the **Tennessee**, came up and was going to clean up on the whole fleet. We poured shot into her from all sides and made her helpless. She surrendered after a two hour fight. My share of the prize was $80.'

"From 1861 until 1862, Reeves served in Company I of the third Michigan from Grand Rapids. In '64 he joined the fifteenth infantry in which he served till the end of the war."

3 -- John Crawford, b-Mar. 9, 1853, d-Aug. 14, 1903, m- Aug. 16, 1885, Ora Bush.

4 -- Libbie, b-Oct. 12, 1856, Living. m-Jan. 16, 1873, H. Alfonso Warner.

5 -- Frank, b-Feb. 5, 1859, Living. m-March 19, 1881, Emma Wilcox; m-Dec. 12, 1900, Minnie A. Elliott; m-June 23, 1911, Amy C. Kingsworth.
January 21, 1927　　　　　　　　H. H. HUTCHINS

41
Rogers & Bird Transportation Co.

In tracing our memory back over the past half century there comes to mind a subject, perhaps small of itself, but which may be of interest in time to come regarding events happening in West Allegan County, and which has been overlooked in recent years, and that is the two steamship lines that were organized to take care of the commerce developed at the mouth of the Kalamazoo and adjacent territory. There were other boats in local trade, both before and after, but they were more in the way of tramp ships, going where and when loads were to be had. These two lines mentioned were the R. M. Moore Transit Co. and The Bird and Rogers Transportation Co. Of the first we plan to mention in an early issue but confine our notes now to the latter named company, the foundation for which we take from personal knowledge but the detail is founded on data received from Mr. Bird in answer to questions.

In 1883 the Rogers and Bird Transportation Company was organized at Saugatuck, Michigan, by R. T. Rogers and Charles E. Bird and they built a boat to run from Saugatuck, Douglas and Ganges Pier (Pier Cove) to Chicago. She was launched in October of that year and was named **A. B. Taylor**, in honor of the local banker. She was 18 feet beam and 106 feet over all, made her first trip March 16, 1884, but without doors or windows in her cabin. The crew consisted of R. T. Rogers, Captain; Grey Moreland, 1st Engineer; Wm. Wilson, 2nd Engineer and Charles E. Bird, Purser.

They got outside about dark and within an hour were in heavy ice and finally ran upon an extra heavy cake. The Captain gave the stop signal and told the crew they could all turn in except the watchman, and they laid there until daylight. Sighting open water off to the west next morning they steamed out to it and laid their course for Chicago, which place they reached at about noon, on St. Patrick's day. They unloaded their freight and took on east bound merchandise and at about eleven at night started on the return trip. When abreast the Chicago light they came to the steam barge **Isabella Boyce**, stuck in the ice. They could not proceed further in the darkness so laid by until morning. When daylight came they found themselves also frozen in and Mr. Bird went ashore on the ice to get a tug to come and help them out. He had much difficulty in getting in touch with a tug, but at the Wells St. bridge he saw one coming down the south branch and prevailed on the captain to go out to their relief. His objection was that he had no iron on his planking and did not want to injure his boat in the ice. Mr. Bird got aboard, however but when they reached the **Taylor** the Captain had backed her out of the ice and was waiting for his return. They started south behind the breakwater, in what was called the basin, breaking the ice, but it was hard work as they were loaded heavily with freight and were low in the water forward. In the mean time the tug had pulled the **Boyce** out of the ice. She came along and passed the **Taylor**, ran a short distance and came to a stop. Then the **Taylor** passed her, and they worked that way until they reached the south entrance and thin ice. They had their troubles until about 11 a.m. when they came to "platter ice," small pieces, like a dinner plate, and the **Taylor** steered for South Haven and the **Boyce** for Grand Haven after blowing each other a good-bye salute. When they neared South Haven they found the **Mary Groh** out in the lake with a broken rudder, towed her to the dock, unloaded their freight and ran on to Saugatuck.

Such was the experience of the little **A. B. Taylor** on her initial trip. How well we all remember that boat. She was a tidy little craft and weathered many a gale during her work on this run. She ran a daily schedule from Douglas, Saugatuck and Pier Cove pier to Chicago during that season, making 88 trips without missing a day, from the Kalamazoo, and only four or five from the pier.

From March 16 to July 3 there was not enough traffic on any trip to pay operating expenses tho from then on the fruit and other cargo increased the revenue materially. That was the year the Rush St. bridge was built and was opened to traffic on July 2, 1884. They docked at the north end of Rush St. bridge, where the Wm. Wrigley building now stands.

The **Taylor** was kept on this run during 1885 and after but in the winter of 1886 she was widened to 20 feet, fitted with new upperworks and supplied with a full cabin.

In 1887 Rogers & Bird built the **Pilgrim**, brought her out as a barge and in 1888, put her in the lumber trade, but freights were scarce, so in the fall they put a full cabin on her and put her on the Chicago run with the **Taylor** -- one direct from Saugatuck and the other from the pier. They landed in one day 35,000 packages of fruit on the Peter O'Conner Dock.

In 1889 they put the **Taylor** on the run from Chicago to Michigan City until the later part of the season when she was sold to Jacob Houghton for the Isle Royal Land and Mining Co. This season they ran the **Pilgrim** in connection with the **Kalamazoo** from Holland, Douglas, Saugatuck and the pier. In 1889 they put the **Pilgrim** on Lake Ontario, on the run from Charlotte (Rochester Harbor) to Alexander Bay, stopping at Kingston, Canada, Clayton, Round Island and Thousand Island Park. On their way home after the close of the excursion season and when about 35 miles from Spectacle Reef, in Lake Huron they found the barge **Allegany** disabled and with her two tow barges floating helplessly, their combined cargo consisting of over two million feet of lumber. Throwing them a line they took them in tow and leaving then in the harbor at Duncan City, Michigan, came on home.

In 1900 they built the **Bon Voyage** for the Rochester, Thousand Island, Ogdensburg Navigation Co. to run from Charlotte to Ogdensburg. She was on the Ontario line until the close of the resort season and from Pier Cove to Chicago during the fruit season.

In 1890 they built the steamer **General Hancock** for the U. S. Government as a survey boat. She was 97 feet ten inches long and 17 feet 6 inches beam and 7 feet 6 inches deep.

In 1893 they built the steamer **City of Holland** for the Holland Steamboat Co. of Holland, Michigan.

In 1894 they built the steamer **Bon Ami**; 123 feet long, 22 feet beam with a small cabin on the after part and put her on the Chicago run. (My recollection is she was made full cabin later.) This boat was owned by Rogers & Bird, five-eighths; A. B. Taylor;, two-eighths; and C. F. Hanchet, one eight, and was held on the Saugatuck-Chicago run until the fall of 1899 when she was sold to Singer and Co. of Duluth.

In 1894 the water was so low in the harbor that Rogers & Bird built the tug **Pup**. She was 52 feet long, 11 feet beam; and 6 feet deep. this boat was used towing boats in and out of the harbor. In 1896 Rogers sold his share in the line to Cal. Whitney. Bird, Taylor and Hanchet continued the line until 1899 when they sold.

Bird sold his interest in the **Pup** to Rogers, who took the machinery out and put it in the tug **Cuco [Cuckoo]** and the hull was sold to be used as a fishing tug.

The **Bon Voyage**; 170 feet long, 31 feet beam, was sold to the Howard line of Duluth, Minn.

The **Pilgrim**; 130 feet over all and 24 feet beam, sold in 1891 to Griffin and Henry of Saugatuck.

The killing freeze in the early winter of 1899, that destroyed the fruit crop of that year and killed many of the peach trees here was the contributing cause of much disaster. The two co-operative fruit packing houses in Fennville were put out of business and many of the growers were practically ruined financially. I have understood that also was the cause of the closing out of the line transportation companies at that time.
Commercial Record
February 18, 1927

43
Ganges Roundup

From the time of the first settlements until perhaps 1880, horses, hogs, sheep and cattle ran at large through the woods and over the countryside in western Michigan. When a person cleared and planted a field, he had to fence it to protect his crops from destruction by loose stock running in the woods. Our parents bought and raised colts, and always had from six to a dozen. It was great sport for us boys to break them to ride and drive. When sent after them, we put two or three nubbins of corn in our pocket and when the colts were found we worked our way carefully around so as not to excite them into a run; for if they started, it might mean miles before we could get near them again. We coaxed the fastest one to come and get the corn.

After it had a nibble of the corn, we laid the ear down on the ground and while the colt was eating it we jumped on its back. We became experts at such tricks. With our old felt hat, we would guide the colt in the direction we wanted it to go, by waving the hat lightly on the opposite side of its head.

We had to get the fastest colt in order to keep the lead all the way home, for if another one could run faster than the one we were on, it would get ahead, and then ours would follow it along with the rest, and no telling where they would go.

One day my father and I started for "The Flats" (now Saugatuck) and when about a quarter of a mile from a cross road west of our farm, we saw a boy coming down that road on a colt, and a flock of them following close behind. Father said, "Who can that be running those colts like that?" I told him it was David (my brother) bringing the colts home. "No it isn't," said he, and I insisted it was, but by that time the question answered itself by the bunch flying past us, with David on the lead colt, with his long hair standing straight behind. His eyes were on the road directly ahead -- which was extremely necessary -- and his little felt hat was first tapping one side of the colt's head and then the other, while the other hand had fast hold of its mane.

On they went -- like the wind -- down one hill and up the other, and out of sight. Father had stopped the team we were driving and stood up in the wagon to look. It being a still day, we could hear the clatter of the nimble feet as the bunch fairly flew on toward home. Then the sound died away in the distance. Father, while looking in the direction of the racing colts, said, "That boy will be killed, we must go right back."

I told him, "No, he won't be killed nor hurt. That is the way he always brings them home." We discussed it further, but finally we went on our journey. Father worried all the way to the Flats and return, just the same, but when we got home, we found David around as usual, and wholly unconscious of the fact that he had done anything out of the ordinary; which in fact was true, for we all did the same.

When more than one of us went for the colts, we took the two fastest, and it was great sport to race back to the barnyard. We became so familiar with horses and colts, that nothing seemed difficult about it.

I would guess that David was about twelve years old at the time mentioned, for I was three years his senior.

44
Early Bands in Allegan County

The first effort at band music here was in the early sixties when Dan and Louis Shead played at a township school picnic at Link's grove, on the lake shore. One played the cornet and the other the baritone and it proved an inspiration to the children who had never before heard music from a brass instrument. Later probably before 1870, Louis Shead organized a band in Douglas, though some of the players lived in Saugatuck. This would constitute the first brass band organized in west Allegan county.

In 1872 a band was organized in Saugatuck with a Mr. Stowe as leader. Squire Newnham carried the trombone and his son Richard L. the E-flat alto. I do not know the other members. This band was weakened when Mr. Stowe went away a little later, but in about 1874 Gus Hay came from Chicago and revived it and under his management it assumed quite sizable proportions. At about the same time a kid band was started by Willie Stimson and Stevie Coates, which finally merged in with the others and formed one band. Hay was said to be the best cornet player that ever took part in a band in this section. He was assisted by A. D. Goodrich and R. L. Newnham on the E and B cornets. Some of the other members were Charles Stimson, two Ebmyer boys and possibly George Gill. Names of the other members not at hand.

About 1872-73 a band was organized in south Ganges and known as the Glenn Cornet band. Henry Bowles late from England was teacher and clarinet player. Arthur Goodrich and Adam Miller were on the cornet. Some of the others were John and Roll Sherman, Frank Tourtellotte. Norman and Ed Fitch, Lesley Fry, Lem and Charley Osborn. Later Joe Miller joined. This was quite a substantial organization and survived for some years. Adam and Joe Miller were Civil War band men, and I think Norman Fitch was. There must have been 15 members or thereabouts.

About 1875 Gus Hay discovered congenial attractions which brought him over from Saugatuck into what was known as the Peach Belt district, three and a half miles west from Fennville, and started a band. A. D. Goodrich came with him and took the second cornet along with his cousin Orvle. Glenn Obrion the tuba, H. H. Hutchins, the bass, and Charley Loomis the snare drums, George and Fred Goodrich and Ed Obrion, with others carried the intermediate parts which brought the force up to perhaps fifteen. After about two years Gus married the lady and moved away and A. D. Goodrich took the lead. Soon he took his departure and Hutchins became leader. The members finally became too scattered for useful work and in 1879 the band disintegrated.

In the spring of 1880 Orvle Goodrich organized what became the first band in Fennville and was its leader. Charley Whitbeck, second cornet, Ira Hutchins tuba, Will Lee B-bass, P. C. Whitbeck bass drum and Eugene Cook snare drum. Walter billings, Matt Orr, George and Fred Goodrich, John, Al and Will Whitbeck and C. G. Abbott carried the intermediate parts. The list as above was the roll some time after its organization and no doubt had been revised some what from the first formation.

At the same time -- 1880 -- H. H. Hutchins organized a band at Grange Corners four and a half miles west and one mile south from Fennville. These boys were started with the first rudiments on the blackboard. Alden and Elmer Johnson took the cornets, H. H. Hutchins, baritone; Glen Obrion, tuba; Charles Loomis, snare, and Theobald Miller bass drums. Memory does not recall the entire list by Frank Loveridge and E. Raplee were members and Hutchins leader. This band numbered perhaps a dozen and came to be quite capable. They played during political campaigns, on steamboat excursions and on all such occasions as called for a band. Finally its members became scattered and it was discontinued, after six or eight years.

During the same period that the Fennville and Grange Corners bands were in working order, 1880 to the close of 1887, there was a very good band in Douglas, but I fail to recall its members except George Dutcher, Horace Welch, Tom Gray and Charley Ball and the parts they filled has gone from me, though there were around fifteen members.

Just when the Grange Corners band had separated, Elmer Johnson in 1888 called the remaining members that could take a part, and began the reorganization of its members. Next year John M. Link came from Joliet, Illinois, and joined. In the following year, 1890, he became leader and under his management it grew to be the largest, best and most renowned band ever in west Allegan county, having a membership of 35. John had a fine musical talent and a great gift as leader and conductor. It was known as the Ganges Marine Band. While Mr. Link was at its head the band prospered, but in 1902 he removed to Chicago and the grand old organization soon fell apart and became a thing of the past.

The only other band here was the Fennville, which was in operation during the several years but has ceased working at the present time.
Commercial Record
August 24, 1928

45
Some Historical Errors Corrected

There is a little confusion of understandings respecting the first settlement of Allegan county. No one questions W. G. Butler coming to the mouth of the Kalamazoo river in 1830; but was he the first settler in the county? Some contend he was.

On the 26th of January, 1839, H. E. Blackman (then a lad of 19 years) arrived in Allegan from Hudson, Ohio, and settled on a farm three miles east of town on the Otsego road. Pine Creek was farther east and between him and Otsego. September 24, 1907, I drove over to his home for an interview. In the talk he said, "Hull Sherwood came to Pine creek from Rochester, New York, in 1829. When he arrived he found the land was not yet on sale. He brought his daughter, Mrs. Scott, and family in 1830 and squatted. In 1831 he brought the family. Later, when land was on sale, he bought there. Mr. Blackman said the Scotts were neighbors and he got the information from them. It is on record that Otsego was settled in 1830 and Hull Sherwood was its first supervisor after the township was organized in 1836. Thus we see he was the first comer in the east and W. G. Butler the first in the west portion of the county, both coming in 1830.

* * *

Another cloudy condition in our history of 100 years ago is the reported town hall and school, hotels, etc., in Singapore. To get the correct data on several matters, this among others, I drove over for a conversation with Mr. Fred N. Plummer, two miles north of Saugatuck (May 17, 1908) with the following result:

"My father, Benjamin Plummer, came to Pine Creek in 1834, built a raft on which he placed his family and floated down to the mouth of the Kalamazoo. Somewhere in my clipping I have read this was the third family to settle there, but this I can not now verify. There was no road cut out below Pine creek at this time so the river was the only means of travel.

"Mr. Plummer built a sawmill on the outlet to Goshorn lake, twelve miles northeast of Saugatuck in 1836. It was a water mill and he ran it about ten years. Mary Elizabeth Peckham taught the first school in Saugatuck township in a room in our house just west of the Plummer mill on a farm owned by my father in about 1836. I think she taught three terms of school there, a term being three months, and she boarded in our home during the time. The house was built on the old-style barn frame plan with big timbers and is now used as a barn. The Singapore schoolhouse was built about 1838 two or three years after she began at our place, after which she taught there several terms and I think until she married."

Now the situation seems to have been this, and I believe it was: There were two little lumber camps about two miles apart, Singapore and Plummer's mill, and neither could support a school so they built a tiny schoolhouse about half way between them and together they could tide themselves over. Until recently it has been known as the Singapore school and by the older settlers is yet. It was built 96 years ago, still stands on the old site, and is now in use for school purposes.

I have it in my mother's writings that while she was in the "big house" at Singapore in 1849 attended religious services in that schoolhouse on the occasion of a "circuit rider" (itinerant preacher) coming there to conduct a meeting. There were no resident preachers here yet in 1850, and aside from local prayer-meetings, usually held in private homes, their only religious services were conducted by preachers who rode a circuit on horseback coming at irregular intervals of two to four weeks.

On the first Monday in April, 1843, at the close of the hard winter, the township of Newark held its first annual township meeting in the little Singapore schoolhouse mentioned. I have often heard my father and others who attended tell of it.

The school, as stated by Plummer, the town meeting and the preaching mentioned all go to show the little community schoolhouse was the only gathering place there for a good many years. The only assembling place within the camp for dances and the like was in the dining room of the boarding house. Besides, hotels and public halls never came into the conversations of the first comers there. Had there been any such they would have been mentioned.

* * *

In my recent letter I gave the mill credit for 12,000 feet daily capacity which was wrong. I had in mind the O. R. Johnson Co. mill of 15 years later where they had introduced two saws of 6,000 feet each and thus doubled their output. All previous mills and many later had but one saw.

Now, since rumors and reports are so unreliable, let's figure it out so we all understand. A log 24 inches in diameter and 16 feet long scaled 400 feet. It would take two and a half such logs to the 1,000 feet; but, to be liberal, we will allow three logs to the thousand. A day's run would call for 18 logs, and 1,000 feet of lumber makes just a good wagon load, so we have six loads for the day's run. The logs were in the boom and floated right up to the mill slide. One man hitched the chain to the logs in the water and took away the slabs and refuse as the timber was sawed. The mill drew the logs in by its own power. There was a sawyer and a setter on the carriage to do the cutting and one man took the lumber away. Then the engineer, who did his own firing. Those five men were all that could be employed within a mill of that sort. Now we will allow one man to haul the lumber away and pile it and a clerk in the store who was usually the bookkeeper also.. That accounts for seven men all told. (The man in the repair shop was not of the mill company crew but was working in his own interest.) When two mills were running there would be 14 men in that work and the shop man and clerk would serve all hands.

There were families there but not all the men were married. Probably two dozen people would compose the population. There were no people whatever in the woods at the start and not many at the end of twenty years. Lumber was the only industry so there was no call for others and no means for their support, if they came. The logs were cut in the woods miles up the river so those men were not in it here. Even Saugatuck had but five or six houses in 1849 as my mother's letter published recently proved.

This condition lasted about twenty years and this place was the only supply center for lumber, shop work, and general merchandise. Settlers had dropped in here and there, scattered about the woods, some as far away as the present Fennville district, Glenn and New Richmond. Not many and very scattering, it is true, but such as there were they depended on Singapore, so the store and shop had a fair patronage; but between the fifties and sixties "The Flats" began to take on proportions. A sawmill, store, shop and of course, a saloon, settled in there which were soon followed by others of like sorts and in due time a hotel. So here it was the people halted for their necessities instead of going on the two miles further through the sand to Singapore for their necessities. As the one grew the other shrank and very soon had to give up. Singapore ceased as a center of trade and was dead, and a thing of the past to the community. Thus ends the glory of the first settlement of west Allegan county. It remained only a landmark.

The little sawmill continued on, however, not depending on local support, but to the community it was no more than any other lumber camp; but by this time the mill property had come into the hands of Stockbridge & Johnson who were known by the firm name of O. R. Johnson & Co. They owned the mill in the early fifties when W. G. Plummer was sawyer there as was shown in my recent letter. The milling seems to have run along at that level until the early sixties when they replaced the little mill with one of the biggest ever erected in this region, capable of cutting 60,000 to 70,000 feet in a day of twelve hours. They continued thus until the pine forests began to shrink away, so in 1875 had it removed north to St. Ignace and Singapore was abandoned to the mercy of the drifting sands. This last is the lumberyards we see in the cuts and photographs. Our Singapore had been dead the past twenty years.

The confusion in the stories of the place came by getting the doings during the thirties and forties all tangled up with those of the big mill. They don't get the cart before the horse; they get the horse right into the cart, which is worse.

* * *

By 1861 seven of the eight towns comprising the original township of Newark had organized and been set off and only town three north of sixteen west remained under the original name. In that year it organized under the name of Saugatuck (river's mouth) and "The Flats" adopted the same.

I am not criticizing anybody. Those stories grow in the repeating and all we know is what someone has said or written. If the report is in error that is no fault of ours. All we can do is to quote others, right or wrong.

It so happens that I have passed nearly four-fifths of the past century (1830-1930) right here and have lived the life so do not have to depend on hearsay for much of my information. Lumbering and milling for many years was as common to our lives as present occupations are to those of this day. I have no possible object in building up or tearing down. My only ambition is to leave a true and unbiased record.

Now reader, if this seems reasonable, it might be well to file it away for the benefit of those to follow. That is exactly what it is written for. In the near future I plan to give you a line on "The Slaughter of the Pine" comprising an account of the method of lumbering, and of lumber camp life.
March 19, 1932   H. H. HUTCHINS

46
The Slaughter of the Pine

When we stand in the heart of a great virgin forest and note the universal form of the trees with their tall, clean trunks upon which not a side branch nor a blemish appears and the tops all high in the air forming a canopy, as it were, that creates a perpetual shade below, one is struck with admiration and wonder; but when we consider nature's ways it is more easy to comprehend.

It is common knowledge that sunshine is of vital importance to all vegetation and without it nothing can succeed and that principle applies directly to the growth of our forests. Trees standing out in the open, with few exceptions, form low bodies and broad spreading tops while the same trees growing in shade will shoot up toward the sunshine to the neglect of side branches. The weaker ones and the lower shaded branches of the more vigorous will die and drop to the ground and here we have the secret, if secret it be, of the long, straight growth of the primeval forest.

This is true of all trees, both hard and soft woods, but there are now no virgin forests standing in our county so far as I know. Their destruction ended 52 years ago, the timber we now have being mainly second growth. The same principle applies to our fruit trees. In some of our old orchards we see trunks twice the height desired and the tops reach above the tallest ladder. Other trees have much dead wood in the under portions of the top, and all this comes from shade. To avoid this condition we must keep ahead of nature and do the cutting ourselves.

* * *

A history of the slaughter of the last block of pine in western Allegan county will be typical. In the fall of 1878 the O. R. Johnson Company had a block of pine they wanted cleared off and my father took the contract to stump the lot and put the logs afloat at the mouth of the Dailey Bayou creek, three miles to the high banks or rollway.

The first work was to build housing accommodations for 60 men and stables for 26 teams and five yoke of oxen, then make roads, bridge a creek, put down a crossway of 20 rods over a swamp and clear off the highbanks rollway for room to store the logs until high water in the spring when we could break the jams and float the logs down the river. I was to act as supply man and bookkeeper while father took charge of the woods.

A saw gang calls for a good timber man and two sawyers. Following each saw gang comes a skidder with an ox team to assemble the logs ready for loading and his swamper to clear roads and made ready for the skidder. Then follows, five horse teams to take the logs to their destination. Ten men and six teams make up a crew and five trips were required of each team, as a day's work. The loads ran from 1,200 to 1,500 feet each depending on the logs and condition of the roads. We had five crews on this job.

The sleighs had three-inch shoes with five-foot tread and tracked a wagon. The bunks were heavy and extended out over the sides of the sleighs. Man were necessary to keep the roads in repair and from two to four were required on the rollway to help unload and keep the logs straight in the jam down the high bank. The scaler took the measure of each load and placed it to the credit of each teamster. Then with a heavy mallet that had a three inch X cap on its face he stamped the ends of each log. The swamper also cut an X cap on the side of the logs with his axe. These were called water marks. Each company having logs in the river had its own mark to enable the river men to identify their logs in the big boom at Saugatuck where they were finally mixed up and had to be sorted out.

The winter of 1878 and 1879 was without much snow so we were in debt on the job in the spring. We didn't run a full crew at any time and part of the time none at all. In 1879-80 conditions were all that could be desired. Sledding was just right and by New Year's the accounts had gone out of the red and we were doing well.

About this middle of January, father was taken sick went home and was not on the job again. I turned the supply team over to another and took supervision in the woods in addition to the books.

The contract called for nothing under one foot top diameter and two-thirds sound timber, so the scaler docked the scale to what he reckoned the log would saw out. There were not many such, it being mostly sound timber.

I am guessing the bank at the rollway was 150 feet from the creek to the top of the bank and rose at a very steep angle. The logs were rolled down the hill into the creek, which was frozen over and required an experienced man to so direct them that they would come to rest in an even line as they built up the bank. When a layer had reached the level ground above, skids were used to carry the next lots over, and so on and they would go bumping and bounding down the hill, though when rightly started they would land in good order. Layer after layer was built up until the pile extended out six or eight rods beyond the bank. That resulted in a great pile of logs eight or possibly ten rods over the top and 125 to 150 feet high, like an immense pile of cord-wood all placed in perfect order parallel with the bank. If memory serves me correctly we had seven of those piles on that rollway besides quite a lot stored on a lower level. We took just a little under 5,000,000 feet of logs from the lot during the winters of 1879 and 1880.

The opposite bank of the creek was a low, flat river bottom that during the spring thaw was overflowed to a depth of three feet or more. We were on hand as soon as the ice broke up in the creek, with a log raft secured to the tree over on the flat, and a windlass attached facing one of the jams. An inch rope was wound on the windlass and two men to operate it, with a third man in a boat to take the line over and hook to a promising log in the face of the jam. Then the windlass was put to work and the log pulled loose and out. That would cause others to follow and quite a break would be the result. The biggest break I ever saw we estimated at 40,000 feet came tumbling down into the water. It was a wonderful sight.

Some one in the crew had to be a good log rider, one who could walk out over the floating logs and work them down stream when they caught on some submerged snag and banked against each other and closed the whole channel. I could walk them all right when close together, so one day I decided to ride a log, along with another driver, down to a jam that had blocked the creek a half mile below. All went well until my log struck a submerged snag and stopped suddenly, but I didn't. Well, I "got my suspender buttons wet" waded ashore, emptied the water out of my boots, and started for camp three miles away, thankful that I didn't get "my collar button wet." That was the beginning and ending of my log riding.

Our camp for that job stood in the middle of the tract we were lumbering off. It was a log house about 18x30 feet with rough boards for floors and roof with one room for kitchen and dining room and a small room partitioned off in the north end for sleeping room for the three lady cooks. Attached to the south end was a similar structure for the men's lobby. They slept in the attic under the roof. The beds were of the old-fashion straw-tick sort and were placed on boards laid on pole benches. Two dining tables were each made of four boards one by sixteen feet, planed on top, of course.

One of the teamsters soon took on the trick of missing trips. He would get in from the fourth just in time to load over night but a little too late to finish the last trip.

I notice the scaler's report but had said nothing, since sometimes things happen unavoidably, in which case we allowed full time, but his omissions were repeated almost too regularly and I was about to remark it to him when one of the other teamsters asked me if that man was allowed full time for those days. I satisfied him he was not, and that that must stop. The man went out satisfied, but presently the other came in the office and asked if he was working by the day or by the trip. I told him that plate at the table, the bed in the chamber, and the stall and feed in the barn, the sleigh and the skidder's time called for five trips, and if he could not make it please drive right down the hay road and let someone take his place who could. After that he had no trouble in doing a full day.

Complaints came to me that someone was robbing harnesses, taking good parts and leaving his own weak ones instead. I told it before the crowd in the lobby and said, "Tomorrow morning I want all harnesses back in their right place. I suspect who it is, and will prove it by comparing parts and the guilty men will take the outside air." Needless to say we had no more of that.

Sleighs loaded over night will freeze down solid and must be loosened or there will be trouble. One of our own teams was strong and true and when told to go, things moved. I noticed that frequently when they were loaded over night something broke next morning and time was lost for repairs. I told the driver it would be better for the job, if he traded places with one of the swampers. Such breakage was his own fault. If he didn't know how to drive horses, get out of the way and let some one take the lines that did.

We had small tea bells on all harnesses to warn empty sleighs so they could get out of the road so loads could pass and warn the sawyers of the approach of a team. Also when a tree began to crack one of the sawyers would call out, "Timber-r." One day James Fosdick was going out with a load and heard the falling cry, looked and saw a tree just starting his way. He jumped off the load and started back. The team saw it too and sprang ahead. The tree fell across the load right where Fosdick had been sitting. (That was like the darkey when asked if his mule ever kicked him said, "No suh, he nebber kick me. Sometime he kick right war I just been.") In this case the sawyers didn't realize they were so close to the road and on account of the wind failed to hear the bells.

* * *

One day while I was busy in the books a vigorous young man of about 180 pounds weight came in and applied for a job. I asked if he was a swamper and he said he didn't know what that was but he had done lots of chopping in his home down in Indiana. I directed him to a gang in the woods and told him Billings would tell him what to do. In about an hour he came back and said Billings sent him in for a cross haul. I told him to sit down, and I said, "These woods men are a fine lot of fellows, but they have their jokes for new men at the business. Now don't get excited and I will explain the work of a swamper. He estimates the loads in the vicinity, clears out a good place for the skidder to assemble the loads, and cuts roads for horses to travel. Then he goes to the opposite side from where the sleighs will stand while loading and clears a track for the oxen to work crosswise of the sleigh in rolling the logs on. This last is called the cross-haul." He was all interest until I told him this last, when he sprang to his feet and started for the door. I caught his coat and told him to "take it easy. Your time is going right on, and I will fix it with Billings. Dinner will soon be ready and we can start right." Finally I got him "cam-med" down, so when the men came in he was quite docile. There were about forty men in by the time Billings came, He asked in a loud voice why I didn't send out that cross haul? He needed it. They all knew there was a joke on, and became very quiet and all attention, when I said to Billings, "Now listen. I have put in the past hour faithfully to keep a cross-haul from going out there that you wouldn't have got over for a month. I sent this man out for you to direct and you sent him off on a fool errand of your own and I will expect you to pay the lost time (which I didn't mean). I have explained to him the swamper's position, cross-haul and all, and now you can follow him." There was a roar, for they all liked to get a joke on Billings. They shoved and pushed him about a bit when it all quieted down. Billings and Con. Henline got on well the rest of the winter.

That job was completed in the winter of 1880 and with it the last of the virgin pine succumbed to the slaughter. I wonder how many there are now living who took part in that work in western Allegan county. I can only bring to mind two besides myself.

Sometimes when a tree was falling through the tops of other trees, limbs were broken off and hung up in the air. If the wind was blowing through the tree tops we had to look out lest they become loosened and come down and hurt someone. One such club came down and broke a saw off close to a sawyer's hand.

* * *

During the last winter we had a thermometer that registered 33 degrees below zero. One morning it went down out of sight. Lanterns exposed a short time burned so low it looked as though it was going out for lack of oil. We all remained in by the fire that forenoon.

To make sure the snow would last out on the road until the job was done I made a tank 4x4x16 feet rigged like a street sprinkler and had two men with team go as soon as the last team came off the road at night and with a large pump at the creek for water supply they worked all night wetting the road. Repeated several nights the road became solid ice and lucky it was, otherwise the snow would have thawed away in exposed spots and we could not have finished.

This last was one of the biggest jobs worked in this region. However, the size of the camp depended on the amount of timber to be moved and the time limit for the work. Sometimes men would build one or more one-room shacks where they cooked, ate and slept all in the same room until the job was done.

The railroad here ran its first train in the spring of 1871. That made an easy outlet for lumber located back from the river and quite large mills were set in along the line. New Richmond, Fennville, Clyde Center (now Pearle), Shermantown (Bravo) etc., Saugatuck, Douglas and Singapore; also Allegan drew quite large quantities of pine from the district to the west of town.

I have before me a list of 29 sawmills that operated in the west half of the county during the lumbering period (1835-1880). Two thirds of the number, and by all odds those of large capacity, were here during the last ten years. The get-rich-quick bug was rampant and our forests were depleted as fast as man and power could accomplish the slaughter. The doleful echo of this stampede was that, with the exception of small lots owned by local residents, the entire output was grabbed by outsiders having the wherewith to tie up large tracts and like the "dog-in-the-manger," kept others off until, at their convenience, they could strip the timber from the stump and reap the lucre. Then they flew with loaded pockets to more congenial parts without one word or act of gratitude for the loot they had been able to grab. Laws that will permit such an outrage on natural resources are subject to severe criticism.

While Singapore had mills, one after another, longer than any other location, the old O. R. Johnson mill in Saugatuck was in operation longer as a unit than any other in this section. It was doubtless the first in Saugatuck and surely was the last there. It changed ownership but was the same mill all the time. Griffin & Henry were the last owners and it was kept in operation some time after the forests were denuded, picking up stray logs and taking in small lots as picked up here and there, odds and ends as it were, but this last can hardly be counted in on the period of the slaughter.

March 22, 1932   H. H. HUTCHINS

47
Rural Telephone

[Historical Paper Read at the Annual Convention of the Michigan Independent Telephone Association, March 22 and 23, 1906 at Ann Arbor, Michigan.]

The Growth of an Independent Co-operative Company

The Saugatuck and Ganges Telephone Co., Ltd., was started in 1895 by a few fruit growers combining with local steamboat men for the erection of lines reaching into the fruit sections of the western part of Allegan county from shipping points. About two dozen telephones were first installed, each subscriber paying the entire cost of his connection. It soon became necessary that we associate ourselves and elect officers for the management of the little system, which was done in 1896. A provision in the by-laws was that each subscriber pay for all material required for the maintenance of the telephone, and that each should bear his pro rata share of the cost of the maintenance and operation of the system.

The management has since agreed that where several desire to connect to our centrals by party line the company will run the wire to the vicinity and allow the subscriber to connect thereto free of line charge.

All supplies and instruments are furnished at actual cost and the work is done by experts in the employ of the management at as low a rate as possible, looking forward to the benefits to be derived from the ability to reach as many as possible of the members of the community.

The system is purely co-operative and no dividends accrue, sufficient charges only being made for service to cover maintenance and operation.

Officers are elected from among the shareholders annually, which places control in the hands of people who have no object in the matter other than efficient service at as reasonable a figure as possible.

The growth and efficiency of the enterprise are too well known here to call for comment and to extend thanks to any one would be merely self congratulation, since it is the outgrowth of an enterprising community who operate it according to their own liking, through managers elected annually from among their own number and who are residents of the community.

When the little plant was first started no one knew anything about telephone matters and but very few in the community had ever talked over a wire. Accordingly, the general impression was given out that there would be no cost after installation. Switchboards were placed in stores and business places at the five centers -- Saugatuck, Douglas, Ganges, Fennville and Glenn. The attendants agreed to do the switching for nothing, as it would be fine sport, and the instruments were supposed to be as free from troubles as the piano in the parlor or the colt in the pasture. The first lot of telephones were installed by the aid of the local telegraph operator and an expert from the factory set up the switchboards. Things ran smoothly during the fall of 1895 and the following winter, but in the spring of 1896 a dark cloud soon followed by a hurricane, filled with Old Cain, rolled up over old Lake Michigan, accompanied with a terrific electric storm. Well, our lines are mostly grounded and any telephone man knows the rest.

Before six months had passed our attendants began to think it better to answer telephone calls when they could not sell goods, so the subscribers grumbled because their calls were not properly attended to. At the same time the fellow who had been obliged to leave his business to "see if he could find the trouble with the phone" began to "sit up and take notice" also. Another matter developed, that of having a head and a tail to this thing. There was no one who had authority over it and it was running wild, so a meeting of those who had donated to the enterprise was called and it was decided to organize. Three bright fellows were chosen to draft a set of by-laws. This, being of minor importance, only delayed the meeting twenty or thirty minutes, but we appreciated the fact by this time that there must be some expense attached, so a clause was inserted providing for a pro rata charge for maintenance and operation, as mentioned above. After the usual ordeal of criticism and changing -- among which was a clause providing that all matters should be referred to the shareholders for final disposition -- we all signed the articles of association which had been prepared by a local attorney and after adopting the by-laws, the meeting proceeded to elect a board of five managers.

One of the first observations of the new board was that we would be under the necessity of paying our exchange attendants a stipulated sum and that we must employ an expert to look after trifling matters which seemed to creep in to disturb the perfect working of the instruments. So an assessment of $2.50 was levied on each member, as a sufficient amount to settle all accounts to date. Things ran on in a hit and miss way until January of 1898. By this time our assessments had amounted to about $9 per year for the two and a half years we had been running. This was considered exorbitant and there were rumblings of distrust to be heard from the members and, as the board of directors were serving gratuitously, they decided to let the honors of office fall upon other members, so at the annual meeting an entirely new management was elected. Just previous to this meeting, however, the manager had a new code of by-laws carefully drawn up and signed by three-fourths of the stock, to become operative at once, so that the new board might not be hampered as the old one was by having to refer every important transaction to the stockholders.

At this time there was a deficit of about $300 and it was decided to place the business on the basis of an annual rental of $12, payable quarterly. This sum was supposed to clear the indebtedness and allow the board sufficient funds with which to run the plant and clear up all accounts. It would doubtless have met all expectations had not the fact developed that many of the pole lines were already overloaded, and more wires waiting to be strung, so that much work had to be done, and expense for material had to be met, and at the end of the second year of the new management we were about $700 deeper in the hole than when they took the reins of government. They were all good business men in their own line and strictly honorable, so our little community settled down to the conclusion that it took money to run a telephone plant as well as any other enterprise, and they voted it to be the sense of the meeting of shareholders that the board place the rental at $15 per year, which was done immediately by the new board and we have dropped out of the fence corner gossip.

At the $15 annual rental we have practically cleared our indebtedness -- that is, we have sufficient amounts now due to finish doing so -- and have added many improvements in the meantime. Our expense account has been swelled in the work of correcting errors in first construction and in reconstruction made necessary by over growth; in other words, in getting experience in a new business.

Our principal advantage in co-operative ownership lies in our peculiar situation. This being a fruit growing section, it is important that our subscribers, who are mostly fruit growers, have free access to all the local marketing points, since much of their output is sold at the surrounding stations, and telephone connection with but one of the stations would be of little advantage, while a toll rate would become burdensome. As our company is mostly made up of fruit growers we can, by this plan allow ourselves the use of the entire system by paying a sufficient rental to maintain the plant, while an outside company would be obliged to charge toll between stations for interest on the investment.

In our five exchanges we have about 200 subscribers in winter and 250 in the summer months, or an average of about 50 to the exchange when all are working. Our rates are $2 per month for three months, $1.75 for six months, $1.50 for nine months and $1.25 annual rental.

By the friendly toleration of the large companies who control the long-distance lines passing our section we are enabled to reach outside points over their wires and at the same time maintain our local institution to our own liking.

Were it not for the peculiar conditions, our perishable crops and the consequent necessity for free access to our surrounding shipping points, both by rail and water, I could see no advantage in co-operative ownership and management.

H. H. Hutchins

48
My History in Business

[Letter to his son Lee, written in 1928.]

My first start in a business way, on my own, was after I moved to the old place to help my father out in his work. He wanted me to work the place on shares. I told him I had no precedent upon which to plan a share rate that would warrant me in the adventure. he said he would give me a third, so I took it. About the middle of the season I saw I was losing and told him I would have to throw it up. He said he would give me half and guarantee me two dollars a day for myself and team, the same I was offered to go on the road for DenBliker of Kalamazoo, selling fanning mills in Missouri, so I stayed. Well, I lost $600 and did not get the $2 a day and hired the money at the end of my two years stay there. I went into the fruit package sales business. Did very well until one year I had a fire in Fennville that net a loss of around $400 and another by way of embezzlement in Glenn, and expense in delivering goods which competition forced and gave my note for some $1300 to settle with the company. I worked that out in the same business and quit. In 1894 the house burned and like a fool I built too big. Probably I put in $1000 more than was necessary, but I paid it. In 1890 I bought the Knox 40 acres (I am not sure of the year but I could look it up) set 2000 peach trees and when the freeze of 1906 killed them with all I had on the home place I had to lose the 40 with a cash expenditure of $2200 book account. I lived off the telephone work and let the place lie idle until 1908 when I began pulling out the old orchards and setting new. I set 1000 peach with apple fillers and when the peaches were just in bearing a freeze killed them, but I kept setting apples and pears until 1914. I set the west pear orchard and devoted my energies to their growth. Now the orchards are 18 to 14 years old, but I get no crops. In 1908 I set solid peach, but in 1910 I transplanted peach to make room for apple fillers, so the first of the apples were set in 1910, of the young stock. In all I have lost over 9000 peach trees, mostly just as they were coming in bearing and after all the cost had been incurred but little profit gained.

Earlier I did get orchards in bearing. In 1894, the year the house burned I cleared around $1500, and the next year $2100. That is how I built the house, but in 1896 I had 10,000 bushels of peaches and lost $600. That was a panic year and we had to shake the fruit off the trees to save them. In 1897 we had no fruit. In 1898 we had just about enough to pay the expense of the two years but the following January, if I remember the right month, we had a freeze that killed lots of trees and we later lost all. I set again and the freeze of October 10, 1906, killed them also.

The succession of losses, most of which were not in the line of mental failure, but from action of the elements, and financial fluctuations, is all I have to brag about as a result of my 75 years of effort on this terrestrial globe. The upshot of it all is I pulled on the wrong string at the start, got into the fruit line and was fool enough to presume I would hit it off finally and collect a competency.

Had I taken some other line I might have done worse. Who knows?

Dad

Meditations of H. H. Hutchins

(Written on the seventieth anniversary of his birth, Dec. 14, 1923, and read at the pioneer gathering at the Allegan County Park, Ganges, Aug. 2nd, 1924.)

Fennville, Mich., Dec. 14, 1923.

Tho I don't myself remember, this is what they told to me—'twas the fourteenth of December back in eighteen fifty-three that a youngster came to see them at their home beside the lake, and whose lifetime forms the subject of the tale we undertake.

Not a dollar in his pocket to defray the cost of board. nor a pocket for the dollar, and he wouldn't say a word. None knew what to call him for he didn't give his name, so they called him Henry Hudson, just to place him in the game.

Seventy years have passed us—just our three score and ten since that urchin made his debut in the realm of mortal man. The forest then prevailing here has all been cut away and the wild life it then sheltered is tradition in our day.

The wolf, the fox, the deer, the coon, the squirrel and the bear, the mink, the turkey and the duck, the bird song in the air, the owl, the hedgehog, chipmunk, all, are things we see no more, the hunter and the red man, too, are in the times of yore.

The plow was drawn mid stumps and stone by oxen moving slow, the wheat and grass were cut by hand, corn planted with a hoe, the grain w s cut with cradle and the sheaves were tied by hand, the cythe was used to cut the hay, hand rake and pitchford manned.

The mower came to cut the hay 'bout eighteen sixty-three, the reaper then attached to it to haste the harvest bee. Revolving rake, then sulkey rake were next upon the job, twine binders, too, came in their turn to aid the harvest mob.

The threshing then was done by flail, or tread by horses feet, the fanningmill would take the chaff from barley, oats and wheat, the tread power came, with cylinder to speed the threshing time. the eight-horse sweep soon followed it with fan and all combined.

And then we had the tractor here that first was run by steam, soon followed by the newer kind that fires by gasoline. The thresher, too, is all complete and blows the straw away, and so a winter's work before is run off in a day.

Our roads lay winding thru the woods o'er corduroy and hill, with mud knee deep betimes, or sand, to try the frontier will. Surveyors came, the lines were run, and tax for roads was paid, the lines were cleared, the swamps were filled and crowning turnpikes made.

Our carriage was the wagon gear with spring poles for a seat, 'twas drawn by oxen in those days, few horses would one meet, but as the woods were cleared away and crops began to grow the horse became the motive power and oxen had to go.

To warm their homes and cook their food they knew naught else but wood. The fireplace, too, with mantle shelf was counted very good. Brick ovens did the baking while the dinner in the pot was cooked upon the chimney crane swung o'er the coals red hot.

The wool was taken off the sheep and grandma spun the yarn, then mother knit the mits and socks and found the holes to darn. The clothes were cut and made by hand by those about the home, no store goods then could there be had for no such thing was known.

No coal oil lamp, no kerosene, and no electric light, to aid the early pioneer to find his way by night, for science and discovery had not up to his day progressed beyond the tallow dip with which to light his way.

The tra c on the lake as noted seven decades agone was carried on in sailing ships, of which we now see none. The cabin of the pioneer with latch string on the door has gone the way of all the rest of which we see no more.

The school tax then was rated by the number in the school, and parents paid upon each child the portion set by rule, so when there were no children in the household to attend, the school tax was omitted from this neighbor's tax stipend. greater portion of the school tax on the list, and likewise, too, the teacher, for she had to board around, so

And so it was the duty of the house that numbered most to pay the where the largest fam'ly was her longest home was found.

And where the tax became too great, or teacher didn't suit, the children stayed at home that term and were not in the count. That left the rest of those who did attend the classes thru so much the more to pay the lack of those who thus withdrew.

The subjects taught in public schools of seventy years ago were readin, writin, 'rithmetic, and that's as far's we go. When grammer was soggested at a somewhat later time the noise that it created made it seem almost a crime.

And so it was with algebra, and each succeeding class, "no one could use the knowledge and the tax would be a loss." The teacher too objected in a most emphatic way, fofr she didn't know the subject an the knowledge wouldn't pay.

'Twas eighteen thirty eight you see, the first to Ganges came and built his house beside the lake to which they gave his name. with neighbors few and far between improvements came quite slow so not 'till eighteen sixty two did Fenn's mill whistle blow.

And railroad trains were far away 'till eighteen seventy one, the telegraph 'bout seventy six its lines here first begun, the telephone was not at hand 'till eighteen ninety five, 'twas in the present century the auto did arrive.

But now we have trunk lines galore to speed us on our way, both as to conversation and to rush our busy day. With railroads and the auto car, and talking thru the air, and aireoplanes to fly aloft for hire at trancients fare.

So when our thoughts go creeping back our three score years and ten and note the many changes wrought between this day and then, the question comes—no use to guess—what will the changes be when seventy years have rolled around from nineteen twenty three?

Index

Abbott, C. G. 25,83
Adam 45
Adams, John 28
Adams, Mrs. Sarah Jane 37
Adelaide 45
Aliber, John A. 26
Allegan 7,8,10,12,14,16,18, 20,22,26-29,31,32,36,37,39, 40,45,46,48,49,50,59,68,74, 76,79,83,88.
Allegan County 17-18,27-28,36,38,77
Allegan County Pioneer Society 28,51
Allegan house 48
Allegan Journal 20
Allegan-Singapore road 50
Allegan township 17,
Allegany 81
Allen, John 17,28,29,30, 36,37,49,60
Alpha 68
Ames, Capt. Horace 68
American Express Co. 66
American Fur Co. 18
Ammerman, Daniel 28
Anderson, John 28
Andrews, Elvira 48
Andrews, Rufus 23
Anthony, Cornelia 76
Arabella 22
Ark 71-72
Astor house 75
Atwater, Clifford 57
Atwater, Lydia 77
Atwater, Stephen A. 25,44, 52,54,55,77,78,79
Aunt Betsey 15,45
Austin, Truman D. 29,30
Avery, A. B. 48

Bailey, Jacob 17,28,49
Bailey, Kate 79
Bailey, Leonard 17,28,49
Bailey mill 27,38,49
Baker, Urial 28
Bakker, Hendrik 30
Ball, Charley 83
Ball, Orrin 29
Ballard, Mr. 26
Bank of Lancaster (Mass.) 11,12
Bank of Singapore 10,11, 12-14,74,77
Baragar, Abbie 41
Baragar, Alicia 41
Baragar Helen (Van Natten) 37
Baragar, Henry 30,42,46
Baragar, Mrs. Henry 60
Baragar, Mary 37
Baragar, Peter 37,38,44
Baragar, Rebecca 44
Barber, George 64
Barber, Martin L. 28

Barden, J. H. 46
Barker, Justice 77
Barker, Mary J. 77,78
Barker, Willis 77
Barnes, Lucius A. 28,29
Barron, J. F. 67
Barrons, Mr. 33
Barton, Harriet A. 50
Bates, Sarah 43
Battle Creek 24
Beals, Mr. 58
bears 34,51
Bell Co. 63
Benton Harbor 16,62
Bidwell, Barnard 23
Billings, Alfreda 41
Billings, Alzeda 41
Billings, Ann 44
Billings, Azella 41
Billings, C. T. 30
Billings, Charles 10,18,38, 57
Billings, Charles C. 37
Billings, Charles Townsend 44,50
Billings, Darius 10,18,19,25
Billings, Eugene 41
Billings, H. D. 5-6
Billings, Hannah M. 37
Billings, J. D. 6,18
Billings, James 37,41,44
Billings, James W. 41
Billings, John 31,32,37,38, 51
Billings, John Darius 37
Billings, John H. 44,60
Billings, John Henry 27,29, 37
Billings, Jonathan Hosias 37
Billings, Maria 44
Billings, Mary (Townsend) 37
Billings, Mary 44
Billings, Mary E. 37
Billings, Peter Henry 37
Billings School 41
Billings, Walter 26,31,38, 44,83
Bird & Smith 18
Bird, Charles E. 64,80
Bird, Henry 64
Black river 16,48
Blackman, H. E. 7-8,9,31, 83
Blackman, James 32
Blackmer, Mr. 58-59
Blakesley, Hattie E. 79
Blakesley, Henry L. 57,77, 79
Blanchard's shingle mill 18
Bolks, Rev. 29
Bon Ami 81
Bon Voyage 81
Bonfoey & Hulbut 59

Born, B. B. 8
Boston company 9
Bouws, Harm 30
Bouws, John 30
Bowker, Asa 9,12,60
Bowker family 37
Bowker, Norman 60
Bowles, Henry 82
Bowles, R. 48
Boyce, Isabella 80
Braman, Amos S. 41
Braman, Tommy 41
Bravo 26,58-59,61,88
bridges 18,19,39,73
Brinkman, Hendrik J. 30
Brittain, Capt. R. C. 64
Bronson 18
Bronson, Titus 18
Brown, Andrew 48
Brown, James R. 37
Brown, L. P. 29
Brownson, Joel 28
Brunson, Dr. E. E. 39,64
Burwell, Myra Jane 43
Bush & Dutcher 55,56
Bush, James D. 45,46
Bush, Ora 80
Bushnell, Henry 54,78
Butler, Emily (Loomis) 12, 38
Butler, William G. 7,8,9,12, 14,15,16,18,27,28,37,43,53, 69,83
Buys family 48

C. J. & M. 77
Cady, D. H. 48
Campau, Louis 18
Carter & Stockbridge 14,69
Carter, Artemas 70,71
Carter Brothers 10
Carter, James G. 11, 12
Carter, Mr. 9,11,73
Carver, Capt. R. 68
Casco township 17,22,28, 29,30,38,48,53
Chaffee, Ira 46,68
Chaffee, Ira 23,45
Chase, John 29
Chase orchestra 26
Cheshire township 28,29
Chicago 8,15,20,22,23,26, 39,45,54,55,61,64,68,71, 76,77,80,81,82
Chicago and Michigan Lake Shore railroad 21, 39,55
Chicago and West Michigan 39,59
City of Holland 81
Clapp, George T. 47,67
Clark, Hovey K. 28
Clawson, Capt. 72
Clement Brothers 59
Clyde Center 46,59,88

Clyde township 17,27,28,30, 49,59,78
Coates, Capt. L. B. 68
Coates, Dr. 50,73
Coates, Stevie 82
Coates, T. S. 60,73
Coates, Timothy 29,53
Cobb, Alice (Weed) 43
Cole, Cyrus 27,31,38,73
Cole, Henry 37
Cole, Mrs. 37
Cole, S. 37
Collins, A. C. 26
Collins, Harley 38
Collins, Joseph 38
Collins, Sprague 38,73
Collins, W. H. 38
Commercial 15,19,26,64
Commercial Record 68.81, 83
Comstock, H. H. 11
Conger, Mr. 21
Cook, Eugene 82
Cook, Mr. 26
Cook, Mrs. Pamela 50
coons 33
Corner, William 25
Costain, E.B. 45
Cowles, Henry 41
Cowles, Sarah Jane 41
Crane, Frank 34
Crane, Mrs. J. H. 79
Crane, John H. 67
Cranson, Mr. 24
Crary, Isaac 28
Crates, W. 48
Crawford, Arba N. 38,47
Crawford, Benjamin 32,78
Crawford, Joel and Jemima 38
Crittenden, Mr. 7
Crosby, R. R. 11
Crouse, Jonas S. 21
Cuco [Cuckoo] 81
Curtis, Randall 60

Dailey bayou 85
Dailey, Roswell 30
Dalton, A. P. 22
Darling, R. 68
Davidson, Henry 30
Davis, Ezra L. 58
Davis, Mrs. Lyman 49
Davis, Mr. 59
deer 22,34-35
Delvin, William 60
Densmore, Barber & Co. 20
Densmore, Ed. 18,19
Densmore mill 18
Detroit 27,28
Dickinson, John T. 67
Dingleville 17,48,70
Domby, Paul 23

92

Dorr township 28,29
Doughty, Rev. B. F. 40
Douglas 19,21-22,39,44,45, 60,73,80-83,88,89
Douglas M.E. church 22
Dresden, Josephine 23,68
Dressel, W. A. 8-9,32
Drought family 22
Dudleyville 21
Dunbar 45
Dunn, Geo. E. 19
Dunning, Amos 28
Dunning & Hopkins 18
Dunning mill 18
Dutcher, George 45,83
Dutcher mill 20
Dutcher, Mr. 56
Dutcher, T. B. 21
Dutcher, William F. 21
Dutcherville 21
DuVal, George 44

East Allegan 44
Easton, Sloan 28
Eaton, Chandler 58
Eaton, Crosby 48
Ebmeyer & Smith 18
Ebmeyer's shingle mill 20
Ebmyer boys 82
Eckford, Henry 76
Eckford township 76
Ederedge, Mr. 24
Eggleston, Mr. 59
Eldred, Munford 28
Eldridge, Joseph 25
Elliot, Hank 15
Elliott, Capt. 45
Elliott family 22
Elliott, Minnie A. 80
Elliott, Mr. 19
Ellis, Postmaster 16
Ely, Alexander 7,28
Ely, Elisha 28
Emerson & Co. 57
Emerson, Mr. 78
Ensfield, C. E. 26
Ensign, Caleb 23
Eve 45
Ewing, Charles 57
Exchange Hotel 49

Faben, John 48
Fairbanks, Benjamin 30
Fairbanks, Isaac 17,29,30
Fairchild, Mr. 15-16
Falcon 22
Fenn & Emerson 55
Fenn & Loomis 25,55,78
Fenn & Perkins 78
Fenn, Albert H. 79
Fenn, Christian 77
Fenn, E. A. 51-54,55,77-79
Fenn, Elam 77
Fenn, Frank 80
Fenn, Irene 57,79
Fenn, Jason 77
Fenn, John Crawford 80
Fenn, Libbie 80

Fenn, Thomas 77
Fenn's Mills 21
Fennville 6, 8,14,16,20,21, 26,27,39,41,42,45,50,54-58, 61,62,74,76-79,83,84,88,89
Fennville Baptist Ch. 54
Fennville Canning Co. 67
Fennville Fruit Co. 67
Fennville Fruit Exchange 67
Fennville Herald 24
Fennville house 50,57
Fennville M.E. church 55, 57,58,78,79
Fennville schools 41-42
ferry 18
Fiegert, Mrs. S. G. 26
Field, Wells 28
Fillmore township 17,28,29, 30
Fish, Arthur 72
Fish, Mrs. 71,73
Fisher, Henry 55
Fisk, Joseph 28
Fitch, Ed 82
Flint, John 48
Fosdick, James 87
Foster, Samuel 28
Fountain, Capt. Richard 68
Frederick 23
Frost, Mr. 58
fruit farming 46,60-63,90
Fruit Growers Co., Ltd. 67
Fruit Shippers' Assn. 66,67
Fry, Harrison 50
Fry, Lesley 82
Fuller, Delos 41
Fuller, Horace 41
Fuller, Nellie 41

Ganges 26
Ganges Baptist Church 40
Ganges M.E. Church 40
Ganges Marine Band 83
Ganges schools 38,40-41
Ganges township 5,6,8,17, 18,22,23,24,26,27,28,30,37, 38-42,44-48,59,82,89
Gardner, James 46
Gem 68
Gerber, Daniel 21
Gerber, Mr. 20
Gibbs, William A. 8
Giddings, Jane 48
Gidley, A. P. 60
Gidley, Abe 41
Gidley, John S. 60
Gil, George 82
Gilman, Sarah 46
Glenn 23,47,61,67,84,89
Glenn Cornet Band 82
Glenn M.E. Church 47
Globe 20
Goodeve, Charles 38
Goodeve, J. B. 30
Goodeve, John 38,73
Goodeve, L. B. 30
Goodeve, Sarah (Collins) 38

Goodhart & Co. 6
Goodrich, A. D. 22,45,82-3
Goodrich, Arthur 82
Goodrich, Asa 57
Goodrich, Dr. C. B. 39
Goodrich, Chauncey 39
Goodrich, Flora (Loomis) 13,34
Goodrich, Dr. 22-23,46,73
Goodrich, Fred 82
Goodrich, George 82
Goodrich, H. H. 6-7,47
Goodrich, Hannah (Brayton) 39
Goodrich, J. R. 67
Goodrich, Mr. 67
Goodrich, Orvle 82
Goodspeed, Nathan 29
Goshorn lake 16,17,83
Grand Haven 19,75,80
Grand Rapids 31,46
Grand Rapids Eagle 6
Grange Hall Corners 8,83
Gray, T. & Co. 20
Gray, Thomas Sr. 19,21
Gray, Tom 83
Great Western 45
Green, Mitchell & Co. 49
Griffin & Henry 81,88
Griswold, I. P. 55,57
Groh, Mary 80
Grovener, Rev. C. P. 40
Grover, Sarah Knox 41
Gunplains township 28
Gwynn, John 68

Hahn, Charles 50-51
Haile, Amos C. 23,45
Haile, A. H. 17
Haile, Charlie 23
Haile, Fred 26
Haile, James C. 14,38,45, 53,73
Haile, Jimmy 44,45,50
Haile, William 26
Hale, A. H. 29,30
Hall, B. F. 26
Hall, D. H. 5
Hall, David 32
Hall, Fred 68
Hall, Homer 5
Hall, Jack 32,42,55
Hamlin family 48
Hamlin, O. C. 30
Hanchet, C. F. 81
Hancock, General 81
Harmon, Rev. Austin 40
Harrington, George 30
Harris, James 14,49-50
Harrison Electric Co. 64
Hawkhead, Mr. 48
Hawkhead P.O. 48
Hawley, Ed 67
Hay, Gus 82-83
Hayte, Mr. 27
Hazelton, Brooks 46,59
Heath, E. H. 30
Heath township 28,29

Heath, George P. 16,18
Heath, James 29
hedgehogs 9,32,33
Helen Mar 45
Henderson, J. T. 23
Henderson, James 41
Henderson, Jim 33
Heneveld, Geert 30
Henline, Con 87
Henry's tannery 19
Hill, Mr. 13
Hinkley, Jonathan 29
Hinsdale 68
History of Allegan County 12,45
Hoisington, Solomon 54,78
Holden & Loney 59
Holland 10,16,20,23,59,72, 73,79
Holland Steamboat Co. 81
Hollister family 48
Holt, D. B. 68
Hoover, Al 37
Hopkins township 28
Hopper & Bennett 59
Hoppertown 59
Hotel Butler 18
Houghton, Jacob 81
Howe, Simon 29
Hoy, Michael 30
Hudson, H. B. 44
Hudson, Henry 32,42
Hudson, Laura C. 42,57
Huff, George 56
Hughes, George F. 30,47
Hull & Collins 58
Hulse, Mr. 56
Hutchins, Alvin 32
Hutchins, David 27,32,41
Hutchins, Edward 62,67
Hutchins, Emery 50
Hutchins, Harrison 5,14,17, 23,26,27,29,37,38,39,42, 60,61,69-73,81
Hutchins, Henry Hudson 5, 64,67-69,82,83,88,90
Hutchins, Horace 50
Hutchins, Ira 57,83
Hutchins, L. C. 69-73
Hutchins lake 34,39,50,73
Hutchins, Lee 90
Hutchins, W. W. 32,55,57
Hutchinson, J. E. 67
Hyatt & Anderson 59
Hyde & Eaton 59

Iddles, Thomas 48
Industry 68
Indians 5,7,8,14,35,43,69

Jackson, Daniel 28
Jane 22
Jenkins, Winchester 31
Johonnett, Edward 11
Johnson, A. A. 10,13,49
Johnson, Alden 83
Johnson, Elmer 83
Johnson, O. R. 22,46,88

Johnson, Mrs. O. R. 70
Johnson, O. R. & Co. 10, 15,19,20,59,74,84,85
Johnson, Ole Peter 71-72
Jones, James 68
Judson, J. B. 18
Junke, Caroline Augusta 50

Kalamazoo 18,20,22,38,68, 69,75,90
Kalamazoo 81
Kalamazoo county 7,8,28
Kalamazoo Harbor 68
Kalamazoo lake 8,9,11,12
Kalamazoo river 7,9,10,14-17,20,27,36,37,39,40,46,67-75,83,84,85,88.
Kalamazoo Telegraph 6
Keirnan, James 49
Kenter, Ed. 48
Kenter hill 8,73
Kenter, V. A. 6
Kenter, Verne 27
Ketchum, Mr. 76
Kibby, Alice (Squires) 34
Kibby, Mrs. Will 34
Kimball, Cottom M. 28
Kingsley, Harvey J. 67
Kingsworth, Amy C. 80
Kirby, Mrs. Cornelia Lepper 76-77
Klomparens, Albert 30
Klomparens, Harm 30

Lackie family 22
Lacomby, Mr. 55
Lake Huron 81
Lake Michigan 9,17,23,45, 71-72,74,89
Lake Ontario 81
Lake Shore & Michigan Southern railroad 20
Laketown township 7,16,18, 28,29,30,38
Lamoreaux, Ebenezer 60
Lamoreaux, Daniel 60
Lamoreaux, Isaac 60
Lamoreaux, Issac H. 60
Lamoreaux, John Gilbert 54,56,60
Lamoreaux, Martha 42,50
Lamoreaux, Thomas 60
Lane, Marcus 29
Lavinda 45
Lee township 17,28,30-31,38
Lee, Will 83
Leggett, Daniel 28
Leighton township 28,29
Leonard, Mrs. Miranda (Clark) 37
Lepper, Sarah (Wilder) 76
Lewis, Charlie 33
Lewis, George W. 29
Lewis, N. W. 8,33
Lewis, Will 33
lighthouse 12,15
Lindsley, James 29

Link, Charles M. 14,22,24, 25,43,44
Link, John M. 83
Link's grove 82
Littin, M. H. 6
Logan, William 29
Lonsbury, Lucy 42
Loomis, Alexander 37
Loomis, Charley 82-83
Loomis, Josiah and Rebecca S. 37
Loomis, Levi 12,13,27,29, 30,33,34,37,38,41,46,54,55, 61,78
Loomis, Lyman 34
Loomis, Mrs. Lyman 41
Loomis, Marion 27,55
Loomis, Sallie A. (Skinner) 38
Louisa 22
Lovel, Cyrus 28
Loveridge, Frank 83
Loveridge, Judson 41
Loveridge, S. W. 46
Loveridge, Seth 41
Lubbers, Gerrit 30
Lucas, John 30
Lukes, Hendrika 73
Lukes, John 72,73
Lutz, John 30
Lymon, Fred 41

Mack, Charley 26
Mack, Richard 49
Macks landing 18,22,54
Macsaube 8
Macsaube, Joe and Louie 8
Mager Curba 68
Maid of the Mist 45
Manlius 6,36
Manlius township 17,18,27, 28,29,30,32,36,37,38,39,42, 49,54,78
Mann, Ralph R. 17,28,29, 30,36,37,49,53,60,
Manning, Mr. 48
Mansfield, Jerry 47
maple sugaring 35,36,40
Marsh, H. F. 60
Martin township 28
Mason, Stevens T. 28
Matthews, David W. 30
May, Frederic H. 21,45
McCormick, James 18,27, 30,31,36,38,41,61
McCormick, Maria (Billings) 44
McDonald, Crawford 21
McDowell, Mortimer 47-8
McDowell's pier 23
McDowell, Timothy 17,29, 30,48,53
McLaughlin, James 11
McLaughlin, Mrs. 37
McLouth, E. H. 48
McMillan, J. J. 45
McVea, Charles 64
Meeker family 37

Meeker, William C. 60
Michigan and Ohio railroad 20
Michigan Central 20,32,45, 68,76
Michigan Tradesman 28
Milwaukee 12,14
Miller, Adam 8,82
Miller, Frank 68
Miller, Jake 8
Miller, Joe 83
Miller, Theobald 82
Mills, Francis 44
Miner, William S. 28
Mix, Elisha 28,29,53,54,78
Moderator 10
Monterey township 28
Moore, H. D. 18,20
Moore, Horace B. 20,21
Moore mill 21
Moore, Robert M. 21,
Moore, R. M. & Co. 25,64
Moore, R. M. Transit 79
Moreland, Grey 80
Morley, Frank 62
Morrison, Mary Elizabeth (Peckham) 40
Morrison, S. A. 8,11,14,16, 18,20,22,43,53
mosquitoes 52,70
Moulton, Mr. 13
Mullen, Mr. 40
Munger, Rev. Harvey 40
Murphy, John 28
Morse, E. B. 34
Mount Vernon 68
Munger family 48
Myers, Jay 10

Nash, D. 59
Nash, Eugene D. 58
Nash, Shelby 59
Nash, Will 59
Neerken, Arend J. 29,30
New Casco 47
New Richmond 6,18,21,28, 39,59,61,69,84,88
Newark 20,68
Newark township 14,17,18, 28,29,30,31,36,39,42,48, 83,85
Newnham, Richard L. 82
Newnham, Squire 82
Nichols & Sweet 68
Nichols, Mr. 15,24
Nichols, Stephen D. 11,12, 14,18,43,69

Obrion, Glen 82-83
Octavia 14-15,71
Oliver, George 59
Oleson, Capt. 68
Olsen, Nelson 20
One-Eyed John 43
Orr, John 31
Orr, Matt 83
Orr place 73
Osborn & Co. 6

Osborn, Charley 82
Osborn, L. W. 48
Osborn, Lem 82 Otsego 31
Otsego township 17,28,83
Overisel township 28,29
Owen, W. H. 67
Ox-bow 9, 10

Packard, William 47
Packard's Corners 47
Packard's pier 22
Palmer, J. W.
Palmer, Mrs. James 50
Parish, Mr. 20
Parrish, Ralph 28,30
Parsons, John 29
Parsons, Johnson 36
Payne, J. S. & Co. 21
Payne, John S. 23,26
Peach Belt 38,82
Pearl 26,46,59,88
Peckham, Mary Elizabeth 16,84
Peckham tannery 23
Peorl, Simeon O. 59
Pere Marquette 39
Perrottet, A. H. 22
Perrottet, Mr. 8,23
Perrottet pier 22
Perrottet, Theodore 22
Phillips, B. W. 49.53
Phillips, William S. 46
Pier Cove 8,22-25,34,39, 40,44,54,61,78,80,81
pigeons 5-6
Pike, Simon 29
Piles, Joseph 59
Pilgrim 81
Pine creek 7,8,11,15,37, 48,83
Pine Plains Tavern 16,49,50
Pine Plains township 17,28, 29,30
Pioneer 45
Plainfield township 17,28
Platt, Daniel 30
Platt, Mr. 37
Plummer, Andrew 48
Plummer, Benjamin 16,22, 23,48,53,83
Plummer, David 48
Plummer, Daniel A. 10,17, 28,48-49
Plummer, Fred N. 9,16,74, 83
Plummer, Hannah (Ames) 48
Plummer mill 16,18,23,83
Plummer, Mr. 23
Plummer, Nathaniel D. 49
Plummer, W. G. 10,74,84
Plummer, W. H. 22,23
Plummerville 21,22,23,48
Plummerville pier 22,23,46
Poage, James A. 29,30
Poorenkamp, Reinderd 30
Portage township 8
Porter & Co. 18,45

Portrait and Biographical Record 17
Potter, Martha 77
Pratt, Martin 25
Prouty, Alonzo 7
Prouty, Jeanette E. 8
Prouty, Leander S. 7,8,10,12,27,28
Prouty, Mrs. 7
Pullman 59-60
Pup 81
Purcey family 22
Purdy, Erastus 46
Purdy, Mr. 22
Purdy, Philetus 46
Purdy's landing 18
Putnam, Dyer C. 21

Rabbit river 18
Raplee, E. 83
Raplee, Thomas 18,29-31
Raymond, Mr. 26
Raymond & Abbott 24,55,78
Reamer, Dan 43
Red Banks 69,70,71,71,73
Reed family 48
Reed, J. L. 56
Reeve(s), James 79,80
Reid, Andrew 24
Reid, Capt. Robert 44,73
Reynolds, William B. 47
Rice, H. B. 30
Richards, Charles 24
Richardson, Wm. 68
Richmond 14,36-7,39,49,60
Richmond bridge 18,49
Robinson, Capt. 46
Robinson, F. W. 55,78
Rockwell, Giles 26,46
Rockwell, William 46
Roe, John 36
Rogers & Bird 26,80-81
Rogers, R. T. 80-81
Rosbock, Gabriel 30
Rose, M. F. 48
Rosenaw corner 49
Rossiter 46
Rossiter, John 71
Round, Jonathan O. 28
Rouse, John 29
Russell, Jonathan 28
Rutgers, Geert 30
Rutgers, Gerrit 30
Rutgers, John 30
Rutters, James 29

Sackett, James W. 60
Sadler, John 29
Salem township 28,29
Saugatuck 7,8,10,11,12,14-20,22,23,25,38,39,42,45,47,48,61,67-69,73,74,80-83,85,86,88,89
Saugatuck and Ganges Telephone Co. 64,88-90
Saugatuck Fruit Exchange 67

Saugatuck house 18,19
Saugatuck Township 16,27,28,30-31,38,44,84
Schoo, H. H. 46
Schorno, Anton 30
Schovel, Capt. S. R. 68
Scott, Chauncey 7
Scott, Giles 28
Scott, Mrs. 7,83
Scott, Thomas 29
Sea Star 68
Seminole 79
Seymour, Banner 38,73
Seymour, L. A. 47
Shaeffer, John 41
Shawnessy, Peter 72
Shawnsy, Patrick 71
Shawnsy, John 71
Shearer, J. L. 28
Shead, Dan 82
Shead, Louis 82
Shed, Dan 6
Shed, Lew 18
Sheffer, William 24
Sheffer family 48
Shepard, Paul 29
Sherman, Alonzo 58
Sherman, John 82
Sherman, Roll 82
Sherman 58
Shermantown 88
Sherwood & Griswold 55
Sherwood, Eber 28
Sherwood, George 19
Sherwood house 19
Sherwood, Hull 7,28,83
Sherwood, Mrs. Kate 50
Shorno, Smith 29
Short, Mr. 14
Sieber, Will 57
Signor, David 57,60
Silver creek, 20
Singapore 8,9-16,17,18,19,26,36,37,39,40,46,67-75,83,84.85,88
Singapore school 10,16,17,84
Slayton, Nathan 30,38
Slayton, Washington 72
Smalley, George G. 30,49
Smeed, Addie 41
Smeed, Mrs. James 60
Smeed, Jay 41
Smeed, Nelson 41
Smeed, Sophia 41
Smith, A. O. 18
Smith, George N. 30
Smith, Henry 68-69
snakes 51-52
Snell & Cobb 59
Snell, Ransom 59
South Haven 10,15,21,22,26,44,61,80
Spencer, A. G. 68,69
Spencer, Gordon 34,68,69
Spencer, Jillet 41
Spencer, M. B. 9,10,18,19,69,74

Spencer, S. G. 68
Spencer mill 18
Squires, Mr. 25
Squires, Sidney 24
St. Germain, Baptiste 71,72
St. Germain, Jim 14
St. Germain, Joe (Joseph) 14,71,72
St. Ignace 10, 15,85
St. Joseph 7,16,22,38,75
St. Pierre 43
Stevens, F. L. 58
Stevens hotel 50,58
Stillson, Alvin H. 8,14,18,41,44
Stillson, Kate 27
Stillson, Mrs. Sophia 27
Stillson, Samuel 27,44
Stimson, Charles 82
Stimson, Willie 82
Stockbridge & Carter 69,74
Stockbridge & Johnson 85
Stockbridge, Francis B. 9,10,14
Stone, George 45
Storm 68
Stoughton, Congressman 15
Stout mill 46
Stowe, Mr. 82
Stowe, Mrs. E. J. 60
Stratton, Jonathan 60
Strayer, Michael 29
Streeter, Mr. 34
Supple, John 55
Sutherland, Marcius 24
Swan creek 27,32,46,52
Sweet & Ferguson 59
Sweezey, John 28
Symmons, O.C. 25

Taylor, A. B. 81
Taylor, A. B. 80-1
Taylor mansion 73
Taylor & Co. 22
Taylor, John 23
Teed, John 29
Teed, Mr. 54
telephones 63-65,88-90
Tempest 68
Ten Cate, Derk 30
Tennessee 80
Terry, Eli 77
Thayer, Eutheria 48
Thayer, Orletus 48
Thayer, John 47
Thomas brothers 48
Thomas, Dan 57
Thomas, Dr. 12,17
Thompson, Benton 24
Thompson, Sam 24
Thompson, Sirenus 28
Thorn, Mrs. Nettie 37
Three Bells 23
Three Sisters 68
Tippiecanoe 45
Titus, A. B. 15
Todd ranch 34

Tourtellotte family 23
Tourtellotte, D. D. 54
Tourtellotte, Frank 82
Town, Oka 28
Trio 23
Trowbridge, C. C. 45
Trowbridge township 28

Underwood, Samuel 11
Updyke, David 30
Utell 45

Valley township 28
Van Raalte, Dr. 16,72
Veeder, George 38,60
Veeder school 41
Veldhuis, Gerrit 29
Voorhorst, C. J. 29
Vredenberg, Isaac 29,30

Wade, D.A.R. (Jacobs) 46
Wade, Frank W. 21
Wade, Fred 64
Wade, Issachar 46
Wade, J. P. 9,11,12,14,15,16,25,43,46,
Wade, Jonathan 9,12,21
Wade, Lotta 46
Wade mill 21
Wade, Mrs. 16
Wade, Snell 46
Wadsworth, Clarissa 48
Wadsworth, Dwight 62
Wadsworth, E. D. 6,37,41
Wadsworth, J. W. 30
Wadsworth, James 14,27,29,31,37,38,41,44,48,73
Wadsworth, John 41
Wadsworth, Leon 62-63
Wadsworth, V. R. 14,17
Wallin, C. C. & sons, 20
Wallin, Frank B. 16,20,22
Wallin tannery 5,16
Wallinville 16-17,21,48,70
Walter, Caroline 50
Walter, Charles 50
Walter, David John 50
Walter, Lizetta 50
Walter, Henry 50
Walter, Julius 50
Walter, William 50
Walters & Sprague 59
Watson township 28
Ware, John 28
Wark, James 67
Warner, H. Alfonso 80
Wayland township 28
Weaver, L. 26
Weaver, S. H. 30
Webster's pier 22
Weed, Ames 43
Weed & Co. 21,67
Weed, Arthur 44
Weed, Cephas 43
Weed, Charley 43
Weed, E. E. Co. 44
Weed, Elmer 43
Weed, Elisha 43

Weed, Elnora 72
Weed, Eoline 43
Weed, Frank 43,44
Weed, George 43
Weed, John 72
Weed, Joshua 43,44
Weed, Lorenzo 43
Weed, Louisa 43
Weed, Orlando 17,22,30,43
Weed, Perry 43,44
Weed, Theodore 43
Weed, William 43,44
Weed, William & Co. 44
Weeks, Alonzo 28
Weeks, Corydon 28
Welch & Crawford 58
Welch, C. B. 67
Welch, Horace 83
Wells & Bartlett 16
Wells & Johnson 18
Wells, Ed. 70

Wells-Higman Basket
  Manufacturing Co. 67
Wells-Higman Fruit
  Package Co. 26
Wells, Mr. 70
Wellsville 70
West, T. M. 28
Western Allegan County
  Telephone Co. 64
Western Allegan Pioneer
  Society 25
Western hotel 60
Wheelock, B. f. 60
Whitbeck, A. L. 67
Whitbeck, Al 83
Whitbeck, John 83
Whitbeck, Will 83
White, Calvin 28
White, Mrs. Wallace (Inez
  Weed) 44
White Oaks 46

Whitaker, Mr. 76
Whitbeck, Al 83
Whitbeck, Charley 83
Whitbeck, John 83
Whitbeck, P. C. 83
Whitbeck, Will 83
Whiting, George 59
Whitney & Strong 19
Wilcox, Emma 80
Wilcox, Gil Blas 28
Wilcox, Capt. Wm. R. 68
wildcats 8-9
Wilder, Mrs. Carrie
  Newark 76-77
Wilder, Cornelia 76
Wilder, Daniel S. 76,77
Wilder, Dewitt C. 76
Wilder, Elijah 76
Wilder, Isaac W. 76
Wilder, John 76
Wilder, Lewis C. 76

Wilder, William N. 75,76
Wilder, Oshea 10, 12,28,
  76-77
Wilder, Oshea & Co. 11,12
Wilder, Sarah A. 75,76

Wilder's Creek 76
Wilderville 77
Wilkinson, John 48
Wilkinson, Mrs. John
  (Maria Weed) 43
Williams, Ed 50,58
Williams, T. 68
Wilson, Anna C. 26
Wilson, Sarah 44
Wilson, Thomas 46
Wilson, Capt. W. P. 26
Wilson, Wm. 80
Winn, R. G. 50
Winslow, Milo 28,45
wolves 32,34,50-51
Woodworth, W. A.

* * * * * * *

Also Available from PAVILION PRESS:

Built on the Banks of the Kalamazoo traces the history of boats built along the river, 1830 - 1989, from Indian dugouts and flatboats to modern craft. The first volume of the Saugatuck Maritime Series. Profusely illustrated. 288 pp., softbound.

Buried Singapore: Michigan's Imaginary Pompeii, the story of a lumbering community on the Kalamazoo River, 1836-1875. Now Michigan's most famous ghost town. Large format, 64 pp.

Lucius Lyon: An Eminently Useful Citizen An early surveyor, delegate to Congress from Michigan Territory, the state's first senator, land speculator and early farmer, Lyon was one of pioneer Michigan's most useful and important citizens. 352 pp., source notes, bibliography, hardcover.

Tales of Saugatuck, retold in a popular illustrated series. Volumes to date include:
The Day the Elephant Died and Other Tales of Saugatuck
The Popcorn Millionaire and Other Tales of Saugatuck
The Wreck of the Hippocampus and Other Tales of Saugatuck
The Letters of William G. Butler and Other Tales of Saugatuck

By Kit Lane

The Saugatuck and Ganges Fruit Region A facsimile reprint of an 1875 promotional piece put out by the Lake Shore Agricultural and Pomological Society. Includes a history of the area, a census of fruit farms, the owners and products. 24 pp., Indexed, saddlestitched.

Allegan County: A Bibliography A listing of books written about Allegan County, fictional books using the area as a setting, and publications written by those who have called Allegan County home. Illustrated, softbound.

And much more --

At your local book store, or send for catalog and price list:

PAVILION PRESS P. O. Box 250 Douglas, Michigan 49406